THE TRANSFORMATION OF CULTURE

CHRISTIAN SOCIAL ETHICS
AFTER H. RICHARD NIEBUHR

THE
TRANSFORMATION
OF
CULTURE

CHARLES SCRIVEN

FOREWORD BY JAMES WM. McCLENDON, JR.

HERALD PRESS
Scottdale, Pennsylvania
Kitchener, Ontario

Library of Congress Cataloging-in-Publication Data

Scriven, Charles.
    The transformation of culture : Christian social ethics after H. Richard Niebuhr
/ Charles Scriven ; foreword by James Wm. McClendon, Jr.
      p.   cm.
    Bibliography: p.
    Includes index.
    ISBN 0-8361-3101-0
    1. Niebuhr, H. Richard (Helmut Richard), 1894-1962. Christ and
culture.   2. Christianity and culture.   3. Anabaptists.   4. Social
ethics—History—20th century.   5. Christian ethics—History—20th
century.   I. Niebuhr, H. Richard (Helmut Richard), 1894-1962.
II. Title.
BR115.C8S37   1988
241—dc19   87-33935
                                              CIP

THE TRANSFORMATION OF CULTURE
Copyright © 1988 by Herald Press, Scottdale, Pa. 15683
    Published simultaneously in Canada by Herald Press,
    Kitchener, Ont. N2G 4M5. All rights reserved.
Library of Congress Catalog Card Number: 87-33935
International Standard Book Number: 0-8361-3101-0
Printed in the United States of America
Design by David Hiebert

88 89 90 91 92 93 94 95 96 10 9 8 7 6 5 4 3 2 1

To
Marianne, Jonathan,
Christina, and Jeremy
with love.

Contents

Foreword by James Wm. McClendon, Jr......................9
Acknowledgments.......................................13

CHAPTER ONE
Anabaptism and the Problem of Christ and Culture 17
  Introduction • 17
  Christ and Culture According to Niebuhr • 18
  The Way of the Anabaptists • 20
  The Thesis in Historical Context • 26
  The Revival of Anabaptist Social Doctrine • 30
  Recent Concern with the Problem of Christ and Culture • 31
  The Bible, Ethics, and Tradition • 32
  Testing the Thesis • 34

CHAPTER TWO
What Was Niebuhr's Real Question? 37
  Introduction • 37
  Niebuhr on the "Enduring Problem" • 38
  Niebuhr's Total Perspective: In Search of Further Clarity • 48
  A Revised Statement of the Problem • 60

CHAPTER THREE
Christian Social Doctrine at the Center:
Gilkey, Haering, and Macquarrie 65
  Introduction • 65
  Langdon Gilkey • 66
  Bernard Haering • 76
  John Macquarrie • 87

CHAPTER FOUR

Liberation and Political Theologies:
Gutierrez, Ruether, and Metz 98
    Introduction • 98
    Gustavo Gutierrez • 98
    Rosemary Radford Ruether • 107
    Johannes Baptist Metz • 116

CHAPTER FIVE

The Bible as Benchmark: Hauerwas, Bloesch, and Yoder 126
    Introduction • 126
    Stanley Hauerwas • 126
    Donald Bloesch • 136
    John Howard Yoder • 146

CHAPTER SIX

The Social Ethics of the Cross:
The Radical Vision After Niebuhr 159
    Introduction • 159
    The Authority of Christ • 161
    Three Virtues:
        The Self and the Community in Radical Perspective • 167
    The Church and the Surrounding Culture • 180
    A Recapitulation • 192

Notes 195
Bibliography 217
Index 221
The Author 224

Foreword

Who is Charles Scriven to challenge the legacy of the Niebuhrs, a legacy that surely constitutes the most impressive contribution any family has made to American theology in the century now ending? Reinhold Niebuhr—preacher, prophet, theoretician, chastened liberal—left behind a heritage of "Christian realism" still influential a generation after his death. His younger brother, Richard—quieter, more introspective, more polished—drew smaller crowds and won less acclaim, but his impact may finally be the greater. In a series of epoch-making scholarly writings, H. Richard Niebuhr set a standard for thought about church and society that has not been surpassed by any successor.

Now one of the striking features of this Niebuhrian legacy is its challenge to the nonviolent peacemakers of radical Christianity. Both Niebuhrs were at one time drawn to some form of pacifism. Both eventually rejected it. When they did so, conscience compelled them to argue against their former convictions—and thus to derogate the standpoint of those heirs of the Anabaptists who heard Jesus' "resist not evil" (Matt. 5:39) and "love your enemies" (5:44) as irrevocable commands to follow the nonviolent way. Eloquent and articulate, the Niebuhrs made many young baptists (Mennonites, Baptists, Adventists, and still others) ashamed of their own long heritage of peace.

It has fallen to Charles Scriven, a fresh voice out of the West, to take up H. Richard Niebuhr's challenge to biblical social ethics with its strong peacemaking emphasis. A gentle warrior indeed, Scriven begins with frank admiration of the great theologian's ethical analyses, though he is sometimes obliged to indicate inconsistencies and gaps in the Niebuhrian arguments. But, asks Scriven, how is the Niebuhrian demand for a faith that *transforms* culture (rather than flee from it) best fulfilled in today's post-Niebuhrian world? Theorist by theorist and school by school, he examines Niebuhr's successors in Christian social theory, seeking those who can point the way. Protestant idealists and existentialists, old Catholic moralists and new Catholic liberationists, militant feminists and militant evangelicals are examined here through their best representatives. And they are cross-examined along with Scriven's ultimate favorites, the heirs of Anabaptism.

Interestingly, there is evidence that the standpoint Scriven reaches in this investigation was at one time the standpoint of H. Richard Niebuhr himself. This was apparently true when he took up the famous debate with Reinhold ("The Grace of Doing Nothing," 1932). It was still his point of view when he wrote his contribution to the collection called *The Church Against the World* (1935). Changing times and the pressure of others' views (not least those of his more famous brother) may have contributed to Richard's gradual turn to a rival point of view by the time of his death. Yet second thoughts are not always better thoughts, and it is good for those who would be fair to H. Richard Niebuhr and his heritage to take account of this side of his mind as well.

For this other side imparts a strange twist. Scriven shows here that it is exactly the Anabaptist scholars Stanley Hauerwas and John Howard Yoder who best deserve to be called the heirs of H. Richard Niebuhr and his transformationist social ethics. It is these who display the power of Christian communities that, seeking first of all to be true to their own calling to be the church, nevertheless exhibit the power of cultural transformation—a power that renounces violence. The Niebuhr brothers ultimately concluded, each in his own way, that violence was inevitable and in that sense necessary. However, these heirs of the Radical Reformation—Hauerwas, Yoder, and Scriven himself—point the way to a social stance that engages and transforms human culture, rather than evading or conforming to it. Yet that way does not abandon Jesus' own means and ways. Contrary to what generations of mainline Protestant and Catholic seminary students have been drilled to believe, are these the real transformationists?

Along the way this book raises some hard questions that it cannot resolve. It deliberately tackles ethical theories of great prestige and sometimes of long endurance, theories that will not easily be dismissed. For the book's argument demands of the convinced standard Niebuhrian nothing less than an intellectual conversion, a turn to another way of construing the facts, another paradigm, another rendering of the world. By itself, I believe, it can hardly bring about that conversion. Yet its argument is always fair, its facts accurate, its conclusions coherent.

If those who maintain the former beliefs read this book and maintain them still, it will not have been for lack of fair argument, nor for the author's lack of loyalty to the deepest insights of H. Richard Niebuhr.

—James Wm. McClendon, Jr.
Church Divinity School of the Pacific
and the Graduate Theological Union,
Berkeley, California

Acknowledgments

As I reflect on what I have written, I sense an indebtedness that stretches back to childhood when my parents and first teachers trained me in love and set me on the way to service in the church. I will here single out and name, however, only the persons who have contributed most directly to the particular reflections that follow.

I am enormously grateful to James Wm. McClendon, Jr., the teacher who influenced me most while I was a student at the Graduate Theological Union. From the day I first began thinking about "Christian social ethics after H. Richard Niebuhr," he has been my exacting critic as well as my cordial friend. I will gain much if he continues to touch my life in these important ways.

I am grateful, too, for the careful reading given to these pages by John Noonan of the University of California, Berkeley, and by Shunji Nishi and William Spohn of the Graduate Theological Union. I continue to benefit from the questions and insights they shared with me.

I did much of the work on this study at Walla Walla College, where until recently I was teaching. Both administrators and faculty of the college (especially those in the School of Theology) encouraged and helped me. I may here single out Gerald Winslow, whose conversations with me made substantial impact on what I say here (though not enough of an impact to bring us to full agreement).

Remarks of this kind customarily end with exclamations of deepest gratitude to the members of one's own immediate family. I heartily adopt the custom. Having completed these several years of work, I know what stress my wife and children have been through, what patience they have displayed, what support they have provided. And I cannot say too extravangantly how much I appreciate and love them all. To Marianne, and to Jonathan, Christina, and Jeremy, I am pleased to dedicate these pages.

—*Charles Scriven*
Takoma Park, Maryland
September 1987

THE TRANSFORMATION OF CULTURE

CHAPTER ONE

Anabaptism and the Problem of Christ and Culture

INTRODUCTION

Christians belong unavoidably both to their religious communities and to the wider culture of their regions, their countries, their civilizations. For their religious communities Jesus Christ is not only Savior, he is Lord. He is the touchstone of outlook, the supreme authority for the shaping of character and conduct of life. For their wider cultures, on the other hand, Jesus Christ is but one influence upon outlook among others. The persons and communities these cultures embrace display a variety of loyalties, some involving indifference, some hostility, to Christ. Insofar as these cultures unite the existing diversity, these commitments inevitably conflict to some degree with commitment to Jesus Christ.

This poses a dilemma for Christians. They are subject to the authority of Christ, his power and right, that is, to determine their views, actions, and dispositions. Yet they are also inescapably subject to the influence of the wider culture. They grow up with its language and are affected by its beliefs and social practices. The dilemma, then, is that Christians find themselves shaped by cultural influences other than Christ while believing that Christ's influence must be supreme, his authority ultimate.

This raises difficult questions. What, for example, does it *mean* to call Christ the ultimate authority, or Lord? How are we to understand the relation between his authority and the influence of the rest of culture? In what ways should a community whose foundation is Christ differ from the wider community of which it is part? How should it understand the contribution it will make to the wider community?

These are the kinds of questions H. Richard Niebuhr addressed in the book *Christ and Culture* and other distinguished writings. In what follows I am going to treat his work as a fixed landmark from which to investigate these questions further. In particular I will look into how Christian social doctrine has developed in the period since Niebuhr's death in 1962.

In my investigation I will constantly refer to how Niebuhr characterized the issues, particularly in *Christ and Culture*. This book's ground-breaking analysis and enormous influence justify making it a beginning point for a modern treatment of the subject.

The focus of this first chapter is the thesis we will explore. A brief review of Niebuhr's book will provide the necessary background for an initial statement of it. We will flesh it out further with a sketch of sixteenth-century Anabaptism. This movement of the Radical Reformation is integral to the thesis. That to this day it remains quite unfamiliar justifies outlining its basic ethos in considerable detail. We will attempt to clarify the thesis still further by putting it in historical context. Then we will notice several reasons for thinking it timely and plausible, and suggest finally how we will develop and test it in the chapters to come.

CHRIST AND CULTURE
ACCORDING TO NIEBUHR

Niebuhr's own account of the problem we are examining employs a now familiar five-part typology to display the variety of Christian perspectives on the relation of Christ and culture. One of these, the Christ-against-culture type, stresses the opposition between Christ and society at large. Various monastic orders and sectarian movements exemplify this approach.

Another perspective—in Niebuhr' s terminology the Christ-of-culture type—plays down, or fails to notice, any marked differences between the way of Christ and the way of the world. What is seen as best in the prevailing culture is taken to be Christian. Niebuhr cites Gnosticism in the early church and nineteenth-century liberal

Protestantism as illustrations of this type.

In contrast to these extreme positions are those characteristic of what Niebuhr calls "the church of the center."[1] All of these construe culture as built upon what God has created and pronounced good, so God's Son cannot be its simple enemy. All acknowledge the depth and universality of human sin. All stress the primacy of grace and the necessity of obedience.

What is central here is that while Christ is not *identified* with the features of the prevailing culture, neither is he *separated* from culture. Obedience means not withdrawal from one's society, but response to God's love "rendered in the concrete, actual life of natural, cultural" humanity.[2]

Among the "three distinguishable families" of the church of the center, one is linked with Thomas Aquinas, among others. It attempts to combine appreciation for the ethics of present culture with appreciation for a Christ whose way is higher and more demanding. It aims at synthesis—in the medieval period it approved both "natural law" *and* the New Testament counsels esteemed in monastic life. This is what Niebuhr names the Christ-above-culture type.

Another family among the Christians of the center is epitomized, for example, by Martin Luther. This one urges that the values of Christ's kingdom differ radically from the values of the world. Yet even though the world is corrupt, Christians must live in it, for it is within culture that God sustains his people. Thus his followers—themselves sinful yet forgiven through Christ—must engage in the work necessary in the world. Even the violence of the world, so strange to the ethos of the New Testament Christ, is legitimate if used for the benefit of others. This perspective is deeply paradoxical and Niebuhr appropriately christens it the Christ-and-culture-in-paradox type.

The third family of the center has been championed by Augustine, Calvin, and Maurice. It envisions the conversion of all of culture through Christ. While recognizing the corruption of human life, it trusts in God's sovereignty. It thus believes in the possibility of universal cultural renewal. Although this renewal occurs through the work of Christ, Christ gives no new law. He does not *supplant* the ethics of culture, but *regenerates* it by focusing human thought and emotions on the right object, the God of *all* the universe. On this view, Christ is neither *against* culture, nor *of* it, nor *above* it, nor *in paradox* with it. He is the *transformer* of culture.

Niebuhr finds merit in each of the five types he investigates. In the end he says that a more extended study would not yield a "conclusive result" identifying *the* Christian answer. No thought of a disciple "can encompass the thought of the Master."[3] In spite of this, however, the last of the five types is for Niebuhr clearly the most adequate. The transformationist motif, unlike the others, receives no criticism at all in his book.[4]

After a rough tracing of Niebuhr's views, we can now state in brief form the thesis here developed and defended. I will argue that Niebuhr has rightly favored the image of transformation as a clue to the proper relation of Christ and culture. Through Christ God seeks to renew the human world—now corrupted but in principle good because he has made it and has pronounced it good.

I will argue, on the other hand, that an Anabaptist conception of *how* Christ transforms culture is theologically more adequate than other conceptions, including the Augustinian-Calvinist one to which Niebuhr himself is partial. Put briefly, the claim is simply this: the true Niebuhrian way is the Anabaptist way.

Before making good on this claim, however, we must make sense of it. We must know what it is to have an Anabaptist conception of how Christ transforms culture. In order to know this, we must attend to at least the outlines of the Anabaptist story and the Anabaptist ethos.

This topic was for a long time elusive, owing to centuries of neglect and misunderstanding on the part of historians. We may benefit now, however, from a twentieth-century revival of scholarly interest in Anabaptism that has greatly enhanced our understanding of it.

THE WAY OF THE ANABAPTISTS

The story of Anabaptism began in Switzerland, though beginnings independent of this occurred later in South Germany and in the Netherlands.[5] These beginnings show the type of conflict out of which the Anabaptist way emerged.

In 1519 Ulrich Zwingli came to the Zurich cathedral and began preaching straight through the New Testament. He focused on ethical questions, not, as Luther did, on questions of personal salvation.[6] His aim was to conform church practice with the scriptural pattern.

To this point the city council had supported him. But when the council refused for political reasons to let him celebrate communion in a new way, Zwingli accepted its decision. He believed that patient education would eventually change the council's mind.

In this he betrayed his acceptance of the medieval pattern of union between church and state. Some of his followers thought, however, that he had "cast down" the Word of God and "brought it into captivity."[7] These dissidents began to meet for Bible study and discussion of their differences with Zwingli. They soon were reflecting on what a true church should be. They emphasized the lordship of Christ and the need for a return to apostolic ways.

On January 21, 1525, the council banned independent Bible study groups. That very day a dozen or so of Zwingli's followers gathered in a Zurich house. Before the evening was through there was a baptism—of the adults who were there, not of infants.

This signaled a radical denial of Zwingli's state-church arrangement and affirmed that loyalty to Christ may mean opposition to the magistrates. Not only was this a break with their teacher, but also with the whole "magisterial Reformation," as the movement of Luther, Calvin, and Zwingli has come to be known. For all these Reformers held on to the medieval Catholic idea that church and government were linked together. The Anabaptists, or "rebaptizers," said no.

From the day of its birth Anabaptism was a missionary movement. Soon the first Anabaptist fellowship grew up in a nearby town and from there spread further. Government authorities resented this, and began persecuting Anabaptists. In the end they killed many of the movement's finest leaders. To Anabaptists, however, the costliness of mission was no surprise but part of their distinctive outlook.

We may turn now in some detail to the main features of this outlook. Our aim is to illuminate a thesis, namely, that the true Christian way of social transformation is the Anabaptist way.

At least one writer has understood the phrase *solidarity with Christ* to be the key to the various strands of Anabaptist dissent from the magisterial Reformation.[8] It is, in fact, an apt summary of all the basic Anabaptist convictions. Consider, to begin, the movement's conception of Christ. Here, as in other doctrines, Anabaptist writers did not display sheer uniformity of opinion. Still, we may with minimal oversimplification sum up their position as follows: Christ is the Jesus of the Bible story now exalted, now the Lord and Liberator of his people; he is embodied on earth in his church; he will soon complete his victory over evil through a final apocalyptic transformation of the world.[9]

Consider now the idea of solidarity. It suggests trust, loyalty, likemindedness, union, and shared life. According to Anabaptism, these are precisely the marks of a proper relationship between Christians and the Christ.[10] So if we understand the term *Christ* as these dissenters did, the phrase *solidarity with Christ* really does epitomize their outlook. The main features of that outlook turn out, indeed, to be ramifications of this single, summarizing motif.

Discipleship

At the center of Anabaptist conviction was the idea of discipleship. This meant, on the one hand, radical identification with Jesus, including the story of his people, of his own career on earth, and of the first years of the church that rose in response to his resurrection. As noted in recent scholarship,[11] the Anabaptists thus took Scripture to be the highest authority for Christian existence.

In this they were like the other Protestant Reformers, except they applied their biblicism in a more radical way. Luther doubted whether Scripture supported infant baptism, yet held on to the practice anyway. A leading Anabaptist, on the contrary, called for discarding "the old ordinances of Antichrist" and holding "to the Word of God alone" for guidance.[12] On the issue of the Lord's Supper, Zwingli subordinated the Bible to the decision of the city council. The Anabaptists said, however, that no authority but Scripture could be the norm for Christian practice.[13]

For Anabaptists the culmination of the Bible story was Jesus Christ. Within all of Scripture, his authority was supreme.[14] Thus one Anabaptist could say that the "content of the whole Scripture is briefly summarized in this: Honour and fear God the almighty in Christ his Son."[15]

The other side of discipleship was actual obedience of Christ, actually following his example.[16] Anabaptists criticized Luther for playing down the necessity of moral reformation among Christ's followers.[17] True Christians, they said, are "regulated and ruled" by Christ, seeking "to fulfill his whole will and his commandments."[18]

New Life

With discipleship we may match another feature of Anabaptist solidarity with Christ: the experience of new life in Christ. Luther began with a crushing awareness of being a lost sinner, but feelings of guilt did not particularly bother the Anabaptists.[19] What galvanized them was the liberating experience of Christ now renewing their lives. In his work on earth Jesus overcame the devil[20] and through the Spirit he now overcomes the devil in his followers as well. He delivers them and sets them free so they may be of the same mind and character as he is.[21]

Persons who do not exhibit the fruits of Christ's liberating power do not have genuine faith. The Spirit, said Hans Denck, "equips and arms the elect with the mind and thoughts of Christ." Then he added: "For whoever believes that Christ has liberated him from sin can no longer be the slave of sin. But if we continue in the old life we do not truly believe."[22]

Here solidarity with Christ means more than commitment to obedience. It means receiving from Christ the power to obey. In Christ "who strengthens us" we are able to live the "way of righteousness," wrote Bernhard Rothmann. Without him, "we can do nothing."[23] Some took the theme of new life in Christ to the point of claiming they were without sin.[24] Most made no such claim.

No Anabaptist, however, believed that impenitent, unchanged persons could be called Christians and remain members of the church.[25] No Christians are perfect as Christ was, said Hans Denck. But if they are true Christians they do "seek exactly the perfection which Christ never lost," The seeking, paradoxically, is itself a gift from Christ.[26]

Witness

A main element in the new life of discipleship, according to Anabaptists, was witness. For these Reformation radicals (in contrast to their magisterial counterparts), the command of Jesus to go, teach, and baptize was addressed *to them*. This command was not for their leaders only, but for every believer.[27] They were all to shed their light. Together, as the church of Christ, they were to be "a lantern of righteousness" so human beings everywhere might "learn to see and know the way of life," so "all war and unrighteousness" might come to an end.[28]

Witness was witness to *Christ*, witness by *obedient disciples*. Thus the church's way of life may differ sharply from the way of life dominant in surrounding society. Schooled in the teachings of the Gospels, Anabaptists emphasized the contrast between the kingdom of God and the kingdom of darkness. They urged that the values of the former put the true Christian profoundly at odds with the values of the latter.[29] Solidarity with Christ meant nonconformity, separation from the world.

Anabaptists thus rejected the typical notion in their day that the church was the nation at prayer. The medieval idea that church and state are a sociopolitical unity remained alive in the thinking of Luther, Zwingli, and Calvin (and even some Anabaptists).[30] Anabaptists in general, however, anathematized it. It presupposed that everyone was Christian, despite the Scriptural doctrine of the two kingdoms. Furthermore, it required the members of the church to compromise their allegiance to Christ.[31]

A symbol and key illustration of such compromise was for Anabaptists the Christian use of the sword. The link between church and state had made church members into soldiers. But the way of Jesus was the way of peace. *Its* weapons, as Menno Simons wrote, are "not swords and spears, but patience, silence, and hope, and the Word of God."[32] True solidarity with Christ, true witness to Christ, meant obeying his command to resist no evil with the sword.[33] Since it was characteristic of the state to rely upon the sword, the church had no business being its partner.[34]

The Anabaptists recognized the danger of making such a witness. The danger simply fit the Anabaptist idea of solidarity with Christ. Jesus suffered torture and death. And so, Anabaptists believed, may his disciples. The enemies of God's kingdom may arm themselves with fire and steel, but true disciples do not shrink back. As one Anabaptist martyr said, Christ's sheep "hear his voice and follow him withersoever he goes."[35] They follow him, moreover, not only in going where he goes but also in forgiving as he forgives. They forgive even their persecutors, as Christ did. And this, said Menno Simons, is *how* they "conquer their fate, their opposition."[36]

Community

Another main feature of Anabaptist solidarity with Christ was the shared life of the community which is now his body on earth. The church was to the Anabaptists a voluntary fellowship of those who had freely consented to follow Christ and to share the joys and sorrows of faithful witness.

The rite of the Lord's Supper, as they understood it, likewise underscored this conviction. It was "a sign of the brotherly love to which we are obliged," an "expression of fellowship." No one could participate who was unwilling "to live and suffer for the sake of Christ and the brethren, [for the sake] of the head and the members."[37] To belong to the church was to be in solidarity with one another, to show concern for one another.

One meaning of such solidarity was mutual aid. Members of the community were to look after the needs of one another. They were to see themselves not as *lords* of their possessions but as "stewards and distributors."[38] Besides concern with the *physical* well-being of the community, however, they were to show concern for its *spiritual* well-being. Solidarity with Christ's body meant not only mutual aid but also mutual discipline and forgiveness. The brother or sister who sins openly, said the Anabaptists, must be reproved. If resolutely unrepentant, that person must be excluded from the community.

Discipline in whatever form, however, was to be redemptive. Whoever repented—no matter how serious his offense—was to be forgiven. The church must receive that person "as a returning, beloved brother or sister."[39] The fundamental thing, after all, was mutual support in Christian life and witness.

Apocalyptic Consciousness

As we saw earlier, for Anabaptists solidarity with Christ meant identifying with his story. In this story we find a vivid sense of coming apocalyptic transformation. We find the themes of urgency, of judgment on the present age, of hope rooted in the trust of God. These same themes appear prominently in Anabaptist writings. One writer said that since the "day of the Lord is nearer to us than we expect," his followers should prepare themselves "in daily worship, piety, and the fear of God."[40] Menno Simons said the rulers and institutions of the present age would soon appear as "earth, dust, wind, and smoke."[41] Being in solidarity with Christ meant sharing his heightened sense of eschatology. This, indeed, was another main element of the Anabaptist outlook.[42]

Our sketch of Anabaptism has shown its emphasis on discipleship, new life, witness, community, and apocalyptic eschatalogy. We may note finally that in all of this, Anabaptists believed they were recalling the vision of the apostles. With the idea of church and society as one—an idea dominant, they believed, since the time of Constantine[43]—Christianity had fallen from the apostolic standard. In saying that the true church lives out today the way and mission of the apostolic church, they were making, they said, "a new beginning upon the rule from which others had departed."[44]

THE THESIS IN HISTORICAL CONTEXT

Having attended to the Anabaptist story and ethos, we may return now to the thesis. My claim is that Christ transforms culture, as Niebuhr says, but that the proper *mode* of transformation is understood best by the Anabaptists. On this last, of course, Niebuhr disagrees, though in a tantalizingly ambiguous way, to which we will later attend. For now it suffices to notice that he links Anabaptists[45] with the Christ-against-culture type. According to Niebuhr, they belong to that strain in Christian history which has been thoroughly anticultural. They seek a kind of perfection, a kind of obedience to Christ "wholly distinct from the aims that men seek in politics and economics, in science and arts."[46] In cleaving to Christ, so Niebuhr tells us, they sunder themselves from culture.

What to make of this charge is central in all that will follow. The vision it encapsulates is commonplace, as indeed it has been from nearly the beginning of Christian history. Celsus, the pagan critic, chided the early Christians for being unhelpful to society, since they would not fight with the king in war. Origen replied that Christians give better service in the church than in fighting the enemy, or even in holding office. In declining "public duties," said Origen, Christians "reserve themselves for a diviner and more necessary service in the Church of God—for the salvation of men."

The reply suggests the idea that the church serves the world simply by being the church. But in explaining how the church makes its contribution, Origen displayed the inchoate posture of chaplaincy—the church giving its blessing to the state.

This understanding of the church already portended the acceptance of a view of social responsibility like that of Celsus himself. Christians stay pure by refusing to bear arms, yet assist the king by petitioning the help of God for his warriors. "We do not indeed fight under him, although he require it," Origen wrote. "We fight on his behalf, forming a special army—an army of piety—by offering our prayers to God."[47]

Early Christianity had envisioned a community whose Lord was Christ and whose way was a witness to him. It would rule out violence as a means of social reform. However, the ambiguity of Origen's position, which at once rejected and endorsed government violence, was altering the original position. As the church grew and included nominal members, the process continued. Church members identified ever more closely with the permanent life of the world.

At the beginning of the fourth century Constantine became emperor. He had fought his way to power in a bloody civil war under the standard of the cross. When he achieved supreme rule of the Roman Empire, admirers proclaimed him the champion of Christianity. Under Constantine, all offices of the state, including military offices, became available to Christians, who continued to forge an ever closer link with their society. By the time of Augustine, Christians had become accepted and influential members of the prevailing culture.[48]

Augustine—a paradigm for Niebuhr of transformationist thought—reflected in his ethical discourse the changed form of Christian social life. Augustine believed that the difference between the divine city and the earthly—his terms for those who "live according to God's will" and those who do not[49]—was somewhat obscure. In the "present transitory world," he said, these cities are "interwoven."[50]

In saying this Augustine was simply acknowledging a fact. The two cities *were* mixed by then. For example, Christians and not only pagans were among society's political and military leaders. But more than this, Augustine was himself committed to the interweaving process. He was, in another figure, a key participant in the attempt to wed two cultures, the Greco-Roman and the Judeo-Christian.

He himself had been influenced by both cultures. He grew up under a Christian mother and studied Latin literature. He was a reader of works by Cicero and Plotinus and a hearer of sermons by the Christian pastor Ambrose. So it is not altogether surprising that he sought to reconcile early Christianity with the "necessities" of political life. After all, these had long concerned writers in the Greek tradition.

Thus Augustine spoke, as Aristotle had, of the "just war."[51] He even set forth its code.[52] He said that Constantine both "worshiped the only true God" and "was victorious, above all others, in the wars which he directed and conducted." Despite Tertullian and Origen's interpretation of the New Testament, he defended the practice of capital punishment.[53]

In giving hurried notice to the development from Celsus to Augustine, we have seen an outlook much at odds with the later Christocentrism of Anabaptism and its attendant separation[54] from the world. Augustine did not simply idealize existing Roman civilization, but he did connect Christ more closely than before with the prevailing ways of life and social institutions.

Augustine repeatedly quoted the psalmist's affirmation, "As for me, my true good is to cling to God."[55] The love of God is thus the focus of moral aspiration, but it is the mediator Jesus Christ who illumines the pathway to God. "As God," Augustine wrote aphoristically, "he is the goal; as man he is the way."[56] Yet it was possible now to follow the mediator's way while winning victories at war. Christ clearly had a different kind of authority here than in Origen or Tertullian or the New Testament.

Niebuhr charges Anabaptism with being anticultural, unresponsive to human social needs and goals. We have seen now that Celsus reproached early Christianity in similar fashion. In time Christians after Celsus adjusted their convictions so the reproach no longer held—at least not in the same way.

What emerged was a social doctrine in which discipleship, with its emphasis on the self-giving, nonviolent Jesus as a pattern to be emulated,[57] adjusted itself to what were considered the realistic demands of social and political life. We may recall that in four of Niebuhr's five approaches to the problem of Christ and culture, this adjustment remained basically intact. It has remained for the most part intact to this day, judging by the recent treatments of Christ and culture.

For illustration now of how pervasive this so-called realist perspective has remained, we may note among twentieth-century theologians Reinhold Niebuhr, H. Richard's influential brother.

In his classic 1935 account, *An Interpretation of Christian Ethics*, he argued that the ethic of Jesus provides a basis for criticizing existing moral views. It cannot, however, be the foundation of a truly adequate Christian social ethic, for the latter must acknowledge "the conflict between the idea of love and the necessities of natural life."[58]

Or we may consider Karl Barth, whose ethics was an elucidation, he said, of the divine command. In a part of his *Church Dogmatics* first published in the early 1940s, Barth said that it is Jesus who shows us the will of God. What distinguishes Christians from other people is that they keep his commandments. "Obedience to God always means that we become and are continually obedient to Jesus," he wrote.

He went on to expound New Testament passages about "following" Christ and taking him as our "example."[59] In reference to 1 Peter 2:21, for instance, he invoked the context to show that following Christ means attending to his approach to unjust violence. It means suffering persecution "without returning evil for evil but rather requiting evil with good."[60]

Nevertheless, in reflections on the protection of life published some ten years later,[61] Barth allowed Christian participation in war. He even endorsed punishment by death for extreme offenses, such as "brutal" tyranny or high treason during war.

Barth was a writer eager to give full authority to Christ. He was equally eager to reproach easy assent to war and capital punishment. This fact only underscores the staying power of the kind of social doctrine that became prominent by the time of Augustine.

THE REVIVAL
OF ANABAPTIST SOCIAL DOCTRINE

My thesis is that Christ is the transformer of culture and that Anabaptism knows best his way of doing so. We have clarified the thesis by summarizing both the account of Christ and culture and the type of Christian existence in terms of which it is stated. We have placed it in the context of what Christians have thought before.

The thesis is certainly no truism. To many it will seem clearly false. Indeed, in a 1966 preface to his collection of readings on the relation of church and society, George Forel stigmatized the "separation pattern" as now "obsolescent."[62]

What seemed obsolescent in 1966, however, has since then been making a comeback. This fact alone saves the thesis from being merely bizarre. In this century, many Mennonite heirs of the Anabaptist way have been attempting to rehabilitate the separation pattern. They are doing so by discovering its shape among the Anabaptists themselves and by interpreting it as a *radical form of social responsibility*. Among the leaders in this effort has been Harold S. Bender, longtime editor of the *Mennonite Quarterly Review* and coeditor of *The Mennonite Encyclopedia*, and Guy F. Hershberger, author of several works on Anabaptist ethics, including *War, Peace and Nonresistance* and *The Way of Cross in Human Relations*, published in 1944 and 1958.[63]

The pioneering efforts of these and other scholars have come to increasingly influential fruition in the work of John Howard Yoder. Yoder is a Mennonite historian and theologian whose prolific writings have earned him the respect, if not embrace, of many Christian thinkers outside his own religious community. The ecumenical *Christian Century*, for example, called his best-known work, *The Politics of Jesus*, one of the finest religious books of the 1970s.[64]

The recipient of this goodwill is solidly Anabaptist in outlook. Yoder's basic ethical claim involves rejection of the usual opinion—classically expressed by Reinhold Niebuhr—that the life and teaching of Jesus cannot be normative for social ethics. He urges that in order to be faithful to its roots, Christian moral thought must attend resolutely to the New Testament story of God's incarnation in a human being. According to this story, he says, the "will of God is . . .

concretely knowable in the person and ministry of Jesus."[65]

Yoder says, furthermore, that through the incarnation, God did not ratify "nature as revelation." On the contrary, he "broke through the borders of [humanity's] definition of what is human, and gave a new, formative definition in Jesus."[66] This means that Jesus is the criterion not just of personal ethics but of social ethics as well. In his actions, teachings, cross, and resurrection, the man Jesus provides the normative pattern for Christian life. Furthermore, this pattern is socially and politically relevant today. (This is the thesis worked out at length in *The Politics of Jesus.*)

For Yoder nothing can lead the Christian out of conformity with the way of life Jesus himself displayed. The *basic* issue in Christian ethics "is whether to set up beside the Jesus of the canon and the creeds some other specific sources and contents of ethical obligation."[67]

Both the power of Yoder's argument and its bearing on our thesis justify attending at considerable length to his views. For now we may simply observe that these "obsolescent" views are eliciting a broad and respectful notice. My thesis invokes a heritage of social teaching usually rejected and often execrated, but it connects with matters about which there is growing curiosity.

RECENT CONCERN WITH THE PROBLEM OF CHRIST AND CULTURE

At the root of this curiosity lies the tension between Christ's authority and the influence of the wider culture. Many writers throughout Christian history have given study to this tension. In recent decades, however, it has been an especially riveting concern. Nineteenth-century Protestant liberals stressed the immanence of God in nature and in history. They saw God as present within an evolutionary development to higher forms of life and culture.

The horrors of World War I, however, challenged this easy optimism. The revolt against liberal theology appears most explicitly in the writings of Karl Barth.[68] God, said Barth in his commentary on the book of Romans, "must never be identified with anything which we name, or experience, or conceive, or worship, as God."[69]

In thus affirming the radical transcendence of God, Barth underlined the difference between God and his creatures. The negative implication of this was that God is judge of finite existence. God is not to be identified with it.[70]

The Social Teachings of the Christian Churches,[71] the masterwork by Ernst Troeltsch, was first published before World War I. It provided a perspective and a vocabulary in light of which many later scholars—notably H. Richard Niebuhr himself—carried out their inquiries into the relation of Christ and culture.

But in an age reeling from violence and greed, it was the Barthian theme of the judgment of God that spurred such inquiries. We see this theme in the writings of Bonhoeffer, Tillich, and the brothers Niebuhr. Among prominent strands of more recent Christian social thought, we see it still: in German political theology, for example; in the liberation theology of Latin America; in the feminist theology in the United States. What is common to all of these is a word of judgment on what now is and a call to a truer way of being Christian in the world.

That Yoder is eliciting a broader hearing for the Anbaptist way than ever before accords, then, with the direction of much of twentieth-century theology. It may indeed be an appropriate outgrowth of theology's response to the century's agony.

The commitment to nonviolence is the most striking aspect, perhaps, of the Anabaptist emphasis upon the tension between the way of Christ and the way of the wider culture. Even here Yoder and the modern Anabaptists are not alone. Many writers not themselves the direct descendants of Anabaptism have been exploring and defending Christian forms of nonviolence. Jacques Ellul, the French sociologist and theologian, has been doing this,[72] and so has Martin Hengel, the German biblical scholar.[73] The American theologian Stanley Hauerwas has been doing it,[74] and before him the distinguished activists Martin Luther King and Dorothy Day were doing it—with their lives as provocatively as with their writings. All of this underscores again the connection between the present thesis and interests now very much alive.

THE BIBLE, ETHICS, AND TRADITION

We have noticed reasons for thinking this is the right season to set forth and defend a thesis such as I am proposing. Historians have opened our eyes to what the Anabaptist movement was. Its heirs are creating a modern and noteworthy interpretation of Anabaptist social doctrine. And its ethos meshes with the recent, prominent theme in theology of real tension between Christ and the wider culture. Two other considerations further buttress this idea.

The first is the present interest within Christian circles in the relationship of the Bible and ethics. The Anabaptists had a strong sense of the authority of Scripture, especially the Jesus story, for the shaping of Christian life. While the Bible has always figured strongly in the moral traditions of Judaism and Christianity, there has been increasing concern to bring biblical studies and religious ethics into dialogue.[75]

Several ways of conceiving the relation of Scripture and ethics have emerged in recent discussion. Some writers, for example, have urged that there is a "unitary biblical ethic" (Carl F. H. Henry)[76] which is the wholly adequate foundation for Christian character and decision-making. Others have doubted the relevance of biblical ethics for moral life today. Jack Sanders, for example, emphasizes the connection between the moral vision attributed to Jesus and the imminence motif in the New Testament. He claims that on the whole the New Testament provides no help in shaping an ethics valid for a world that goes on and on.[77]

Some, less sanguine than Carl Henry about the supposed unity of the biblical ethic, have argued nevertheless that the Bible story should shape Christian life. Stanley Hauerwas, for example, maintains that the Bible's moral authority consists precisely in shaping, through the story it passes on, the identity and character of the people of God. This identity and character, he claims, will be distinctly different from that of peoples who do not similarly attend to Scripture.[78] Others have emphasized that the Bible is a central (but not exclusive) resource for learning right principles of action.[79]

It is not germane at present to consider this discussion in detail, though we will return to it in coming chapters. What matters here is this: the debate is lively and the disagreement substantial. Our present concern clearly involves the relation of the Bible and ethics. We have thus connected it to a problem that is at the heart of current discussion in Christian ethics.[80]

Another consideration links our thesis with present interest, and that is recent philosophical studies concerning the force of traditions on human understanding. In the early part of the century, Martin Heidegger effectively argued that our culture inescapably shapes our worldview. We can never have a fully detached, spectator relation to an object of study. Whether in ethics or natural science or whatever, we are *already* caught up in an understanding passed along in the language, beliefs, and social practices we have inherited.[81]

A later figure, Hans-Georg Gadamer, has made similar points. He attempts to show how human beings can grow in understanding through openness to what the cultural heritage reveals—through openness, that is, to the authority of tradition.[82]

If we turn from the continent to England we notice Wittgenstein, whose later philosophy exhibits a similar outlook. He had once said that true propositions describe how things are.[83] In the *Philosophical Investigations* he rejects this. In saying, "This is how things are," one may think that "he is tracing the outline of a thing's nature." In fact, claims the later Wittgenstein, "one is merely tracing round the frame through which we look at it."[84]

How we look at things depends on our language. Moreover, how we talk depends on our social practices. Even speaking a language "is part of an activity, or of a form of life."[85]

These points significantly discount the possibility of a morality independent of the religious tradition of the community that holds it. This view is still widely accepted,[86] but what we have just been noticing raises this question about it: How can religion be singled out as an element of a community's tradition whose impact on morality can be overcome? Since we are dealing here with a moral vision rooted precisely in a religious tradition, this question and the insights behind it will certainly have a bearing on our discussion. Even now, though sketchily outlined, they rescue the ethical Christocentrism with which my thesis is bound from sheer outlandishness.

TESTING THE THESIS

By now we have noticed the dilemma from which our inquiry springs. While belonging to cultures in some degree at odds with Christ, Christians are to make Christ Lord, the supreme criterion of life. How, then, ought they understand the relationship between the one who is their Lord and the cultures of which they are inescapably a part? How ought they differ from, and contribute to, the wider human community?

We have, in the second place, marked down a thesis. We have filled it out with a sketch of the Niebuhrian analysis and Anabaptist vision in which it is stated. We have acknowledged developments in the Christian church's social doctrine in light of which the thesis may seem merely deviant. We have further advanced reasons to take it seriously in spite of this. What now remains is to show how we will develop and test the the claim in the chapters to come.

The concern here is with theological ethics. Since, however, the parts of theology presuppose one another, what we say will touch on a broad range of Christian doctrines, especially the doctrine of the church. Still, the focus will be on theological ethics.

As with any theological discussion, how we proceed will affect crucially the conclusions to which we finally come. We need now, however, to distinguish the general question of method in Christian ethics from that of our procedure for this particular project. Throughout the pages to come an underlying and sometimes explicit theme will be that of *method*. How are we to go about ethical investigations claiming to be Christian? A perspective on this theme, and a defense of that perspective, will emerge during the study. Our present concern is the more limited one of saying how this particular study will proceed.

We will, first of all, undertake to achieve greater clarity about the problem itelf. The next chapter considers Niebuhr's own analysis. We will look at a broad range of his published works, especially, of course, *Christ and Culture*. Although the typology and Niebuhr's own attraction to the transformationist motif will figure prominently in the chapter, our special focus will be on *how he conceives the question*. We will first set forth and analyze the conception in *Christ and Culture*, and then, using his other works, try to arrive at a more adequate statement of the problem of Christ and culture.

In the next three chapters we will explore the problem further by examining selected writings on social ethics by nine theologians of today: Langdon Gilkey, Bernard Haering, John Macquarrie, Johannes Metz, Rosemary Radford Ruether, Gustavo Gutierrez, Stanley Hauerwas, Donald Bloesch, and John Howard Yoder. Without claiming to unfold the entire vision of any of these authors, we will consider certain of their positions in order, first, to place prominent recent treatments of Christian social doctrine under the light of Niebuhr's own achievement. At the same time we will see how these treatments clarify the question we are asking and how they contribute insight toward an answer to that question. Finally, we will notice the diversity of current views in light of which a new proposal would have to be evaluated.

A sixth and final chapter will present a constructive elaboration of the thesis. The aim will be to show why the Anabaptist way is the true Niebuhrian way and also to spell out the meaning of this claim in more detail. In doing this I will make two uses of our survey of recent Christian social doctrine. I will appropriate the wisdom of the writers to develop and refine my own vision and use it also to bring out potential objections to that vision. In part the chapter will consist in the attempt to meet these objections.

Although this entire proceeding is highly revisionary, I must emphasize before going further that it is in no way hostile to Niebuhr. It will involve, to be sure, criticism of Niebuhr's picture, but it will also betray an indebtedness to him as important as its indebtedness to the Radical Reformation. This will become immediately evident.

CHAPTER • TWO

What Was Niebuhr's Real Question?

INTRODUCTION

Only in culture, with its language and practices, beliefs and institutions, can human life develop and flourish. Christians as surely as others depend upon it for their very humanity. Indeed, if we may slightly modify one of H. Richard Niebuhr's own remarks,[1] Christians are in culture as fish are in water.

Yet what nourishes human life also imposes burdens upon it. Culture supports a variety of outlooks and ways of being human, engendering not only pleasing diversity but also painful conflict. It is this conflict that gives rise to what Niebuhr called the problem of Christ and culture.

As we noted earlier, Jesus Christ is for Christians the proper object of final loyalty and the proper criterion of character and conduct. Yet the wider culture—of which Christians are part and on which they necessarily depend—embraces persons and communities who uphold other ideals and urge other loyalties. The general cast of the wider culture clashes to some degree with what Christian conviction upholds. The result is a dilemma. Followers of Christ can neither endorse their cultures fully nor reject them altogether. Thus they must ask not *whether* to participate in cultural life, but *how* to do so and *why*.

These words tell roughly what the problem of Christ and culture is about. H. Richard Niebuhr took the questions connected with it to be "the essential problem of Christianity."[2] His book *Christ and Culture*, published in 1951, made the title phrase a commonplace in the theological vocabulary. In this chapter we are going to use his book to gain a more finished comprehension of what the problem is. This will prepare the way for later substantive proposals concerning it.

The chapter will be, from beginning to end, a Niebuhrian reflection. We will first examine *Christ and Culture* itself, noting and evaluating its conception of the issue. We will turn next to some of Niebuhr's other books and articles. We will invoke the main themes of his entire vision as a means of clarifying and correcting what he says in *Christ and Culture*.

The goal will be to abstract from the main body of his works a conception of the problem adequate to Niebuhr's total theological perspective. Our analysis here will illuminate the explorations taken up in later chapters.

NIEBUHR ON THE "ENDURING PROBLEM"

We may start with Niebuhr's own focused treatment of the issue. In the opening chapter of *Christ and Culture*, "The Enduring Problem," he attempts to clarify the question that absorbed Troeltsch. Troeltsch had been eager in his discussion of Christian social doctrine to connect the Christian ethos positively to the life and tasks of society.[3] Some, he knew, doubted whether there was such a connection.

Niebuhr, who shares Troeltsch's concern, acknowledges this doubt at the beginning of his analysis. From the days of the early church onward, he says, critics have charged that Christ is the enemy of civilization. They have accused him of encouraging contempt for life in the present. They have reproached him for admonishing his followers to rely on grace instead of challenging them to accomplishment. They have said that his way, which questions all earthly loyalties, threatens civilization by being intolerant and divisive. They have said that his message of forgiveness conflicts with the claims of justice.

Niebuhr goes on to observe that Christians themselves have had questions about how Christ relates to culture. They have long debated this problem, whose "many forms" include questions "of reason and revelation, of religion and science, of natural and divine law, of state and church, of nonresistance and coercion."[4]

He emphasizes that the issue concerns how Christians should regard the authority of Christ vis-à-vis the commitments of culture.

> When Christianity deals with the question of reason and revelation, what is ultimately in question is the relation of the revelation in *Christ* to the reason which prevails in *culture*. When it makes the effort to distinguish, contrast, or combine rational ethics with its knowledge of the will of God, it deals with the understanding of right and wrong developed in the culture and with good and evil as illuminated by Christ.[5]

At the outset Niebuhr's analysis contains several elements worth noting. The first is an ambiguity. In cataloging the typical criticisms of Chrisianity, he writes as though the issue is whether Christ is the friend or foe of civilized life as such. Later, however, the problem of Christ and culture is said to involve "the relation of these two authorities"[6]—the relation, that is, between the influence of Christ and the influence of the culture at large.

In other words, the discussion first evokes the question: Is Christ concerned at all with cultural life? Then it evokes another: What is the relation between his moral authority and the moral authority of the culture in which the Christian lives? We will want to get a clearer sense of what his question really is.

The second element to note concerns another ambiguity, Niebuhr's contrast between Christ and reason. In the sentences just quoted, Niebuhr distinguishes the revelation given in Christ from "the reason which prevails in culture." Here reason is relativized somewhat, linked to the reigning cultural outlook. Then, however, Niebuhr distinguishes the moral knowledge derived from the Christ story from what he calls "rational ethics." He uses this term without qualification, suggesting a neutral, as opposed to relative, moral standpoint. Here, too, we need a clearer idea of what he is saying.

A third element is his use of the terms *Christ* and *culture* in a way that separates one from the other. The "revelation in Christ" contrasts with the reason dominant "in culture," as though Christ, the Word made flesh on earth, were not himself a part of culture. This also is something to consider more before we finish.

We may turn now to Niebuhr's treatment of the terms in the book's key phrase. He attempts, first, a "definition" of Christ. In so doing, he observes that Jesus Christ is "the key to . . . understanding . . . themselves and their world, the main source of the knowledge of God and [humanity], good and evil, the constant companion of the conscience, and the expected deliverer from evil."[7] This Christ, he allows, has been variously interpreted. Yet there always remain the "original portraits."[8] We can always compare and correct the differing interpretations in light of these original portraits.

Christians are thus secure against having nothing to say toward a definition of Christ. Even so, what they do say about him will necessarily be inadequate. He was a person whose essence cannot be fully expressed in propositions. In any case, our thinking itself is relative to the standpoint we occupy in church, history, and culture.[9]

Niebuhr attempts, nonetheless, to say something about the "essence" of Jesus Christ, focusing to begin on his virtues or "excellences of character."[10] One of these, magnified above all others by Protestant liberalism, is love. Harnack said love is the root and single motive of Jesus' moral life. Niebuhr reacts to Harnack by insisting that it is misleading to speak of Christ's love without linking it with his devotion to the one God of all the universe. God, not love, is for him the one absolute good. And the virtue of love is "*the love of God and of the neighbor in God*, not the virtue of the love of love."[11]

Niebuhr considers both the synoptic and Johannine versions of the love commandment. He argues that nothing, not even liberalism's much-prized "human soul," has value for Jesus apart from God. For Jesus, *worth*—even the worth of neighbor—"is worth in relation to God." Despite Harnack's claim, it "was not love but God that filled his soul."[12]

Another classic view has been associated with Albert Schweitzer. It sees Jesus primarily as a man of hope, oriented entirely by the expectation of supernatural consummation. Niebuhr grants that hope is important to Jesus, but again reproaches what he sees as a failure to connect virtue in Christ clearly with God. At bottom, his was not hope in a dogma about the shortness of time or hope for a transformed nature. It was a hope "in God and for God." It was his sense of "sonship to God," not an eschatological belief, that was "the key to Jesus' ethics."[13]

Still another virtue of Jesus—the master virtue according to Bultmann—is obedience. For Bultmann this is not conformity to an ethical standard given by God. It is Jesus' faithful assent to what he himself, as a free and responsible person, sees his duty to be. Niebuhr objects, however, to Bultmann's failure to find "real content in the gospel idea of obedience." In fact, he writes,

> The Jesus who is radically obedient knows that the will of God is the will of the creator and Governor of all nature and of all history; that there is structure and content in His will; that He is the author of the ten commandments; that He demands mercy and not sacrifice; that He requires not only obedience to Himself but love and faith in Him, and love of the neighbor whom He creates and loves.[14]

Jesus knows, moreover, that God, through the gifts of love and faith, makes obedience possible. All of this means that in Niebuhr's view, one cannot adequately portray virtue in Jesus apart from its relation to God. His obedience was an obedience *before God*, the God whose will and way we learn from the story in Scripture.

Niebuhr similarly analyzes other virtues of Jesus. His faith is faith in God, not faith in human beings or human institutions. His humility is humility before God, not "inferiority-feeling" before men.[15] Thus what stands out among Jesus' virtues is his "unique devotion to God," his "single-hearted trust in him." This devotion and trust is symbolized by the affirmation that he is Son of God.

The *Christ* in the phrase *Christ and culture* is thus the one who points us away from finite values to the Maker of all things. And because he loves this God "with the perfection of human *eros*," he is in perfect unity with God. He thus regards men and women as God does, "with the perfection of divine *agape*, since God is *agape*."[16] He is the "focusing point" of God's movement toward *us* as much as he is the "focusing point" of *our* movement toward God.[17]

With *culture* Niebuhr has in mind that "total process" and "total result" of human activity called *culture* or *civilization* in ordinary speech. Culture "is the 'artificial, secondary environment' which [human beings] superimpose on the nature. It comprises language, habits, ideas, beliefs, customs, social organization, inherited artifacts, technical processes, and values."[18] It is the "social heritage" individuals receive and use and pass along.[19] It is something human effort achieves. It comes into being to serve human purposes and goals.

Niebuhr then points back to the problem he means to clarify. He says the traits he has listed are those of a "culture which lays its claim on every Christian, and under the authority of which he also lives when he lives under the authority of Christ."[20]

We noticed before an ambiguity in Niebuhr's view of what the problem of Christ and culture is. Sometimes it concerns whether Christ is friend or foe of culture as such. Sometimes it's how to understand the "relation of these two authorities."[21] By saying that the authority of both Christ and culture impinges on every Christian, Niebuhr here evokes the latter of these conceptions. If we combine this conception with Niebuhr's remarks about the two key terms, we get something like this:

On the one hand, there is the authority of that person who, through his life and ministry and fate, points us unambiguously to the one supreme good, the Creator God. In so doing, he displays unambiguously the love of this God for creation.

On the other hand, there is the authority of the "man-made and man-intended." This includes everything—whether language, customs, artifacts, ideas, or values—that is humanly superimposed upon nature. The problem is, how ought we conceive the relation of these authorities?

John Howard Yoder has written a largely unsympathetic critique of *Christ and Culture*. He charges Niebuhr with treating Christ and culture as though they were entirely separate from each other.[22] We found in Niebuhr's initial description of the problem of Christ and culture evidence that could support this allegation. We find it, too, when we apply his definitions. There is Christ on the one hand. There is culture on the other.

However, even though Niebuhr does appear to separate the two, it is on his own terms absurd to do so. For in Niebuhr's picture, Jesus Christ lived on earth as a flesh-and-blood person. He was a definite human being with a definite character and history, even though he is truly the Son of God.[23] This means that he was himself a cultural figure, a participant in cultural life. If he was human, then he employed language, entertained ideas, held beliefs. He embodied customs and played a role in social institutions. He used artifacts, mastered technical processes, and adhered to values. In short, he inherited and contributed to the social heritage. That is, he inherited and contributed to culture as Niebuhr defines it.

We must acknowledge, then, a certain confusion in Niebuhr's account. But there does remain, I will argue, a *working* conception of the problem, distinguishable from the *stated* one, that is coherent and illuminating.

Consider his exposition of the *Christ-against-culture* perspective. He does, we must grant, begin with an unsuitable description. This perspective, he writes, "uncompromisingly affirms the sole authority of Christ over the Christian and resolutely rejects culture's claims to loyalty."[24] This is puzzling since Niebuhr's definitions of the key terms imply that the authority or influence of culture inevitably affects us all. Moreover, the one who has "sole authority" over the Christian was himself human, according to Niebuhr. And since this *means* that he participated in cultural life, one cannot appeal to *him* as the basis for rejecting culture altogether.

Some of Niebuhr's remarks, however, suggest that he has something else in mind. We see this especially in his treatment of Tertullian, whom we are told displayed the *Christ-against-culture* attitude "in radical fashion."[25]

As background for remarks about Tertullian, Niebuhr says that Christian writers of the earliest period typically interpreted Christ as having founded a "new society" very unlike the "old society."[26] This conviction came to expression, for example, in the doctrine of the two ways. According to *The Didache*, there is "one of life and one of death, but there is a great difference between the two ways."[27]

Tertullian exemplified this outlook. For him Jesus Christ was absolute authority, the enlightener of the human race. He was the declarer of the Father's will, the Lord through whom we worship God. He espoused a "rigorous morality of obedience" to Christ's commands. This included, Niebuhr tells us, "not only love of the brothers but of enemies, nonresistance to evil, prohibitions of anger, and the lustful look."[28] Tertullian thus pictured the surrounding society as corrupt and degrading, studded with idols, and abounding in sensuality. It was a constant threat to Christian loyalty to Christ.

Tertullian denied that Christians are "useless in the affairs of life." They live in the world, engage in commerce, and till the ground. Yet he urged them to withdraw from activities and occupations inconsistent with Christ's will. They have no business, for example, seeking political power. They ought also to avoid military service, since Christ "in disarming Peter, unbelted every soldier."[29]

Tertullian, furthermore, was deeply distrustful of Greek philosophy, as well as of the theater. He was thus a foremost exemplar, as Niebuhr sees it, of "the anticultural movement" within the history of the church. He was of a piece with others who "present Christianity as a way of life quite separate from culture."[30]

This way of putting the matter is not exactly suitable, as we have begun to see. Tertullian employed language and artifacts in his writing. He played a role in the church, which was a social institution. He exhibited values strongly held. It is true that he opposed reliance on the wisdom of philosophers, recoiled from political power and military service, and condemned the theater. But that does not, according to Niebuhr's definition of culture, make him anticultural nor the advocate of Christian life apart from culture. It makes him, rather, the foe of certain *ways* of being cultural, of certain *expressions* of cultural existence. He was not antagonistic to culture per se. Rather, he advocated a different cultural option.[31]

In his evaluation of the *Christ-against-culture* position, Niebuhr notes some of these very considerations. We all—Tertullian included—live in necessary dependence upon culture. We cannot think or speak, for example, unless we have a language. Even radical Christians, therefore, "are always making use of the culture, or parts of culture, which ostensibly they reject."[32] Niebuhr's point is that no thoroughgoing *Christ-against-culture* position can be consistent. While this is certainly true, the very idea of "Christ against culture" is logically impossible given the definitions of the terms. The phrase literally makes no sense. Niebuhr, however, does not appear to recognize this.

If this is so, the term *Christ-against-culture* cannot be an entirely adequate name for a type of Christian social doctrine. We may still ask, however, what he is really trying to tell us. A clue lies in a further criticism he directs against Tertullian and other champions of separatist Christianity.

Christians, says Niebuhr, have always depended on the surrounding culture in order to fill out their understanding of Christian existence. The words of Jesus did not answer all the questions of daily life, so early Christians learned from Jewish-Hellenistic ethics. Benedict could not find scriptural support for all his counsels concerning monastic life, so he, too, resorted to wisdom not written in the Bible. Tertullian and Tolstoy illustrate the same tendency.

"When Tertullian recommends modesty and patience," says Niebuhr, "Stoic overtones are always present. . . . When Tolstoy speaks of nonresistance, Rousseauistic ideas are in the context." Then Niebuhr adds, "Even if no use were made of another inheritance besides that derived from Jesus Christ, the needs of the withdrawn community would lead to the development of a new culture."[33]

Alluding to his previous listing of the traits of culture, he explains that human achievement, social organization, and attempts to realize value are all involved. Thus even a community of the *Christ-against-culture* type would manifest a cultural existence. Here he seems to agree that Tertullian was not the enemy of culture as such but the champion of a particular cultural option.[34]

We have taken a step toward seeing how in the full course of his exposition Niebuhr understands the *Christ-against-culture* position. We will now consider the use of the term *culture* in his chapter on this position.

Here is a position, he says, that affirms Christ's "sole authority" and "resolutely rejects culture's claims to loyalty."[35] This admittedly is strange as it stands. The authority of Christ is itself a cultural phenomenon, and so not something totally distinct from "culture's claims to loyalty." But a remark we find later in the chapter helps. Having discussed Tolstoy and then virtually repeated his opening characterization, he then says it would be easy to multiply illustrations of the *Christ-against-culture* type of thinker. They would be, to be sure, a diverse group from many Christian traditions. Still, their "unity of spirit" would be apparent. It would be apparent, he says, in their "common acknowledgment of the sole authority of Jesus Christ and their common rejection of the prevailing culture."[36] The *prevailing* culture. With the help of this adjective we see that in this context, *culture* signifies *the dominant way of life*.

We saw earlier that, according to Niebuhr's definitions, Christ is part of culture. Thus any conceivable community of his followers itself expresses a form of cultural existence. Now we can hold on to these conclusions and still make sense of remarks by Niebuhr that might otherwise remain puzzling.

Niebuhr says, for example, that the most popular books of Tertullian's age "present Christianity as a way of life quite separate from culture."[37] We must take this to mean that they present Christianity as a way of life unmistakably different from the prevailing one. There is support for this, not just in the term *culture* itself but also in a later explanatory remark.

Whatever the theological differences among these books, Niebuhr tells us, the Christian life is seen as "life in a new and separated community."[38] Elsewhere in the chapter he uses phrases such as *withdrawn community* and *exclusively Christian community*[39] to describe the form church life takes in the *Christ-against-culture* point of view. According to Niebuhr's original treatment of the term *culture*, life in human community is by definition cultural. It is thus clear that the perspective we are here considering embodies itself in a distinct *type* of cultural existence.

If, then, this is not truly a *Christ-against-culture* perspective, how may we characterize it? Under Niebuhr's own description this perspective sets Christ in opposition, not to culture per se, but to the dominant way of life. It sees Christ's authority as final for Christians in such a way as to require clear divergence from broadly accepted patterns of behavior and modes of thought. It requires, too, sheer refusal to participate in certain social institutions, such as the military, even if non-Christians should deem them absolutely indispensable. It is a type of Christianity propounding what Niebuhr calls "the radical answer"[40] to the problem of Christ and culture. In intention, at least, it brooks no compromise between the New Testament witness to Christ and the way of the world.

By noting the types of social doctrine Niebuhr identifies, we are trying to advance our understanding of the problem of Christ and culture. To do this we do not need to treat all the types in detail. We will come back to a fuller exposition of the *Christ-the-transformer-of-culture* approach, but we will first consider briefly the key phrases in the rest of the typology.

We will first apply what we have noticed about the phrase *Christ-against-culture* to the phrases *Christ-above-culture* and

Christ-in-paradox-with-culture. Given Niebuhr's definitions, they, too, lack a clear meaning. We can understand them only by interpreting the term *culture* to mean *prevailing* culture, or dominant way of life.

Given the definitions, the phrase *Christ-of-culture*, is certainly sensible. But it is somewhat vague. It might mean that Christ has cultural traits, or is a product of culture, or is part of culture. Such meanings, however, do not illuminate a particular type of Christian social doctrine. Again, in Niebuhr's actual usage the term *culture* means dominant way of life. The defining feature here is thus the *"accommodation"*[41] of Christianity to the prevailing culture.

The analysis of the *Christ-the-transformer-of-culture* type of social doctrine differs from the others. Here the term *culture* apparently means what Niebuhr declares it to mean in his definition: everything man-made and man-intended. He says that writers who exemplify this approach envision through Christ the transformation of "life in the world," of "mankind in all its nature and culture," of human beings in their culture.[42] They see the world as God's creation and therefore good. They recognize, in words Niebuhr quotes from F. D. Maurice, "the sacredness of our life here" and repudiate all "Manichaean notions that the earth or the flesh is the devil's creature and property."[43]

With such conviction central, the transformationists see Christ as the converter of the total process and result of human activity. This image seems capable of illuminating Christian social doctrine. We will be returning to it in later chapters.

Near the beginning of his remarks on conversionist doctrine, however, Niebuhr attempts to distinguish it from that of "radical" thinkers, and here we discover an inconsistency. "Though they hold fast to the radical distinction between God's work in Christ and man's work in culture," he writes of the conversionists, "they do not take the road of exclusive Christianity into isolation from civilization, or reject its institutions with Tolstoyan bitterness."[44]

Notice first that *civilization* is to Niebuhr a rough synonym for *culture.*[45] So he is telling us that proponents of transformationist thought differ from radicals in not rejecting culture. But this claim can only make sense if the word *culture* refers to the prevailing way of life. Yet in the surrounding context, *culture* means everything man-made and man-intended. Niebuhr must therefore mean one thing by this word when he is describing the transformationist approach and another when he distinguishes the approach from its rivals. That he thus resorts to using a key term inconsistently raises a further question. Is *Christ-the-transformer-of-culture* at all a lucid marker for a *type* of Christian social doctrine? Further reflection exacerbates the doubt. Many theological adversaries would agree that Christ *alters* culture, while remaining very much at odds over *how* he does so.

Our goal here is to gain a more finished conception of what the problem of Christ and culture is really about. To this point we have focused on one of Niebuhr's works, a book devoted entirely to the questions with which we are concerned. We can now summarize what we have learned.

Niebuhr says, in epitomizing "the enduring problem," that it is a matter of the relation between two authorities—Christ on the one hand and culture on the other. If we apply the given definitions, however, it turns out that this is an unhappy dichotomy. Culture does have "authority"; it unfailingly shapes us all. But it makes no sense to oppose Christ's authority to that of culture since Christ is part of culture and his authority part of the authority of culture.

In presenting his typology, Niebuhr bears witness to this by abandoning this conception of the problem. His question has to do rather with two broad concerns. First, does Christ value cultural existence positively? And second, how does his authority relate to the way of life presently dominant in culture?

To this point, then, we can say this about the operative conception of the problem of Christ and culture in Niebuhr. As the "focusing point" of God's movement toward *us* and of *our* movement toward God, Jesus Christ has authority over Christian life. How, then, ought Christians esteem earthly or cultural existence? And how ought they regard that authority in relation to the authority of the way of life now dominant in culture?

NIEBUHR'S TOTAL PERSPECTIVE: IN SEARCH OF FURTHER CLARITY

We may turn now, though in less detail, to others of Niebuhr's published works. Rather than dealing with each separately, we will identify the broad outlines of Niebuhr's entire theological position. From writings not yet treated we will attempt to illuminate their significance. In all of this our purpose will be that of filling out and correcting the results of our study so far. The ethical theme of the analysis will befit well a body of thought whose author focused on moral implications of the Christian gospel.[46]

Let us begin with Niebuhr's conception of the human condition in general and follow with his proposals concerning Christian existence in particular.[47] We may mark down to begin his conviction of the "radically historical character" of all human life. In autobiographical reflections published in 1960, Niebuhr says that from "long before" the 1930s this conviction shaped his outlook.[48]

In *The Meaning of Revelation*, published in 1941, this conviction is central to the entire study. Nothing has more deeply affected the twentieth-century outlook, he says, "than the discovery of spatial and temporal relativity." This has brought recognition that the place we occupy in space and time conditions all our knowledge. Our reasoning, too, is so conditioned. Even the concepts we use reflect the "particular society" in which we have grown up.

Thus there is no such thing as "pure" or "universal" reason. We are in time. We are part of a history, part of an unfolding story. Time is in us. The history out of which we come affects not only what we believe but how we see and think. Thus "if reason is to operate at all it must be content to work as an historical reason."[49]

Late in his life, and in different language, Niebuhr makes a similar point. He affirms with George Herbert Mead "the fundamentally social character of selfhood."[50] One becomes a self, he says in his postumously published book, *The Responsible Self*, not in isolation from others but through membership in a human community. It is from our social companions that we pick up our language, our patterns of behavior and thought, our ways of interpreting impressions on our senses, our modes of moral life, and of interpersonal interaction. Thus the self is shaped by what has gone before it. "The categories of historical reason largely determine what it can now know and how it will now respond."[51]

Yet the fact that we are historical beings does not make our thoughts entirely unreliable. We have a particular angle of vision, it is true. Still, we may approach, at least, a knowledge of what is. Our individual interpretations, he says in *The Meaning of Revelation*, may be tested through conversations with companions in our own communities.[52] Moreover, even though we cannot fully comprehend those who do not share our history, we may still with benefit check ourselves against their assessments of us. The wall separating persons in one historical community from those in others is substantial but not impenetrable.[53]

Our second point concerning the human condition has to do with value.[54] According to a 1952 essay by Niebuhr, we usually seek those things that meet our needs, fit our capacities, and enhance our potential. Whatever does so has positive value. Whatever gets in the way has negative value. Nothing can have either type of value *in itself*, but only in its relations with beings for whom it can be good or bad.

Furthermore, in seeking after things that have positive value we are looking for a *center* of value around which to orient our lives. Niebuhr believes that all of us notice sooner or later "that we cannot live without a cause, without some object of devotion, some center of worth, something on which we rely for our meaning."[55]

We may have several such centers of value, or "gods," as he calls them; "our natural religion is polytheistic."[56] We may, for example, make the self a god and also our families, jobs, countries, ideologies, or churches. Less frequently we may deify a single value. Evolutionary ethics, does this, for example, when it fastens upon life itself as the center of value.[57] In any case, Niebuhr claims, we characteristically attach ourselves to a focal value. We have "faith" in these values. We trust them and are loyal to them. Such attachments, or relations, are pivotal in making us the selves we are.

A third crucial aspect of Niebuhr's view of the human condition is his conception of the moral life. The key term here is *responsibility*. Moral life is responsible life. In unpacking this idea we are going to see its close alliance with points we have made about the connection of human being to history and to value. So far what we have noticed above all is the importance of *relations* in the constitution of the self. We have noticed its relation to history and society and its relation to values.

The same motif is at the heart of the concept of responsibility. We are responsible when we acknowledge fully the presence of other selves whose lives, words, and deeds address and challenge us. The self, Niebuhr tells us, following George Herbert Mead, comes to know about itself, to be a moral judge of itself as a result of dialogue with others and of response to the attitudes of others.[58] If in its relation to other beings the self takes this process of dialogue and response seriously, it is a responsible self, a moral self.[59]

Niebuhr's longest treatment of this theme occurs in *The Responsible Self.* This was published after his death and based upon lectures he did not have opportunity to revise for printed presentation. The book is nevertheless a pregnant display of his mature judgments about human moral existence.

Near the beginning he contrasts the "symbol" of responsibility with two other symbols, both immensely influential in Western moral thought. One is the symbol of the self as maker or artist. According to this image—Aristotle and Thomas are two examples of thinkers who relied upon this image—moral life consists primarily in aiming at goals. We are, as moral beings, artisans or craftsmen fashioning ourselves for some dominant purpose or *telos.*

Another main symbol of Western moral thought is that of the human person as citizen or legislator-lawkeeper. This image—of which Kant is a major patron—makes moral life a matter of creating and consenting to law. The right is a present demand, one that deserves respect without reference to future goals.

Both of these symbols are helpful, says Neibuhr, but neither wholly adequate. He thus offers *responsibility* as "an alternative or additional way of conceiving and defining" moral existence.[60]

Central here is the idea of the self as *answerer.* Moral life consists in *response* to the actions and address of the beings with whom the self is in relation. The question now is not, What goal shall I strive for? or, What is the law? It is, rather, What is fitting in light of the entire context?

This image has the advantage of tallying with how our lives actually go. It is not so much in the abstract pursuit of ideals or adherence to laws that we form the selves we are. It is rather in the meeting of actual challenges, in the reactions we give to what actually happens to us. Every day we find ourselves having to *respond* to action upon us. Also, of course, we find ourselves having to *answer* for how we respond.

This brings us to a second advantage of the image of responsibility. It gives prominence to the dialogue, the conversation with our fellows, in which we characterically engage. It shows that in responding to what happens to us, we must give an account of ourselves to others.

How can the responsible moral agent do what is fitting in light of the entire context? Niebuhr would note that all our responding involves interpretation. We identify, compare, analyze, and relate events in our lives so "they come to us not as brute actions, but as understood and as having meaning." Then he would say that the responses we make with the aid of these interpretations are fitting if they suit the "total interaction," or as he also puts it, "the total movement, the whole conversation." Ideally, our responsive actions should "fit into the whole as a sentence fits into a paragraph in a book."[61]

These remarks are suggestive, but somewhat obscure without further clarification. What does it mean to respond with the entire context in mind? It means dialogue, for one thing. It means consideration of what those around us say or would say. It also means paying attention to what really—beneath as well as on the surface—is happening in the events that impinge upon us. Of a sulking child or a nation at war, for example, we need to ask, What response is most appropriate in light of the total circumstances, past as well as present, and in light of what we may reasonably expect in the future?

The interpretation involved in answering such questions is *our* interpretation. So *we*, too, are part of the total context of which we need to be aware in our responding. In this responding we are "surrounded by" the sense we have of our own lifetimes, our own histories.[62] Patterns of interpretation shaped by these histories largely determine the responses we make.[63]

Here it is important to notice that we do not live, as Niebuhr reminds us, in a single, seamless society. We live in many communities—the family, the professional group, the nation.[64] And among these our religious community, the bearer of our "ultimate history," mediates the stories and images most influential on our responding.[65] In truly responsible moral existence, we acknowledge our history fully, knowing that we cannot in any case begin outside of it.[66]

Without giving slavish obeisance to our past, we let it shape us. We seek moral growth not by abandoning it but by seeking ever-deeper interpretations of its significance.[67]

We must thus give special heed to what we may call a shared history, or "shared story."[68] We must note as well what is actually going on around us and converse with those who do not share our history. In so doing, we attend responsibly to the entire context. When our actions suit this context, they have what Niebuhr calls the "character of fittingness."[69] They are appropriate to our whole life story as a sentence is appropriate to the book of which it is a part.

We are noticing the broad outlines of Niebuhr's theological position in order to enhance our understanding of his overall conception of the problem of Christ and culture. Having now considered his view of the human situation in general, we may take up his proposals about Christian existence in particular.

The central premise in Niebuhr's doctrine of revelation is the belief that human existence is radically historical in character. It is no less true of Christians than of others that their thinking betrays their history. Niebuhr acknowledges this in his interpretation of the term *revelation*. It refers, he says, to "something that has happened to us in our history which conditions all our thinking." It is something that gives us an identity, a sense of "what we are, what we are suffering and doing and what our potentialities are."[70] Revelation is that part of the history out of which we come that illuminates the other parts, including the history we are now making. It is that "special occasion" or "moment" providing us "with an image by ... which all the occasions of personal and common life become intelligible" and in light of which we carry on our reasoning.[71]

The key revelatory moment for Christians is Jesus Christ. His story tells not merely of a human life but also of God, who shows himself through that life and thus brings us to know ourselves.[72] In a passage worth quoting at length, Niebuhr writes:

> The preaching of the early Christian church was not an argument for the existence of God nor an admonition to follow the dictates of some common human conscience, unhistorical and supersocial in character. It was primarily a simple recital of the great events connected with the historical appearance of Jesus Christ and a confession of what had

happened to the community of his disciples. Whatever it was that the church meant to say, whatever was revealed or manifested to it could be indicated only in connection with an historical person and events in the life of his community. The confession referred to history and was consciously made in history.[73]

The point Niebuhr makes is that just as the memory of a story framed the outlook of early Christians, so it frames the outlook of Christians today. Theology, he said earlier, "must begin in Christian history and with Christian history because it has no other choice." Now, elaborating on the long quotation just given, he says that the church cannot say truly what it stands for "otherwise than by telling the story of its life."[74]

Hans Frei remarks that Niebuhr's thought is more Christocentric in *The Meaning of Revelation* (published in 1941) than in works published before or after it.[75] It is true, certainly, that other works warn against an attention so focused upon the Son as to exclude the Father and the Spirit or in some other way dim our vision of the one God whom the Son reveals. We may mention, for example, the 1947 essay on "The Doctrine of the Trinity and the Unity of the Church"[76] and the 1960 volume, *Radical Monotheism and Western Culture*.[77] Niebuhr's concerns in these writings, which are somewhat confusingly set forth, will bear further comment in a later chapter.

For now what matters is that even in *The Responsible Self*, the Jesus story is seen as central to Christian understanding. In words clearly reminiscent of ones we have been quoting from *The Meaning of Revelation*, he writes that

> in Christian life Jesus Christ is a symbolic form [or image] with the aid of which [human beings] tell each other what life and death, God and [humanity], are *like*. But even more he is a form which they employ as an *a priori*, an image, a scheme or pattern in the mind which gives form and meaning to their experience.[78]

The setting of this remark shows that by "Jesus Christ" Niebuhr refers to the Jesus of the gospel story. On this story the Christian community relies. With its aid, he tells us, each Christian self "guides and forms itself in its actions and its sufferings."[79]

We now see that Niebuhr's views of human historicity and of

Christian revelation obviously complement each other. So do his views of value in human life and of Christian faith in God. We have seen that value arises when there is a meeting of beings or entities able to assist or thwart the satisfaction of need or enhancement of potentiality. We have seen, too, that human beings characteristically rely on some focal value (or values) in which they trust to make their lives worth living.

The term *faith*, Niebuhr tells us in the 1960 volume, *Radical Monotheism and Western Culture*, refers precisely to the self's confidence in and loyalty to some *center* of value. Faith may be polytheistic, attaching the self to several nuclei of value. But then, in supplying no single, unifying focus, it destroys the self's integrity. Faith may also be henotheistic, centering on a single, though finite, center of value. But then, as in nationalism, for example, it excludes part of the universe from the sphere of what is valued. Thus, indifference, or even hostility, to that part is consistent with it and perhaps demanded by it.

In contrast with both of these, Jesus displayed a kind of faith called "radical" or "monotheistic." Here the value-center is single but not exclusive. Trust and loyalty go to God, "the principle of being itself," the "one beyond all the many, whence all the many derive their being, and by participation in which they exist."

Radical faith is a value relation to the one who himself values and thus establishes the worth of *all* being. In relation to him, whatever is, is good. Faithfulness to God's cause therefore involves "universal loyalty," a reverence for all that is, and a disavowal of ingroup/out-group distinctions.[80] With a faith like this the self achieves integrity. It "cannot remain internally divided as it pursues now one interest, now another, for all its loves are drawn together" in devotion to God and all that he has made.[81] Truly Christian faith is this monotheistic kind since the Jesus who exemplified it is the paradigm of a truly Christian existence.[82]

Niebuhr believes that moral life is responsible life in which we attend carefully to a shared story, to the full significance of what is going on around us, to the conversation we have with others. He also believes that Christian life is a distinctive kind of human existence. What makes it distinctive is the story on which it is nourished. We are beings "guided and formed by images in our minds," and for

Christians the image dominant above all is the one given in "the gospel story."[83]

The key to the story, in Niebuhr's view, is the monotheistic faith of Jesus. In the story Jesus considers himself answerable to God.[84] As the Christian pattern, Niebuhr writes in a 1946 essay, Jesus directs all Christians to the ideal of responsibility *to* God and responsibility *for* all that he has made.[85] More than pointing beyond himself to God, however, Jesus reveals God. He discloses the one to whom we are all accountable. This was the testimony of the early Christian community.

In light of that, responsibility before God means, for Christians, being answerable to "*God-in-Christ* and *Christ-in-God.*"[86] It means being answerable, that is, to the one for whose way and being the Jesus story provides the central clue. If we do not qualify the idea of responsibility in this way, Niebuhr tells us, we cannot in any historic sense call ourselves Christian.

We have seen that responsibility to God thus means responsibility for God's world, and this suggests the idea of the transformation of society. The idea is pivotal through all of Niebuhr's scholarly career. In his earliest published book, *The Social Sources of Denominationalism*, Niebuhr says that the church has a responsibility to transform a divided social order "into a kingdom of our Lord and of his Christ."[87]

In 1939 in his next book, *The Kingdom of God in America*, Niebuhr again urges the ideal of social transformation. In his 1946 essay on "The Responsibility of the Church for Society," he writes that the church is "social pioneer." It gives a "radical demonstration" of faith in God so that eventually all nations may be blessed.[88] Its ultimate objective, he says ten years later in *The Purpose of the Church and Its Ministry*, is "the *increase among men of the love of God and neighbor.*"[89]

The theme of social transformation implies a difference between the Christian understanding of moral responsibility and other understandings. Niebuhr clearly believes there is such a difference, but his discussion of it, though suggestive, is not clear. On the one hand he suggests a puzzling sort of continuity between the Christian moral outlook and that of others. One theme, for example, recurs in his (highly favorable) treatment of the transformationist motif in

Christ and Culture. It is that Christ does not really give a new law or new virtues, but rather, he converts and redirects the law and virtues that exist.[90]

This theme reflects ideas developed in his earlier book, *The Meaning of Revelation.* There, in deference to philosophers such as Socrates, Kant, and Hartmann, he seems to allow that our moral laws are the deliverance of "transcendent" or nonhistorical reason. "We recognize," he says, "that they were written on our hearts apart from revelation."[91] Yet a pivotal claim of the entire book is that revelation is fundamental to outlook, making even reason itself a historically conditioned phenomenon.

He speaks accordingly of a kind of change in the moral law that does take place as a result of revelation. First, revelation heightens the "imperativeness" of the law. We know now that it is the demand of one from whom there is no flight. In transgressing it we go against the very "grain of the universe." Second, revelation makes the moral law more extensive and intensive. We see that it is to be "universalized," for duty goes beyond neighbor and kinsman even to the enemy. Its demands defy all our moral rationalizations. The third and "greatest" change wrought upon the moral law by "God's revelation in Jesus Christ" is that the "imperative" becomes "indicative." Keeping the law now seems to us a genuine possibility. Thus, he says in summary, "revelation is the beginning of a revolutionary understanding and application of the moral law rather than the giving of a new law."[92]

Niebuhr's general theory, held to the end of his career, is that human life is radically historical. Even our reason is historical reason. The passage we have just reviewed suggests that moral reason is an exception to this general theory. Then it suggests that it is not an exception, and we wonder what exactly Niebuhr is saying.

Nor does his own exposition resolve the uncertainty. The first and third "change" he cites as resulting from revelation are in fact changes in *how we regard the law.* They do nothing to show that revelation alters the moral law itself. The second "change"—revelation universalizes the moral law—can be interpreted two ways. We could say that under the impact of revelation our attitude to the law changes. That is, we become willing to apply it in *all* our relationships. But then revelation has not changed the law itself. Or we could say that revelation transforms our belief in, say, "justice for members of the tribe" to belief in "justice for all." Then it has indeed changed the law. But what happens now to the law written on our hearts apart from revelation? Is it no longer written there? And how do we know the universalizing of our laws is what revelation contributes? Kant said the idea that true moral law is universal comes from pure reason alone.

There is, we must grant, confusion here. It might have been avoided had Niebuhr remained entirely faithful to his idea of human embeddedness in history. We find the idea through all his writings, most unmistakably in the mature thinking of his last work, *The Responsible Self*. He holds that our place in time and space conditions our knowledge, our action, and our evaluation. Certainly the images passed along in stories with which we identify condition us.

Often this idea comes through in his reflections on moral knowledge. A passage quoted earlier from *The Meaning of Revelation* describes the preaching of early Christians as the telling of a story. It was neither an argument for God's existence nor, significantly, "an admonition to follow the dictates of some common human conscience, *unhistorical and supersocial* in character." It was rather a confession referring to history and made in history.[93]

Hinted at in this is a denial of unhistorical moral knowledge. A stronger denial is implicit in Niebuhr's 1945 essay, "The Ego-Alter Dialectic and the Conscience." In this essay, Niebuhr connects the experience of inner moral judgment to the special history of the self.[94] As for *The Responsible Self*, we have already seen its claim that moral responsibility *requires* attention to our history, whose influence we cannot in any case escape.

These assertions, particularly when read in light of Niebuhr's general outlook, render baffling his claim that revelation gives no new law. He cannot mean, surely, that the "special occasion" in our history that is revelation for us illuminates everything *except* our understanding of the content of moral law.[95] I submit that in the overall Niebuhrian picture, the claim has no place. Our previous exposition gives adequate evidence already that this is so. An essay published in 1955 under the title "Introduction to Biblical Ethics" further buttresses the point.

Here Niebuhr traces the "development" of biblical ethics. He compares and contrasts the Book of the Covenant in Exodus, the writings of Amos, the sayings of Jesus in the Sermon on the Mount, and the letter of Paul to the Romans. The Sermon on the Mount, he says, "represents the essence of the ethical teaching of Jesus. It was probably designed by the writer of the First Gospel to be an incisive epitome of Christ's commandments to his disciples."

Then, significantly for us, he declares that it was meant as "a guide to conduct, a ... new law for Christians."[96] This flatly contradicts remarks in *Christ and Culture* and *The Meaning of Revelation* more often remembered. Yet it is consistent, as they are not, with his total outlook.[97]

Someone who, despite the general theory we have seen, objects that it is *this* statement about law that goes against the Niebuhrian grain, might wish to invoke the distinction Niebuhr makes between universal views and views *of* the universal. We do "regard the universal," he says, but the viewing is not alike in all human selves. We look from the standpoint of individuals in particular societies.[98] One might argue that in denying that Christ gives us a new law, Niebuhr is being faithful to this claim. The point would be that Christ revolutionizes our understanding of (universal) moral law by giving us a distinctive perspective on it.

In reply, we must first acknowledge that there *are* universal moral concepts—concepts common, that is, to all human communities. Alasdair MacIntyre has pointed out, for example, that the very idea of a human *community* entails that some notion of truth and justice has taken root.[99]

We all do, then, regard the universal in the sense of having our particular perspectives on these and other universal moral concepts. Niebuhr would say, however, that the perspectives we look from are those of our particular societies. They are perspectives shaped, as he would also say, by images and stories. And since from society to society the dominant images and stories differ markedly, our perspectives will differ markedly, too.

We can see this unmistakably if we imagine a moral argument between a feminist and an Islamic fundamentalist. They could both speak of "justice" and yet disagree as to the just treatment of adulterous women. It is puzzling, indeed, what Niebuhr could possibly have meant by ascribing to both of them a knowledge of the universal moral law. If it is simply that they share certain moral concepts, and are thus in some degree ethically bound together, we may agree with the point and object to the language used in communicating it.

The natural interpretation of the claim that persons from widely different backgrounds share a knowledge of the universal moral law is that they substantially agree in moral conviction. But in our world there is substantial, sometimes tragic, *disagreement* in moral conviction. This fact, which Niebuhr's overall theory helps to explain, requires us to deny a general knowledge of a universal moral law. The moral world is not that simple.

We may hold, as Niebuhr presumably would,[100] that the sharing of moral concepts makes edifying communication across the boundaries of particular societies possible, even if difficult.[101] That, however, does not justify the use of language that exaggerates the degree of moral unanimity among these societies. In light of this we may well accept Niebuhr's remark that Christ's Sermon on the Mount was meant as a "new law for Christians." In a world of moral variety it should not surprise us if the word of Christ differs from that of others. *That there is such a difference is what gives sense, indeed, to the whole Niebuhrian theme of social transformation through Christ.*

A REVISED STATEMENT OF THE PROBLEM

After our analysis of *Christ and Culture* we set down a statement of Niebuhr's *working* (as opposed to *stated*) conception of the problem of Christ and culture. Our overall goal is to abstract from the main body of his published works a conception of the problem that faithfully represents his entire theological position.

In investigating that position over the past few pages we have noticed several claims important for the attainment of this goal. One is that particular social circumstances condition our entire understanding, though without cutting us off completely from the possibility of fruitful conversation with those in different circumstances. Another, closely related to the first, is that moral responsibility involves attention to the implications of a shared history. Still another is that faith is a relation of trust and loyalty to some focal value (or values). A fourth claim of importance here is that the Jesus story is the special revelatory occasion illuminating all authentically Christian existence. A fifth (ambiguously attested in Niebuhr's own writings though demanded by their total impact) is that clear differences mark off responsible Christian moral existence from other kinds.

In *Christ and Culture* the working conception of the problem addressed in the book's title is roughly this: Jesus Christ has authority over Christian life. How, then, ought Christians esteem earthly, cultural existence? And how ought they regard that authority in relation to the authority of the way of life dominant in culture?

Now we can identify respects in which this statement of the problem is at least potentially misleading. It fails, in the first place, to convey clearly the variety of ways in which culture expresses itself. In *Christ and Culture* Niebuhr contrasts the authority of Christ with that of a seemingly monolithic culture. He does not, to be sure, deny the heterogeneity of the cultural life within which the believer must have a relation to Christ. But neither does he bring it out.

His general theory, however, clearly implies such heterogeneity. The world obviously harbors a variety of histories shaping a variety of particular societies. It must therefore harbor, in Niebuhr's view, a variety of moral perspectives. The problem of Christ and culture, if we are to be faithful to Niebuhr's total outlook, will have to be understood in light of this.

A second defect exists in what we said after our analysis of *Christ and Culture*. It does not convey adequately the rootedness of *all* moralities in the authority of a shared story. In the book, Niebuhr contrasts Christ and reason. His remarks are ambiguous, but he seems to distinguish between "rational ethics" on the one hand and "knowledge of the will of God" on the other.[102] This suggests that the problem Niebuhr is addressing is one of reliance upon authority versus reliance upon (unhistorical) reason. That would, of course, radically distort the overall Niebuhrian picture, according to which no unhistorical reason exists. All our thinking, whether we are Christians or not, reflects the shared story of which we are part. This point, like the previous one, is not denied in *Christ and Culture*, but neither does it receive unmistakable affirmation.

The book clearly exhibits Niebuhr's belief that Jesus Christ has authority over Christian life. Niebuhr's other works emphatically underscore this point. His doctrine of revelation and his conception of Christian moral responsibility show clearly that the gospel story is the key to authentically Christian identity. It provides the pivotal images for guiding and shaping Christian action and evaluation.

As we have begun to see, we best understand authority in terms of story. At the root of the church's life is a narrative recounting the words, deeds, and destiny of Jesus from the standpoint of Christian faith. Jesus' authority consists at least in this: that his story provides the indispensable guiding images for the words and deeds and sense of destiny of Christians today.

Remembering this and the two main defects in the conception implicit in *Christ and Culture*, we may attempt finally to offer a more adequate statement of the problem of Christ and culture. This will be a statement true to the central elements of Niebuhr's entire outlook and to the direction, indeed, of his development as a thinker. We may organize our characterization by noting first the factors that give rise to the problem and then the features that make it what it is.

Why does the problem exist at all? It exists first because of *the authority of Christ*. The Bible tells the story of Jesus, whom Christians call the Christ. According to Christian faith, he is, as Niebuhr says, the "focusing point"[103] of God's movement to humankind and human movement to God. His words, deeds, and destiny provide the central clue both to the ways of God and to the appropriate human response to God. He has authority in that the commandments he gave and the images connected with his story guide and shape genuinely Christian existence.

Second, it exists because of *cultural pluralism*. There is cultural opposition to the Christian way. This opposition is not monolithic, nor can it in any of its manifestations rightfully claim to be the deliverance of (unhistorical) reason. The world sustains a variety of shared stories, or shared histories. These nourish and authorize a variety of ways of life. This cultural pluralism marks out the Christian way as a distinctive alternative under the steady challenge of rival alternatives. Within a region, country, or civilization, of course, certain commitments broadly shared may unite the existing diversity into a prevailing cultural outlook that is the dominant vehicle of challenge to Christian existence.

These factors together generate the problem that was Niebuhr's deepest ethical concern. Consider now its main features.

First, *the question of Christ's authority in relation to other cultural authorities.* The gospel story is the criterion of Christian existence. Yet other stories, other histories, also impinge on Christian lives. These include, for example, those of one's own family and nation, those of rival religious and political traditions, and those of Western science and philosophy. How should we understand the authority of the Christ of Scripture in relation to these other authorities?

Is the story of Jesus Christ supremely authoritative? If so, is its authority supreme in all respects? If not in all respects, in which? And what would make proposed answers to these questions adequate, justifiable?

Second, *the question of the relation of the Christian community to the cultural life surrounding it.* Niebuhr's stated definition of culture makes it senseless to ask *whether* to participate in cultural life. Posing the question itself presupposes such participation. Still, from the standpoint of the Jesus story, the general cultural life within which the Christian community exists has ambiguous merit. Furthermore, the question of how to relate to it does characteristically arise.

Should Christ's followers, in order to remain unspotted from the world, distance themselves as far as possible from the society around them? Or should they, in order to transform the world, integrate themselves into that society, attempting to live out the gospel story *fully within* its structures and institutions?

Are these really the proper questions? For if it is senseless to ask whether to participate in cultural life, it is equally misleading to mark out the issue with these grotesque alternatives. Complete separation from the surrounding cultural life is impossible. Some integration is inevitable. If, on the other hand, Christ's authority makes complete integration objectionable and some separation commendable, then the question is really *how* to be separate and *how* to be integrated.

That, indeed, is the point to which our investigations have brought us. In what ways, we are wondering, should a community genuinely Christian distinguish itself from the surrounding cultural world? In what ways should it identify with that world and share its life? Put briefly, what precisely is it to be *in* culture *as* loyalists to the cause of Christ?

We now have before us a characterization of the problem of Christ and culture. It revises Niebuhr's own stated characterization, yet, I have argued, remains faithful to the kernel of his vision. I will in the end offer my own constructive proposals in response to the questions the analysis has raised for us. Our next step, however, is to set the problem as now understood in its contemporary context. We will do this by considering the writings of several recent Christian theologians.

CHAPTER THREE

Christian Social Doctrine at the Center: Gilkey, Haering, and Macquarrie

INTRODUCTION

The thesis announced in chapter one that the true Niebuhrian way is the Anabaptist way. The transformation of culture is Christ's true purpose and his true means is the witness of radically obedient disciples. We have just completed an analysis of the problem for which this thesis is a proposed solution.

The next step is to use this analysis in marking out the current theological context of our discussion. From the standpoint of the conclusions reached in chapter two, we will now examine several prominent, recent treatments of Christian social doctrine, all of them written since Niebuhr's day.

Our purpose here is two-pronged. First we want to gain from these treatments the means of filling out *our* proposal in more detail. Second, we want to test that proposal against the wisdom of these other writers.

I have chosen to consider nine theologians: Langdon Gilkey, Bernard Haering, John Macquarrie, Rosemary Radford Ruether, Gustavo Gutierrez, Johannes Metz, Stanley Hauerwas, Donald Bloesch, and John Howard Yoder. I have chosen them both for the quality and influence of their work and for the range of theological outlooks they exemplify.

Within the group are both Catholic and Protestant writers. To distinguish more finely, there is an American in the tradition of Paul

Tillich and Reinhold Niebuhr, an Anglican who is partial to natural law theory, and a German who writes in the spirit of St. Thomas and Vatican II. There is one North and one South American liberation theologian and also a German political theologian. Finally, there are three more Americans: a narrative theologian, an evangelical, and a Mennonite interpreter of Anabaptism. In dealing with each of these authors I will attend only to claims which are pertinent to *my* question. It is in this limited way that I will attempt to do justice to what they have said.

In this chapter we start with three authors who occupy the center in the stream of contemporary Christian social doctrine. All produce careful, provocative analysis. None is extreme, nor does any belong to an exotic school or movement. Two of them, Langdon Gilkey and John Macquarrie, are fixtures of Protestant academic theology. The other, Bernard Haering, is a writer of broad appeal in present-day Catholicism.

LANGDON GILKEY

In our century the issues of religion and culture and of church and society at once evoke the names of Paul Tillich and Reinhold Niebuhr. These two contemporaries of H. Richard Niebuhr have had, as he had, a massive impact on recent Christian thought. Because of this, it is fitting to begin our inquiry into Christian social doctrine since 1962 with a writer deeply appreciative of their work.

This writer is Langdon Gilkey, a professor at the Divinity School of the University of Chicago. He received his theological training in New York City when Tillich and Reinhold Niebuhr were there and their influence on him is quite evident in his writings.

Gilkey's first major work, *Maker of Heaven and Earth*, appeared in 1959 and expounded the Christian doctrine of creation. We will not deal with it here at length. It does show, however, the relevance of the Christian message to the present social order, something characteristic of all Gilkey's writings. He here expresses this concern by interpreting a doctrine that affirms history as a movement toward the fulfillment of God's purposes, not as a meaningless round of cycles.[1]

In 1964 Gilkey's *How the Church Can Minister to the World Without Losing Itself* was published. This book engaged two questions: How *does* the church (in America) actually relate to the cultural life around it? And how ideally ought it to do so?

We will set the stage for what follows with a treatment here of the first question. We will consider the second one later in connection with others of Gilkey's writings.

Gilkey's analysis concerning the actual relation of the church to surrounding cultural life grew out of the classic studies of Ernst Troeltsch.[2] One interpretation of the relation between church and world embodies itself in what Troeltsch called the *church-type* of Christian social structure. Here the church is holy, not in the special moral witness of its members but in its apostolic authority, sacraments, and dogmas. The individual belongs to the church not through voluntary commitment, but through birth into a society with which the church is intimately bound. The church functions as supreme spiritual guardian for society, offering truth, grace, and salvation to all the society's members. In this form the church is essentially conservative, accepting the prevailing social order and sharing in its practices.

The *sect-type*, on the other hand, aspires after the moral perfection exhibited in Jesus' life and teaching. Instead of upholding the holiness of hierarchy, dogma, and sacrament, it upholds the holiness of transformed lives. Instead of accepting and overseeing the prevailing social order, it stresses opposition to the evils in that order. Indeed, in its moral rigor, the sect's tendency, as Gilkey notes, is to reject certain cultural practices altogether. These might include war, for example, or science, or the judiciary.

Over against the *church* and the *sect* Gilkey celebrates the "new form" of Christian social structure typical of American religious life, namely, the denomination. It is like the church in its thoroughgoing intimacy with the prevailing social order. Its members participate in all the society's major institutions. On the other hand, it is like the sect in its emphasis on lay participation and rejection of hierarchy and sacerdotal clergy. It is also like the sect in taking personal virtue and religious experience, instead of liturgy, sacrament, or dogma, to be the loci of holiness. The difference, however, is that denominational virtues do not require separation from the political, economic, and social structures of society.[3]

In summary, Gilkey says that the denomination is "the sect-type *in* Christendom, *in* culture."[4] He then remarks that here the "separated community" has taken on an intentional relation to the world, creating "the present possibility of the transformation of the world of which it is now fully a part."[5] The danger of this form of church life, to be sure, is its vulnerability to domination by the secular culture. Gilkey devotes an entire chapter to describing why and how American Protestantism, both conservative and liberal, has tended in fact to capitulate to such domination. Still, for all its faults, liberal Protestantism has offered a significant if uneven challenge to prevailing culture. It has thus preserved the "one real element of transcendence in recent American denominational life."[6]

Liberal Protestant insistence that the gospel is "relevant" to the structures and moral dilemmas of the whole social order has been basic to this achievement.[7] This insistence is basic, too, to Gilkey's own sympathy with the liberal tradition in American Christianity.[8] He believes that all of life has a religious basis.

The task of Christian proclamation, therefore, is to address the religious basis of society in order to bring about social transformation.[9] Any view that fails to interpret the gospel in these social terms is utterly misguided.

Gilkey's conviction that Christianity should be a transformative agency *within culture* is clear. Now, with his basic orientation before us, we may turn to an elaboration of several themes in his writings that will develop what we have noticed so far. The first concerns the relation between religion and culture in general.

Gilkey's indebtedness to Paul Tillich is nowhere clearer than it is here. He developed his root claim in both an essay on religion and culture called *Society and the Sacred* and an interpretation of history called *Reaping the Whirlwind*. This root claim is that our basic sense of ourselves and our societies is religious. Our private experiences receive their shape largely from the social world, the shared community that generates our meanings, values, norms, and expectations.

These latter, in turn, reflect the myths, symbols, and rituals by which the society expresses its own identity—its sense of what and why it is. In expressing this identity, society exhibits awareness of its relation to other societies, to "wider history." In light of this awareness, its "symbolic structures move quickly to encompass not only

the grounds of its own political life, but also history as a whole."
They evince a perspective on the entire story of humankind, a
perspective authorizing society's morality and grounding its sense of
security and meaning.[10]

These symbolic structures include, for example, the communist
myth in Russia and the myth of progress in America. They are, in a
word, "religious." That is, they deal with what is final and sacred,
what we take most seriously, what assures and guides us at the
deepest levels of our being.[11]

Thus, Gilkey writes, paraphrasing Tillich, "Every society has a
religious substance which it shares and expresses in all aspects of its
cultural life and in which we participate insofar as we are members."[12] The idea is not the obviously false one that we all acknowledge and worship one God. Rather, it is that we all live under the impact of some ultimate perspective. Whether we are Marxist or capitalist or whatever, our ways of life have a "sacral character."[13]

One way of putting all of this is to say that religion is "constitutive of society."[14] Of course, the myths and symbols grounding communal existence may meet with neglect or fall into disrepute. When
in this way a society's religious basis begins to crack, the society itself
suffers disintegration. Its institutions and identity begin to lose the
sacredness necessary to support belief that participation in the society serves a worthy and important goal. The common moral purpose gives way to the increasing dominance of self-interest. The
unity of social life ruptures with the rise of countercultural groups
seeking new ways of being human.[15]

Though it will not serve our interests to develop it now, a main
theme in *Society and the Sacred* is that the American myth of
progress has fallen into disrepute. Further, social disintegration is oc-
curring in America as a result.

Let us now see how Gilkey understands the role of churches,
groups within society whose special concern is religion. In a key
passage in *Reaping the Whirlwind* he makes two broad claims. One
task of churches in society is to reinforce the religious dimension
necessary to a healthy social existence. Churches are "to encourage
and enliven those structures and symbols conducive of security,
meaning, community and self-actualization." They are to play, that
is, a "constitutive" role in society.[16]

A second task of churches is to criticize the accepted religious basis of society, to call society "to new possibilities beyond ... warped and desecrated traditions." This task arises because of the ambiguous nature of religion. It can be the ground "of the demonic in history as well as of history's creative possibilities." We must determine whether to emphasize retrieval of existing myths and symbols (the constitutive function) or judgment upon them (the critical function). This requires first an interpretation of the norms and goal of history, then, in light of that, an assessment of the possibilities inherent in the present situation.[17]

With mention of history's norms and goal we face squarely, once again, the figure of Jesus Christ. We may recall from the previous chapter that the problem this study addresses exists because Christians live amid bewildering cultural diversity. Yet they take Christ to be the final criterion of human existence, the true norm of history, the definitive clue to history's goal.

Gilkey himself of course affirms this. In *How the Church Can Minister to the World Without Losing Itself*, he asks how the church should relate to the cultural life surrounding it. His most basic point there is that the church must accept the Word of God made flesh in Jesus as the source and norm of its life.[18] In *Reaping the Whirlwind* Gilkey describes Jesus as the manifestation of God on earth and thus the norm for human history and illuminator of its final goal.[19] God does not confine his healing activity to Jews and Christians, for God works through adherents of other religions and also through nonbelievers. However, the criterion of this "universal reconciling work" is Jesus. Where judgment and love are evident as they are "known and defined by him," there God is at work.[20]

Gilkey is fully aware of the inevitable interpenetration of the Christian community with the wider culture in which it lives. It is impossible even for a people whose focus is Christ to be perfectly sequestered from the influence of other cultural authorities. As he says in *Society and the Sacred* in one of several essays on cultural pluralism, God's presence always comes to "a given cultural 'situation.'" Then it is "interpreted from and through that situation, and expressed in its terms."[21] Even were this not so, it would be undesirable for Christians to refuse to associate with surrounding cultural life.

Recalling the patristic concept of "covenant with the Greeks," Gilkey suggests that a truly healthy Christianity will take the form of a "synthesis"—his modern synonym for the patristic term—with the culture around it. Failure by the church to embrace such a synthesis may lead to an arrogant imperialism. Its assured final result is "ineffectiveness, emptiness, and disappearance."[22]

The possible "emptiness" of an insular Christianity seems especially to worry Gilkey in *Society and the Sacred*. A central claim he makes is that encounter begets deeper understanding. In one essay he shows how his contact with Buddhism led him to explore implications of his own Christian tradition often covered over, yet, in fact, centrally important. In another essay he writes similarly about Maoism. In both he notes how Christianity in its turn can make a helpful contribution to the other tradition.[23]

Throughout he seems at once to be affirming loyalty to his own particular faith and also to be affirming the truth present in other faiths. He does not intend to relativize Christ. He *does* intend to relativize our apprehension of him, and to open us to the prospect of transformation at the hands of those outside our circle. We may thus, he says, "uncover elements of the final truth—of Christ if you will—unseen through the spectacles of our limited tradition."[24]

Gilkey's main historical backing for these ideas, as we saw, is the patristic "covenant" with the Greeks, or "pagan Hellenism."[25] Theirs was not, of course, a tradition distant from early Christians as Buddhism and Maoism are distant (more or less) from us. It was dominant in the very environs of the patristic church. Like the early fathers, Gilkey himself applies the idea of covenant or synthesis to the church's relations with its *immediate* cultural surroundings.

What he says to justify exchange with Buddhism and Maoism, he says also (though not here at great length) to justify exchange with the "pagan modernity"[26] so influential in our own midst. He remarks approvingly that Reinhold Niebuhr, Paul Tillich, and other leading twentieth-century theologians all used "modern categories of interpretation." They sought deliberately "*not* to combat the secular science, history, [and] psychology" of their age. Their concern, he tells us, was not to combat modern culture per se, but its "false religious dimensions."[27]

By now it is becoming clear that Gilkey does not recommend a policy of synthesis *merely* in order to foster recovery of suppressed or forgotten aspects of the Christian tradition. It is also a matter of acknowledging the boundaries of Christ's authority.

Recall from the close of chapter two that one main feature of the problem of Christ and culture is the question of Christ's authority in relation to other cultural authorities. And the problem concerns not only the authority of rival religious traditions, but that of political, scientific, philosophical, and other traditions as well.

For Gilkey, Christ's authority addresses the *religious* substance of a culture. It addresses the "vision of what is ultimately real, true, and valuable" lived out "in all aspects of its life."[28] In reflecting on what Christianity might contribute to Maoism, he says that it "has no science, politics, sociology, or economics of its own to offer." Its proper business is rather that of "transforming the religious substance of the culture into one of its own shape." It thereby changes "these common aspects of culture into a more perfect realization of what they themselves intend."[29]

One cannot, in other words, invoke the authority of the Christian tradition as support for saying that *this* is what true science or politics or sociology or economics really is. One can only use the Christian tradition to make a *religious* critique of such cultural expressions, exposing distortions of *value, norm,* and *sense of ultimate reality.* One can then show how one may correct these distortions. Examples of such distortions in modern culture are "its rampant individualism, its scientism, its principle of autonomous self-sufficiency, its belief in progress, and so on."[30] Such "religious idolatries" of communal life, not its "cultural forms," are what Christianity must shun and oppose.[31]

The thing to mark here, and mark well, is Gilkey's endorsement of the wholehearted Christian embrace of cultural life in *all* its various forms. The only proviso is that Christians reprove and abhor religious idolatry and anything that gives expression to it. In this way, to use Gilkey's language, the community living under Christ's authority exhibits the "relevance" of the gospel to earthly human life. At the same time it retains its "transcendence" in relation to the present structure of that life.[32]

We have seen Gilkey's concern with this world in his hopeful account of the denomination—the sect *in* society—as a potential agent of cultural transformation. We have seen it in his account of religion and culture and of the church's responsibility to reinforce and criticize the religious basis of cultural life. We have seen it in his notion of "synthesis," with its denial that all cultural life is rooted in religious idolatry.

We see it finally in his reflections on the symbol of the kingdom. Jesus proclaimed the kingdom, Gilkey says, as the "goal of God *for* history" as well as "beyond" it.[33] The kingdom is the direction in which, under God, our life on earth is taking us.[34] Again, the symbol refers "to a redeemed social order and ultimately to a redeemed history," not merely to "redeemed individuals."[35]

The criterion of the kingdom and illuminator of its goal is Jesus. Its concerns, like his, are the preservation of life and the enhancement of community through responsible love.[36] Since, however, the kingdom is a "perfected social community," its norms somehow correspond to, but are not necessarily the same as those exhibited in the personal life of Jesus. This at least is the apparent meaning of a somewhat puzzling passage in *Society and the Sacred*.

Here Gilkey writes about the kingdom as symbol. He says it

> functions in relation to ongoing historical and political life as the individual perfection of Jesus as the Christ functions in relation to the crises, despair, and fragmentary realizations of individual Christian existence. It establishes the ultimate norms, the bases for judgment and for policies in relation to political and communal action, much as the individual perfection of Jesus' life sets the ultimate norms for our own fragmentary good works.[37]

This is redolent in its way of Reinhold Niebuhr's *An Interpretation of Christian Ethics*,[38] as is, indeed, the entire emphasis on politics and social justice in Gilkey's writings. However, where Niebuhr clearly affirms a "conflict" between the ideal of love exemplified by Jesus and "the necessities of natural life,"[39] Gilkey does not. Although this appears to deny that Jesus can be a criterion for political life, we must keep in mind Gilkey's affirmation that the "perfected social community corresponds to the personal and individual perfection of the figure of Jesus."[40]

We may turn to Gilkey's engaging memoir, *Shantung Com-*

pound, for clarifying remarks on this matter. The memoir, published in 1966, describes and interprets his experience in a civilian internment camp in North China during World War II. In this fairly benign camp, the prisoners had the bulk of the responsibilities for organizing social existence. They prepared and distributed food, assigned housing, and gave out work assignments.

One thing Gilkey says he learned during his years in camp is that effective political action involves compromise. It requires the use of force and it discredits most pacifist theory.[41] These points he never disavowed in his later writings. They are Niebuhrian, as *An Interpretation of Christian Ethics* documents.

What is not so clear, certainly not from the standpoint of Niebuhr himself, is how they correspond to the individual perfection of Jesus. Gilkey would presumably say that they do, but he has not shown it. This fact puts into sharp relief a fundamentally important question, namely, whether the Jesus story can really be the basis of an adequate social doctrine. Reinhold Niebuhr answered with a qualified no. Gilkey apparently answers with a qualified yes. However, whether this is really different from Niebuhr's answer is by no means clear.

Gilkey's treatment of Jesus' bearing upon Christian social doctrine is a good point at which to begin a brief critical reflection on his analysis. He says that the symbol of the kingdom establishes Christian norms for sociopolitical existence while the perfection of Jesus' life establishes the norms for our existence as individuals. What does this mean if, as Gilkey himself suggests, it is through Jesus that we understand the values of the kingdom? Certainly the values of the kingdom cannot clash with the values of Jesus! We would expect them to be in accord, for how could a perfect individual life, which shows the kingdom's traits, be anything but normative for social and communal action?

If Jesus' life is normative, then one would surely have to justify the necessity of force and futility of pacifism, for instance, *in terms of that life.* This would be true as well for other claims about Christian political existence. Then, however, the distinction between the kingdom Jesus announced and his own individual life might not do all that Gilkey intends it to do in protecting modern life from the haunting demands of the Nazarene.

Jesus' authority for social ethics is a particular example of a more general issue. What, we may ask, is the *scope* of Christ's authority? Is his thought and action the rule for Christian life in *all* its aspects? Gilkey answers that his authority is "religious," and that we cannot appeal to him as the basis for a *Christian* history or science, politics or economics. He says also that on these matters the wider culture in which the church exists inevitably shapes the Christian outlook. Even though the church may appeal to Christ in exposing religious distortion in these aspects of cultural life, it cannot separate itself altogether from prevailing views. Nor should it try. Only through synthesis with surrounding culture can the church remain both humble and effective in its witness.

This is helpful and illuminating. It is certainly difficult to see how a group intractably hostile to modern knowledge about history, science, and other fields could have a substantial influence upon surrounding cultural life. A church that expects to have transformative impact will surely recognize that Christ's authority touches all of life but does not make us captive to an ancient worldview. Thus it would be perverse and misguided for any Christian community to make an attempt at *total* separation from the world.

But has Gilkey explored this point adequately? Let us grant that the church cannot develop a complete political theory on the basis of Christ's authority. Let us grant that some sort of synthesis with the surrounding culture is necessary. Does this then mean that churchly virtues never require separation from the surrounding political, economic, and social structures? Gilkey suggests this in his analysis of the *sect-type* in culture.

Suppose, however, that the surrounding political structures are totalitarian. They could be and for some Christians are. Does this not tell us that a faithful church may have to refuse participation in certain social structures? How could it fulfill its critical function in society if it did not consider this at least a possibility?

All this makes up a second broad question about Gilkey's analysis. Has he not, in urging the relevance of the Christian ethos to society, failed to give adequate safeguards against undue compromise of that ethos? The answer so far is yes. Whatever we may answer, however, the question itself is undeniably important. Like the first one about Christ's authority for social ethics, it evokes issues that lie at the very center of our interest. They will come up again and again.

BERNARD HAERING

Bernard Haering wrote *The Law of Christ* more than two decades ago. It was a signal of revolution in Roman Catholic thinking. From the seventeenth century onward, the church had written its moral theology with a view to confessors and the sacrament of penance. It had focused upon law and upon questions about specific acts.

As the twentieth century passed its midpoint, Haering was one of several European writers who pioneered a different conception of Catholic morality.[42] They attended to the goals of human life and to the Christian virtues. They considered diversity and change in human culture. They began to see the moral life less as obedience to a code of law and more as personal response to the gracious call of God.

As Haering's three-volume work was appearing, the Vatican II Ecumenical Council began. It was the same year, 1962, in which H. Richard Niebuhr died.[43] Now, some twenty years after all of this, Haering has produced *Free and Faithful in Christ*, another three-volume work of Catholic moral theology. This work bears the influence of Vatican II. It aims at being comprehensive[44] and belongs to the period since Niebuhr's death. For all these reasons it is an appropriate focus for our treatment here of Haering's ethical thought. In what follows we will devote ourselves to it exclusively.

Haering's controlling theme in the three volumes is the idea of "responsibility in Christ."[45] He concerns himself (as he had done before) not only with what acts and decisions are right, but also with what sorts of persons we should be.[46] He says that responsibility is the defining trait of persons truly Christian. True Christians take responsibility for the world, Haering tells us, and they do so in a discerning, innovative, and courageous way.

By itself, however, the idea of responsibility is a rudderless thing, a merely abstract concept. It can neither give direction nor inspire action. That is why, in Haering's exposition, it is always responsibility *in Christ*. What he has in mind is a responsibility shaped by Jesus Christ and a responsibility made possible through "solidarity" with him in the common life of the church.[47]

Near the beginning of the first volume of *Free and Faithful in Christ*, Haering remarks that his title reveals the "identity and main programme" of the entire study.[48] We have seen that "responsibility in Christ" is the central motif of the study. We will explore the concepts of freedom and faithfulness as the main clues to a fuller exposition of this motif. Then we will advance the analysis by considering Haering's ideas in light of the issues we earlier established as central to the problem of Christ and culture.

Haering tells us that his thinking about moral theology was influenced more than anything else by the "mindless and criminal obedience of Christians to Hitler, a madman and tyrant." So it is not surprising that in his view an adequate Christian ethics must stress "creative freedom." Uncritical obedience to governments, laws, or traditions is repugnant and dangerous. God did not make us for mechanical compliance with codes and authorities but for "co-creativity." He made us for partnership with him in the enhancement of human understanding and the making of human culture.[49] If authorities require what is wrong, we are to disobey them. If codes and traditions fall short, we are to purify them.[50] We are beings called to freedom, to moral discernment.

Again, however, it is no merely abstract thing Haering is recommending. The Christian community, he tells us, must be deeply rooted in history and tradition. In its present reflection it does not begin afresh, as though God's will today had no likeness to his will in the past. Moral discernment, he says, quoting James Gustafson, "is in continuity with the past, not discontinuity. It learns from, and is thus informed and directed, without being determined, by the past."[51]

The pivotal element in the Christian past is Jesus Christ, and thus the freedom Christians have is "freedom in Christ." In freedom we go beyond slavish deference to authority and tradition, yet we do so in fundamental loyalty to Christ. He is the pattern, indeed, for our whole manner of life, from our attitude toward God and world to our way with self and one another.[52] Our freedom is thus bound up with faithfulness, or "fidelity,"[53] and we come to the second main clue to Haering's central theme of responsibility in Christ.

Christians find themselves by entrusting the whole of their being to God and making every decision and aspiration a response to God.[54] What God is we know through Christ. In him "the revelation of God has come to its summit and can never be surpassed. Christ is the final word of the Father to humanity." It is only in knowing Christ, therefore, that we learn what true responsibility is. Only in following him can we come to embody it.[55]

Fidelity to Christ is a creative thing, of course. The circumstances we face are not the same as Jesus faced. His life and teaching provide us with broad guidelines, not a static code. It is to these broad guidelines, or "goal commandments," that we must faithfully adhere. Justice and love and mercy are always binding, but they are norms we must apply creatively in meeting present challenges.[56]

In the process we may not only cope well with the challenges, but come to know better the meaning of the guidelines themselves. For the revelation God has given us in Christ is not a "dead heritage." The revelation continues, with the Holy Spirit bringing the faithful by degrees to a better grasp of the Christ-event and its significance for human life. The Holy Spirit, Haering says, "will never teach us anything opposed to Christ's doctrine but will lead the church and humanity gradually to a deeper understanding of it."[57] We grow, then, but we never leave the pathway of fidelity.

All this leaves a distinctive mark upon genuinely Christian morality. We are to be faithful to Christ. Christ was *with* humanity and *for* humanity.[58] He was a servant who bound himself in "saving solidarity" with all people. He tore down barriers of race and class and attended especially to the sick, poor, and oppressed. He loved even the enemy.[59] He sought no advantage for himself and he bore the burdens of others. In these ways he lived out the divine covenant of universal fidelity and was thus a sign of the peace to come. He was a sign of the harmony and fulfillment that is God's design for all creation.[60]

The truly Christian way is therefore a way of saving solidarity. This, indeed, is the "heart of the law of Christ."[61] It requires faithfulness to "our belonging to each other." It bids us to a life of "co-humanity" in which we attain our own potential by honoring and promoting the potential of others.[62] We live now, of course, in a broken place, a world in need of healing. The peace of God is as yet a distant goal. But it is precisely the mission of those who accept the way of saving solidarity to help mend this brokenness and to establish this peace. "God's people," Haering writes, "are his co-actors, his partners in the building up of the city of God by their love."[63]

This is the "covenant morality" to which God calls Christians and by which they become God's "collaborators" in overcoming "individual and collective selfishness" in the world.[64] It is a morality, Haering tells us, with both teleological and deontological elements. On the one hand, it considers the goals of ethical life. Participants in the covenant morality seek the goal of maturity as responsible persons, a maturity marked by freedom and fidelity in Christ. They seek, too, the goal of a responsible society marked by peace, by solidarity, and co-humanity. They are legitimately concerned, therefore, with consequences and creative strategies.[65]

The covenant morality is not, however, a "one-sided utilitarian pragmatism." It does look at goals and consequences, but it looks, too, at obligation, law, right, and wrong. And here the all-embracing thing is love. This is not a vague, unstructured love, but a love whose "countenance and true meaning" Jesus has shown to us in his life.[66]

The deontological element in Christian ethics is this focus on the law of love and the conscious, explicit search "to discover and understand the essential qualities and demands of this love." In attending to this element we learn the rules of the covenant morality, or the rules of love. To some of these there can be no exception at all. This would include, for instance, rules prohibiting rape or torture.[67] Depending on circumstances, however, others may be set aside (or "approximated") for the sake of a higher good.

One example is a rule "we know infallibly" as believers in one God who is Father of all. This is the rule that no person may exploit or manipulate another person nor may any group do so to another group. Here, according to Haering, Reinhold Niebuhr's doctrine of the impossible ethical ideal is helpful. In the public, or economic-social-political, realm we cannot always observe this rule. We have to allow for some "open-ended compromises." Yet the rule represents the ideal toward which we should always strive even though "we can reach it only gradually."[68]

Another example of a rule we may break under certain conditions is the prohibition against the use of violence. Haering does not hesitate to say that according to the life and teaching of Christ, God's love is a "nonviolent love."[69] Faced with the temptation of violent revolution, Christ proclaimed a kingdom that would come "by the power of the Spirit and the power of his word and, finally, by the powerlessness of the cross." Even when he met violence against his own person, he stayed true to his gospel of peace.[70]

Here, indeed, is a central difference between the message of Karl Marx and the message of Jesus. Both sought the liberation of the downtrodden. Both envisioned the unity of all peoples. But Marx believed we can reach the goal by a mechanism of hatred and violent struggle. Jesus, on the other hand, set out to win humanity over by gentleness and nonviolence.[71]

To Jesus, then, Haering attributes the idea of transformation by nonviolence. He also endorses it himself. Only through commitment to "nonviolent means of liberation," he says, can the church promote the "exodus from violence" so necessary in our time.[72] Only through a prophetic presence marked by solidarity with the powerless and a spirit of nonviolence can it be truly "salt for the earth and light to the world."[73] He suggests, too, that if humanity one day attains a "peace mentality," disarming itself substantially and building up "new structures for the protection and promotion of peace" . . . If it does that, it will owe much to the "conscientious objectors" who in witnessing against warfare are "now helping to prepare this event."[74]

In spite of all this, however, Haering says the Christian morality does not rule out violence absolutely but only violence as a "normal means" of resolving conflict.[75] Where it is the "only feasible way to check unjust violence," governments, for example, may resort to it. Christians in government should witness always to "the ideal of non-violent use of power" and "refuse cooperation" when state authorities employ violence in an unjust cause. Where an "extreme need" legitimates it, Christians may cooperate with state violence, though only, Haering says, "with deep regret." They should signify clearly their preference for "nonviolent solutions" and their love for those "whom they have to oppose by violent means."[76]

We can see that on Haering's view the Christian morality allows the possibility of legitimate violence, but that it can never be comfortable with violence. Both these points come through—the second strikingly—in Haering's discussion of violent revolution. He accepts the traditional teaching of Catholic moral theology in this regard. That is, a tyrant or political system may become so intolerably oppressive as to justify a violent revolution if there is a "realistic hope" of change for the better.[77]

But then, at greater length, he raises further questions. Can revolutionaries who have not shown "creativity in the way of nonviolent, solidaric, patient action" be expected to show the right kind of creativity when they gain power? Does not a violent reaction to violent abuse of power betray a vicious circle of violence?

Even as he grants that violent revolution may under certain conditions be permissible, he evokes the memory and method of Jesus. "Those," he writes,

> who raise their voices in protest or discerning criticism and use creative nonviolent strategies, may have to suffer for quite a while. But the question is whether we believe in the power of conscience to convince and to convert. If we have little trust in these realities, our violence will surely not change the world for the better..[78]

Thus, for Haering, believing in that power and having that trust is part of genuine Christian existence. Elsewhere in *Free and Faithful in Christ* he remarks that our being God's handiwork shapes us more than our having been born into a sinful world.[79] We thus have a basis for hope.

This is truly a Christian hope, however, only if it anticipates a world made better precisely through faithfulness to Christ. And on Haering's view, Christ shows the Father's love to be a nonviolent love. Christ transforms humanity, not with force and threat, but with gentleness and the gospel of peace. The traditional Catholic teaching, rooted in the idea of the just war, Haering accepts. The rule against violence is not unbreakable.[80] The overall effect of his exposition, nevertheless, is to make us deeply hesitant about recourse to violence.

We have looked now at freedom and fidelity as the key elements in Haering's idea of moral responsibility in Christ. Fidelity is fidelity to Christ, to the moral pattern he embodied. Freedom is the creative interpretation of what fidelity requires. It takes us beyond slavish, unthinking obeisance to authority, whether secular or religious. And while it roots us, to be sure, in a moral tradition, yet at the same time it makes us critical, discerning, and imaginative.

Now we may round out our exposition by bringing in the questions identified earlier as central to the problem of Christ and culture. We noted earlier the source of the problem. It is that Christians regard Jesus Christ as normative for their way of life, yet live in a pluralistic world opposed to that way of life. This raises, we said, two main questions. First, how are we to understand the relation between Christ's authority and other cultural authorities? And second, how are we to understand the relation of the church to the cultural life around it?

Haering, of course, makes Christ the focus of Christian morality. Christ, he says, is "our Law, our Way, our Life."[81] This in itself suggests pluralism and therefore the issues upon which this entire essay focuses. Haering engages these issues himself in treatments of natural law and of the encounter between gospel morality and human cultures.

On the first of these, Haering attempts to affirm a part of traditional church teaching while also acknowledging human historicity. He believes with Thomas Aquinas that all true moral law is "natural" in the sense that it is "inborn." It is not something we determine, but something we discover.[82] It is thus a "most unnatural situation" to turn away from loyalty to God. Christ embodied God's "original design" for us. Thus, a moral system opposed to the Christian ethic rejects not merely the ethic Christians prefer, but the very law of our creation.[83]

Haering also distinguishes moral knowledge open to the eyes of reason—Aquinas's "natural law"—from the special knowledge available only through the revelation of Jesus Christ. His exposition of this distinction illustrates his sense of human historicity. It also illustrates, we may add, the difficulty of making the distinction at all when one takes human historicity seriously into account.

"It is distinctive of the human being," Haering writes, "that he has history, is history, and makes history." This trait pervades every dimension of human existence and means, among other things, that how we live today reflects the past and shapes the future. One must, Haering believes, acknowledge and deal with this fact in a theory of natural law viable today. Treatises on natural law tend, as he notices, to "absolutize" what is common to a particular group. Their authors betray, in fact, "the social and cultural milieu in which they move." Nor can we count on a "rational procedure" to overcome this ethical pluralism, since rationality, too, "manifests itself differently according to the historical context."

Even if we concede all of this, however, it does not entail "unlimited relativism." It is certainly wrong to impose "time-bound norms" upon others, but there *are* abiding truths—abiding human rights and moral values.[84]

These, he believes, make up a natural law accessible to human beings in general, apart from their embeddedness in a particular tradition. It is a law written on all our hearts, he says, that we have equal dignity and that we are to love and respect one another as free persons. We have only to "read it" in our hearts and to explore it in "shared experience and reflection" with others.[85]

If our approach is right we do this not with the idea of constructing a closed system, but with an openness to new insights. We do it with a "readiness to learn together" in the common quest for truth. Instead of being a closed system, he sees natural law as "an integrated part within the one unfolding revelation that comes to its fullness in Christ."[86]

Our interest here is Haering's understanding of Christ's authority in relation to other cultural authorities. What he says about natural law does, in fact, uphold his central theme of Christ's unqualified moral authority. Christ is God's "original design" for us. He is the very law of our creation. We cannot, in Haering's view, fully know this design, or law, apart from knowing Christ.

Still, there is a basic moral knowledge available to rational beings in general, regardless of their historical background, and this is the natural law. Here the fundamental truth—known, as even Scripture says, by "the light of nature"—is the principle of respect for the humanity of all persons.[87]

Something remains puzzling, however, about Haering's idea of Christ as God's original design for us. Christ came, he tells us,

in order to tear down the barriers between Jews, Samaritans, and Gentiles. He has revealed that before God there is no difference between those born in freedom and those born in slavery and no difference between male and female. But *only those who have a living faith and who live totally under the influence of the grace of Jesus* are able to draw the conclusions and to do the hard and patient work necessary to tear down the barriers of prejudice....[88]

As examples of such barriers, he mentions sexism and the "superiority complex" of the Western world. Interestingly for our purposes, however, the passage does not easily mesh with the claim about natural law. For how could we know apart from revelation the principle of respect for all humanity, while relying on revelation to know our duty to respect slaves, women, and Samaritans? The two points seem obviously contradictory.

Further questions arise regarding Haering's analysis of the gospel and human cultures. In this analysis *culture* does not have the broad, Niebuhrian sense with which we have become familiar. It rather signifies a particular people marked by distinctive skills, beliefs, and practices.

Haering's question is how to establish Christianity among such peoples without recourse to "cultural imperialism." This requires us, he says, to distinguish Christian faith and morality from the "time-bound expression" of it in the language, symbols, and customs of a particular social group. He says that we must certainly avoid estranging people from their own cultures. Still, we must disapprove and seek to eliminate attitudes and practices "which strikingly contradict the moral implications of faith."[89]

As an example he describes a form of sexual exploitation typical of the Bemba tribe in Zambia and supported by tribal myth. The example shows that the attitudes and practices he has in mind may belong to the ethos, or fundamental outlook, of a particular culture. However, if this is true, and if they yet "strikingly contradict" the morality of Christ, certain questions arise. For they must surely also contradict the natural law, which in Haering's view bears so considerable a resemblance to the morality of Christ.

With this, however, the whole idea of a natural law written on all our hearts becomes less plausible, or at least seems misleading. If fundamental cultural outlooks can differ so profoundly, then the moral pluralism in our world is perhaps too marked to permit belief in a natural law. Haering's own discussion, stamped as it is with the awareness of human historicity, certainly cuts much of the ground from under the idea.

Christ's authority, on Haering's view, is final. He is ambiguous, however, regarding the degree of dissonance between the Christian and other moralities. Rather than resolving our questions, he has sharpened our sense of how difficult they are.

Now we will turn to the matter of the church's relation to the cultural life around it. What we have said so far about Haering has been suffused with the idea of social transformation, so we need not develop the point here at length. In faithfulness to Vatican II (to which he often, in fact, appeals), Haering describes the church as a "servant in the world." It is a sign and an agent of peace, a continuation of the mission and presence of Christ on the earth.[90] It is to be these things by prophetically protesting the sins of groups and nations, by participating responsibly in social institutions, such as the state, and by being a model community for the world.[91]

The metaphor of light to the world epitomizes all of this,[92] and the Christ who spoke the metaphor provides himself the pattern by which we fulfill the task. We are light to the world only if through him and in faithfulness to him, we become living signs of the "very goodness and compassionate love" of God.[93] This will involve both courage and discernment. In remaining faithful to Christ we may have to distance ourselves from authority opposed to his ways. We may, for example, have to meet unjust laws with civil disobedience.

On the other hand, we may have to obey even his own commands by "approximations." We may have to carry out the "best possible fulfillment and not always a literal application."[94] For on Haering's view, the fidelity through which we transform the world is not a slavish but a creative fidelity. And we must so construe it as to allow for the freedom which is also part of moral responsiblity in Christ.

Haering has given us a powerful statement, certainly, of what it is to be faithful and responsible Christians in the world. At least two broad questions remain, however, both of which we will pose in terms of his dual themes of fidelity to Christ and creative freedom.

The first, hinted at already, is whether Haering succeeds in his attempt to harmonize the ideas of natural law and fidelity to Christ. We noticed inconsistencies in his exposition that suggest he has not succeeded. They suggest, indeed, that the very idea of natural law may be misleading. The moral pluralism in our world seems too marked, even in Haering's own exposition, to accommodate it. We must conclude, therefore, that the idea of a common human morality requires sharper qualification than he has been willing to grant.

The second question concerns the difficulty of meshing fidelity and creative freedom. How, we may ask, can freedom in Christ be at once free *and* faithful? What keeps fidelity to a tradition from becoming a slavish, unthinking legalism? Haering makes these issues central in his social ethics. However, what he says is not fully satisfying, although this is due in part to the sheer intractability of the issues.

His treatment of Christianity and violence, a topic crucial in any discussion of Christ and culture, is especially so where Anabaptism hovers in the background, as it does here. Haering tells us that in knowing Christ we know God. Further, we know *how* God transforms his world: through nonviolent love. It is not with force and threat, but with gentleness and the gospel of peace. We who are followers of Christ must do our work of transformation in the same way. It is what fidelity requires. However, this fidelity, Haering tells us, is not a wooden, legalistic thing. It is creative. In extreme circumstances it can allow the discerning use of violence in a just cause.

In response to this we may wonder how violence, even reluctant violence, can be faithful to the Christ who revealed God through *non*violent love. What justifies setting aside the nonviolence of God? Does nonviolence cease under certain conditions to be transformative? Did these conditions not obtain in Jesus' lifetime? How do we know when they obtain today?

By no means does Haering wish to support easy recourse to violence. He speaks movingly, for instance, against those who give up too easily on the power of conscience to convince and convert.

On the other hand, he does not adequately address these questions about the consistency of his approach. And this underlines the puzzles that remain concerning the broader question of the relation between fidelity and freedom.

These two criticisms of material are more easily faulted than corrected. It is well, perhaps, to think of them also as challenges. For how the Christian morality relates to other moralities, and how it can be faithful without being legalistic, are matters large not only in importance but also in difficulty.

JOHN MACQUARRIE

John Macquarrie is an Anglican theologian who flatly denies that any jarring discontinuity separates Christian from non-Christian moral striving. The best secular philosophies and the great world religions unite, says John Macquarrie, in teaching "love, compassion and altruism" and in upholding the quest for wholeness, for peace and full humanity. It is true that Christ has authority in the church. This indeed has a "profound effect" on how Christians conceive the good. It does not so much create a new morality, however, as endow the common, "natural" one with a new seriousness and a new dignity.[95]

The theme of continuity between *Christian* aspiration and that of human beings in general appears throughout the ethical writings of this Anglican professor at Oxford. It is a theme he presses far more vigorously than Haering does. It is, indeed, the most striking feature of his approach to the problem of Christ and culture. Also important for his approach to this problem are his ideas about the human person, about the world in which moral striving occurs, and about the ministry and mission of the church. We shall consider all of these in the exposition that follows. However, the theme of continuity—of a natural law acknowledged across ideological lines—will occupy us most.

We cannot show conclusively that the world accommodates our quest for wholeness. Nor can we prove that it supports our moral efforts—that it is not faceless, mechanistic, indifferent.[96] What we cannot prove, however, we can affirm in faith, and for Christians it has become possible to do this through Jesus Christ. In Christ's life and work, Macquarrie tells us, he was "the supreme miracle," convincing us that it is our destiny to grow toward fulfillment. Through him we come to have faith in God and to believe that he "confers, sustains, and perfects the being of his creatures."[97]

Recent conceptions of the human person largely agree, according to Macquarrie, that human beings are able to shape themselves. Instead of having a fixed nature we can alter what we are. We are beings in motion, beings still emerging.[98] This by itself implies the possibility of moral change.

What Christianity adds is a sense of the presence of God, and this undergirds the seriousness of moral endeavor by the encouragement it provides.[99] For if material being and the historical process are the focus of divine love, then the world is the right place for us. It is a hospitable environment for our moral striving.

The Christ who shows us what God is and awakens our trust is human—a figure in our history.[100] This emphasizes a point made in the Old Testament creation story. That is, the God who is present with us uses his human creatures to help "shape the world and advance it into fuller being." It is true that Jesus "focuses" God's activity, pouring out love so strikingly that through him we become aware of God. But he is a "paradigm" for all human existence. It is every person's "destiny ... to become a coworker with God" in bringing creation to fulfillment.[101]

Thus the perspective opened up through Christ encourages the moral quest not only by its avowal of divine support, but also by its affirmation of human responsibility. The quest is not only possible and feasible; it is important.

One can capture all of this, says Macquarrie, in one sentence. "The sense of God's presence, which is the crown of the religious life, reaches over into the sphere of ethics and glorifies it." Macquarrie praises this remark by William Adams Brown first for its recognition that the "awareness of the divine presence" is what determines any "distinctively Christian" conception of ethics. Then he praises it, too, for recognizing that "the Christian contribution is continuous with our 'natural' endowment." Brown says that God's presence "glorifies" what we already know. Macquarrie takes that to mean that it enables us "to understand the moral life in a new light and a new depth."[102]

We have seen how Christian faith, in Macquarrie's view, enhances our enthusiasm for morality. Now we have come to his idea that it evokes a moral outlook "fundamentally akin" to outlooks not shaped by this faith.[103]

Macquarrie does *not* wish to deny the genuine distinctiveness of Christian morality. Though he mostly emphasizes what is common among moral perspectives, he does acknowledge the special "context" in which the Christian perceives the moral life. This includes the "normative place assigned to Jesus and his teaching." It includes worship and prayer, faith, and hope. This context does not, however, result in a "separate moral system."[104]

Here we will consider first Macquarrie's assertion of the authority of Jesus Christ. For Christian faith he is the "paradigmatic" revelation of God, the "decisive" means of God's self-communication to his creatures. He thus determines the Christian way of understanding God.

But he is paradigmatic for human existence, too, and so determines also what human beings should be.[105] The Christian accepts the goal, indeed, of being "fully conformed" to Christ. Through God's "supporting grace," Macquarrie says, following Bonhoeffer, the "pattern of existence manifested in Christ" becomes clear in the "disciple."[106] Thus Jesus is the norm of Christian ethics, though not, Macquarrie says, "as a paradigm for external imitation." He is, rather, "the criterion and inspiration for a style of life."[107]

The precise difference between Jesus as a "paradigm for external imitation" and Jesus as "the criterion and inspiration for a style of life" is not immediately clear. We will have to come back to it. For now we may note that from Macquarrie's viewpoint, attempts to express the meaning of Christ's authority are bound to be difficult. Christ is the "one supreme authority"[108] not just for the individual, but for the whole church. It is to him that we may appeal in determining how to give the Christian faith concrete expression in the world.

However, the full significance of what God has revealed through Christ is by no means easy to establish. For one thing, our knowledge of Christ comes to us through a variety of interpreters whose accounts and ideas sometimes conflict. For another, human reason submits even revelation to its scrutiny. It questions it and excises from its content whatever may conflict with other "well founded convictions."[109] This means that while upholding the supreme authority of Christ, the church upholds other authorities as well.

Here Macquarrie shows his Anglican colors unmistakably. For early in the development of Anglicanism, Richard Hooker and other English divines, struggling against the Puritans, denied the sole sufficiency of the Bible as a guide for Christian life. They appealed also to the authority of reason and tradition.[110]

Hooker and the others did uphold the Bible as one authority in the church's life, and so does Macquarrie. It may "perhaps," he tells us, be the "basic" authority.[111] It re-presents the paradigmatic revelation on which the church is founded and from which it gets its identity. Any theology truly Christian "must maintain close and positive relations" with it. Still, since it is fallible and contains discrepancies even on matters of such importance as theology and ethics, it is not to be absolutized.[112]

Although the Bible is a shield against "individualism and enthusiasm in theology," it is not adequate for this function by itself. One can read almost anything into it, Macquarrie says. That is why yet another authority, tradition, is so important. Tradition is the "communal wisdom" found in the fundamental doctrines of the church, in its creeds, and in the "beliefs of the early councils." It is no rival to Scripture. It is its "necessary complement." By providing a "consensus" regarding the essential teaching of Scripture, it protects against eccentric interpretations and thus helps to preserve the stability and identity of the Christian community.

Setting the tradition aside, as though one could ignore the development that has occurred since New Testament times, wounds the community. It amounts, indeed, to "abandoning" it. "A Christian theology," Macquarrie writes, "can no more fly in the face of the mainstream of tradition than it can in the face of Scripture."[113]

Alongside the authority of Scripture and tradition in Macquarrie's scheme lies the authority of reason. Reason, he says, brings out the meanings of revelation. It organizes the ideas of Scripture and tradition into a coherent whole. It submits what has been revealed to critical appraisal.

In all these ways reason renews the "ancient teaching." It applies this ancient teaching to new conditions, correcting its errors. It thus has crucial importance for the life and practice of the church.[114]

Against those, indeed, who give a "meager place" to reason, Macquarrie invokes Archbishop William Temple's remark. "Revelation can, and . . . must, on pain of becoming manifest as superstition, vindicate its claim by satisfying reason."[115]

We have looked now at the elements of the "three-fold type of authority" in light of which, according to Macquarrie, we can address our questions about Christian existence in the world. The "supreme authority" is Christ, but Scripture, tradition, and reason are the means by which we come to know *him*. In Macquarrie's analogy, they are like the three branches of government in the United States. Together they provide "checks and counterchecks that balance each other and ensure both stability and the possibility of ordered change and progress."[116]

This latter point about "ordered change and progress," or what Macquarrie also calls "development,"[117] is worth remarking further. In doing so we may also illuminate a remark which earlier evoked our puzzlement. Namely, that Jesus is the norm of Christian ethics though not as a "paradigm for external imitation."

Macquarrie's thoughts about development in understanding may be summarized as a dual thesis. First, the Christian understanding of the Christ mandates such development. Second, this development must build upon an unvarying basic principle. Christians can define maturity only with reference to Jesus Christ and his self-giving love, says Macquarrie in his *Three Issues in Ethics*.

Then he says that

> Christ himself is no static figure, nor are Christians called to imitate him as a static model. Christ is an eschatalogical figure, always before us; and the doctrine of his coming again "with glory" implies that there are dimensions of christhood not manifest in the historical Jesus and not yet fully grasped by the disciples. Thus discipleship does not restrict human development to some fixed pattern, but summons into freedom, the full depth of which is unknown, except that they will always be consonant with self-giving love.[118]

Thus the one unchangeable norm of Christian existence must be self-giving love. When in other contexts Macquarrie speaks of obedience or following Christ, he means "the obedience of self-giving"[119] or "obedience to the demand for self-giving."[120] This is basic, fixed.

The question, on the other hand, of *how* self-giving love should express itself remains open. The authentic Christian community, it is true, will cope with the question by attending respectfully to Scripture and tradition. It will do so, however, without absolutizing either. It will employ reason to reflect constructively and critically upon these authorities. And it will seek whatever dimensions of Christhood, whatever forms of self-giving, may now be appropriate.

We saw at the beginning that according to Macquarrie the great religions and philosophies unite in teaching love, compassion, and altruism. This is what he believes the ethic of Christianity comes down to. In affirming the one fixed principle of self-giving love, it affirms the core of moral conviction common to all humanity. If we put this basic moral conviction together with Christian aspiration toward fuller being for all creation, what we have, roughly, is Macquarrie's conception of the natural law. Our obligation to be compassionate and giving, our aspiration toward a richer, more personal humanity—these belong to us all, whatever our religious and philosophical traditions. They are "natural," part of a moral order not created by us but given with our existence.[121]

For Macquarrie this natural law is by no means a set of inflexible rules governing a fixed human nature. He believes human nature is dynamic, still emerging. Accordingly, it interprets natural law in a way that allows for flexibility and growth. No detailed natural law exists to prescribe how human beings in all times and places should conduct their lives. What does exist, however, is a "tendency," an "inbuilt directedness," that belongs to human existence as such. It points us toward a fuller being characterized by love, compassion, and altruism. The direction of this pointing remains constant, although the particular rules and prohibitions we adopt to smooth our way may change. This constant direction to which we feel bound is the natural law.[122]

The obedience of Christian faith is "continuous" with this law. Indeed, Macquarrie (in his *Three Issues in Ethics*) considers it ill-advised to adopt a "Christocentric position" in ethics. We should, rather, base our ethics upon "the common humanity which we all share," since this offers the "most likely" foundation for establishing "secure moral bonds between Christians and non-Christians" in the world.[123]

But Macquarrie believes that despite the close kinship between Christian and other moralities, the Christian morality remains distinctive. On Macquarrie's view it provides a "context of belief and formation that is supportive of the moral life." It offers Jesus and his teaching as a means of helping us "see the law in new depth."[124]

Macquarrie has written a chapter-length discussion of Christianity and violence. As we have been suggesting, this issue goes to the heart of the problem that is our main theme, the problem of Christ and culture. In a moment we will turn to that discussion to see how it may further illuminate Macquarrie's account of Christian ethics. We will also see how it may raise questions concerning this account.

Besides the ethical reflection we've been considering so far, however, the issue of Christ and culture embraces the matter of the church and its mission in the world. What Macquarrie says about this must occupy us briefly before we take up his ideas concerning Christianity and violence.

His basic point here is that the church is the earthly embodiment of Christ, continuing his ministry and advancing his goals. Macquarrie says, indeed, that of all the titles for the church the "most appropriate" is the phrase *body of Christ*.[125] This is not to say that the church has attained the stature of Christ. It is not free from sin. But it is an "association" whose Head is Christ and whose aim is the "transfiguration" of the world into the form of Christ. It thus represents him in the world.[126]

In his *Principles of Christian Theology* Macquarrie works out at some length the details of the church's representative function. He develops a theology of the Word and sacraments as well as of ministry and mission. We cannot attend to all of this, but may note a couple of points that bear particularly upon our interests here.

One of these reflects Macquarrie's view of Christian authority and Christian morality. We must understand the Christ whom the church represents in light of a "three-fold type of authority." The three elements of this authority, again, are Scripture, tradition, and reason. We saw, too, that on Macquarrie's interpretation they together yield a Christ whose morality is basically the morality "natural" to serious-minded human beings everywhere. Thus the values and goals Christians espouse do not differ sharply from the values and goals other thoughtful persons espouse.

The church must apply this, Macquarrie believes, to its conception of mission. In doing so it will cease to be preoccupied as in the past with gaining converts. Indeed, the time is perhaps here, he suggests, to end "the kind of mission that proselytizes, especially from sister faiths which, though under different symbols, are responding to the same God and realizing the same quality of life."[127]

Thus the center of the "missionary task" is in "manifesting and propagating" self-giving love. This may happen without the affected persons or peoples "becoming incorporated into the Christian church or explicitly confessing the Christian faith."[128]

The second point concerns how the church is to fulfill its central missionary task. How is it to go about the propagation of self-giving love? It does this in part, Macquarrie tells us, by being a "conscience" to society. Through its witness—especially the witness of international Christian organizations—the church calls society away from its actual, disordered life. It calls it instead to the authentic communal existence our common morality envisions.

Furthermore, Macquarrie adds, the church fulfills its mission by establishing a Christian presence in society's institutions. This includes, for instance, its government departments, trade unions, corporations, and the like. Through a laity involved in these institutions—often "at the decision-making level"—it serves as the instrument of divine grace in the world, humanizing the social reality in which we are all enmeshed.[129]

To clarify Macquarrie's overall position further, we will turn to his essay on Christianity and violence. The essay appears in the midst of a short book, *The Concept of Peace*. In this book the author defines peace as a costly striving toward wholeness—a wholeness in which all things reach fulfillment and exist together in harmonious interdependence.[130] He stresses that the concept includes not only this goal of wholeness, but also "the process" by which it is achieved. It includes the strife and struggle and suffering involved.[131]

Evoking as it does a scenario of conflict, this understanding of peace inevitably raises the question of violence. Again and again, Macquarrie allows, Christians have condoned violence. Despite this "long history" of support for it, however, the question remains whether violence is ever justifiable for the Christian. Is it ever permissible, in other words, to inflict "death and injury"[132] upon the members of the other side in a conflict?

Macquarrie's answer is yes. His supporting argument is a striking indicator of his position on authority in Christian ethics. Although he considers violence justifiable under certain conditions, Macquarrie does say that today Christians accept it "too quickly and too lightly."[133]

This occasions a vigorous refutation of those who consider Jesus to have been a violent revolutionary. The weight of scholarly evidence goes against this view, he says. In fact, violence is "in flat contradiction" to Jesus' teaching and "out of character with most of what we know about him."[134] Though Jesus was an "opponent" of the established political and ecclesiastical order, he

> was in fact too much of a radical to use the weapons of the existing order and so allow himself and his followers to get locked into the circle of violence. He chose . . . the more costly path of atonement.[135]

Jesus stood, Macquarrie continues, for "a radical change in values, whereas violence can only confirm the existing values and postpone any real change." Violence dehumanizes and begets further violence. Christ's weapons of atonement and reconciliation are the Christian way to break the circle of violence.[136]

In making these points Macquarrie quotes from Jacques Ellul's *Violence: Reflections from a Christian Perspective.* In this work Ellul himself argues unabashedly for Christian pacifism. He claims that anyone who accepts or uses violence "has abdicated from Christianity as a way of life."[137] Macquarrie neither argues with Ellul on this point nor even acknowledges that he makes it. Having rebuked the easy embrace of violent revolution, he says, nevertheless, that "absolute nonviolence" is likewise unacceptable. To the problem of violence there are "no simple solutions," he says. He then proceeds immediately to discuss the circumstances under which "resort to violence may be necessary even to the Christian."[138]

In doing this he invokes the traditional doctrine of the just war (though he dislikes the term *just war*). He summarizes the conditions of legitimate Christian violence as follows. First, there must be a just cause. Second, violence must be the only way left of effecting change. Third, there must be a proper authority. Fourth, there must be a reachable goal. Fifth, the means must be appropriate to the end. Sixth, reconciliation must be considered the ultimate goal.[139]

It is not germane here to consider further either this doctrine or Macquarrie's elaboration of it. What is important here is that Macquarrie does not even discuss how all of this fits with what he has just said about Jesus and violence. How does the just war theory mesh with the idea of stepping outside the circle of violence, making a radical change in values, and choosing the costly path of atonement? It is certainly not obvious how the theory can mesh with it. The fact that Macquarrie does not take pains to try, shows, perhaps, that he does not deem it necessary.

On the other hand, perhaps this *is* consistent with his whole position. He says Jesus is normative, but only as a paradigm of self-giving love. *How* to embody self-giving love remains an open question for Macquarrie. Even Jesus is not the final authority. Tradition reflects growth in understanding that has already taken place. Thus reason can help us continue to grow: the Christ is yet before us.

We will now connect all of this with the Niebuhrian analysis of Christ and culture we have marked out, and then close with some questions. The problem of Christ and culture exists, we said, because there is cultural opposition to the Christian way. On Macquarrie's view, opposition to the way of Christ does not arise from moral pluralism but from failure to live up to the law that is natural to all. As for the relation of Christ's authority to other cultural authorities, Macquarrie again plays down the difference between the Christian and the common morality. He does say that the "context" Christianity provides deepens our moral understanding, but still there is no sharp break with what we know apart from Christ. In its relation to the surrounding culture, the Christian community is to operate within it as a transformative agency. Doing so, however, is not primarily a matter of calling the world to a different morality. It is rather a matter of asking it to live up to the morality it already knows.

All of this verges, perhaps, on what Niebuhr would call the *Christ-of-culture* position in which there is little tension between the church and the world. Macquarrie would rightfully object that he by no means wants to deny the disorder in our personal and social existence. He would say that a call to respect the natural law is itself a call to substantive change.

Still, it is hard to see how Christian morality, when *conceived of* as the natural morality, could avoid reflecting whatever happens to be the prevailing ethos, or at least the prevailing ethos among the intellectual leadership. It will surely be tempting to say of whatever seems right to this culturally dominant group: *this* is the natural morality.

Thus it would not be surprising if a Christian community shaped by Macquarrie's views should turn out to be essentially conservative. It is not clear, however, how such a community could plausibly claim to represent the heritage of the Bible, in which we find constant judgment upon the present order.

There is something to be said, certainly, for the idea that Christian morality reflects convictions common to all. How could one even begin to hear an ethic unrelated to common aspiration? How could a community embracing such an ethic be at all transformative? Surely it is right to stress the necessity of understanding Christ's authority in a way that does not make the Christian ethic seem arbitrary and "unnatural."

But granting the need for continuity between Christian morality and the human moral quest in general, is it true that no jarring discontinuities exist? What justifies the idea that it is only Jesus' self-giving that is normative, and not the *way* he embodied it? By Macquarries's own account, Scripture testifies that in his own self-giving Jesus *refused violence*, preferring the costlier path of "atonement."

If this is not normative, why not? Is it because the theory of natural morality forbids making it so? Is it because we today, due to the insights of tradition and reason, know better than Jesus knew? Why would it not be merely arbitrary to say of Jesus' authority that here it must give way to later authority?

These questions are reminiscent of ones we have asked of the two previous writers in this chapter, underlining the central dilemma of Christian social doctrine at the center. All these writers agree that Christianity must involve itself in the transformation of surrounding culture. All agree that Jesus Christ is authoritative for the pursuit of this task. All agree that some sort of common cause between church and surrounding culture is necessary. Each fails, however, to explain how this latter point justifies the particular limits he paradoxically goes on to place upon Christ's authority. Surely no adequate treatment of Christ and culture can be at ease with such a failure.

CHAPTER FOUR

Liberation and Political Theologies: Gutierrez, Ruether, and Metz

INTRODUCTION

We may say of a society that it has flaws which require us to fine-tune its structures and institutions. Or we may say that it is fundamentally misformed and call for sweeping, revolutionary change.

The three writers we examine in this chapter regard our Western society from this latter point of view. They all see a sharp conflict between the values of the gospel and the values of the modern world. All call for the radical restructuring of our social and political relations. As it happens, they are all Roman Catholic, yet each brings a different perspective to the questions we are considering here.

The first, Gustavo Gutierrez, is a priest from Latin America who identifies with the poor and oppressed of the third world. The second, Rosemary Radford Ruether, is a feminist from North America. The third, Johann Baptist Metz, is a priest from Europe. He is disaffected with the uncritical, bourgeois religion that he says is characteristic of Christianity in the privileged nations.

GUSTAVO GUTIERREZ

As a leading proponent of Latin-American liberation theology, Gustavo Gutierrez is deeply concerned with the radical transformation of society. He is like the other figures of this chapter in this regard. A distinctive mark of his own particular approach, however, is his emphasis upon the claim that the theology of liberation is written from the viewpoint of society's victims. It is a theology, he says, that *begins* in "solidarity with discriminated races, despised cultures, and exploited classes." It is a theology rooted in the plight and praxis of the poor.[1]

This matter of the context, or "matrix,"[2] of theological labor will be the starting point for our exposition of his thought. It has basic methodological significance, according to Gutierrez. It shapes all that he says about Christian existence in the world. Having considered it in more detail, we will turn next to his view of Jesus Christ as the touchstone of Christian thought and action. We will look finally at what all this means for the church and its relation to the cultural life around it.

Starting in the fifteenth century, European civilization established itself in the Americas in the name of commerce and liberty. From one standpoint, it was a movement of noble purpose. From another, it meant only "new and more refined forms of exploitation of the very poorest—of the wretched of the earth."[3] Especially in Latin America, the native peoples and other poor became victims under the ethos and economic dominion of industrialized, capitalist foreign nations.

Meanwhile, the Catholic Church, Gutierrez tells us, was a defensive and timorous institution. It was eager to please the established authorities who themselves had nothing to fear from the church's otherworldly interpretation of the gospel. This had the effect of reinforcing the domination of the poor by the rich.[4]

By the 1930s, however, a new Catholic social doctrine was emerging in Europe, notably in writings by Jacques Maritain. It began to touch Latin-American Catholicism. Although it evoked a concern to correct injustice, it did not, says Gutierrez, radically critique the whole social structure.

About the same time, a socialist current was developing. Its "most outstanding" radical representative, Jose Carlos Mariategui, interpreted Latin-American reality "in creative Marxist terms."[5] Few Christian leaders noticed this development at first, though in time a larger number did. The "revolutionary ferment" in Mexico, Bolivia, and Guatemala during the 1950s and later the "socialist revolution" in Cuba, prepared the way for increasing Christian participation in the socialist liberation movement.

"The year 1965," writes Gutierrez,

> marked a high point in armed struggle in Latin America and
> hastened a political radicalization even of persons who had hoped to
> find other avenues for their revolutionary activity. Camillo Torres and
> "Che" Guevara symbolized so many others—anonymous, commit-
> ted, setting an indelible seal on the Latin American process, raising
> questions and exerting definitive influence in Christian circles.[6]

Shortly afterward, just before the famous meeting of Latin-
American bishops in Medellin, Colombia, in 1968, the theology of
liberation was born.[7] It grew up as Christians already involved in the
"struggle for liberation" began to reflect on their experiences "in the
light of faith."[8] According to Gutierrez, it could not have happened
otherwise—not without the revolutionary movement. It could not
have happened until the "historical liberation praxis" associated with
it had "achieved a certain degree of development and maturity."
For only then was it possible for Christians to live their faith "at the
very heart of the social conflict" occasioned by solidarity with the
poor. And it is this experience, this "spiritual experience," that is
"the very spring and source" of liberation theology.[9]

Any theology, says Gutierrez, expresses a view of faith rooted in
the circumstances of the Christian community at the time. Theology
interprets faith "from a point of departure in a determined situation,
from an insertion and involvement in history, from a particular manner of living our encounter with the Lord in our encounter with
others." Liberation theology is no exception. It has a special history,
namely, the involvement of its makers

> in the concrete historical, liberating, and subversive praxis of the poor
> of this world. . . . It is born of a disquieting, unsettling hope of libera-
> tion. It is born of the struggles, the failures, and the successes of the
> oppressed themselves.[10]

Before the *theology* of liberation, in other words, there were the
persons who have written it. And before their writing of it, there was
the immersion of these persons in the struggle of the poor for justice.
In Latin America this struggle is substantially Marxist, as our exposi-

tion already suggests. The claim about the beginnings of liberation theology thus underscores the Marxist roots of the movement Gutierrez represents.

Liberation theology grew out of insights gained in revolutionary praxis. This, indeed, is how theology *ought* to come into being. The themes this movement considers are the same as those of other Christian theologies, but the approach is different. Here the theologian ponders faith from the standpoint of solidarity with the oppressed.[11] From now on, we should see this as a norm, a requirement of adequate theological method.

The "intellectualizing" of writers who reflect upon the faith from the perspective of the privileged and learned must be "done away with," since it is "only to the poor that the grace of receiving and understanding the kingdom has been granted." The only theology with any promise of adequacy is theology rooted in the practice and aspirations of these people. All theology should be what liberation theology is: a "second act," a discipline that *follows* the "necessary precondition" of involvement in the "liberation praxis" of the poor.[12]

The dominant theologies of Europe and North America today, whether Catholic or Protestant, fail at precisely this point. For they interpret the faith from within the cultural world, not of the plundered and dispossessed, but of the bourgeois middle class. They try to answer questions posed by the modern mentality—liberal in ideology and skeptical or frankly unbelieving when it comes to religion. The bearers of this mentality are themselves the agents of oppression. Any theology which answers to their needs and questions runs the risk of being "the theology of the dominator."[13]

The theology of liberation does not merely address the rift between those who have differences of religious belief but still share basically the same social world and lifestyle. It addresses the rift "between oppressed and oppressors."[14] It brings the message of salvation to bear upon the political conditions that create this rift and attempts to be part of the process in which it is overcome. It works for the building of a new world, a "just and fraternal society."[15]

The justification for doing so, Gutierrez tells us, is that this is what the gospel itself requires. The work of salvation announced and described in the Bible is specifically for this world, which is God's creation and the object of the messianic promises. Here, as the prophets said, a reign of peace will come. Here justice, the rights of the poor, and freedom from fear of enslavement will be established.[16]

This, indeed, was the hope and commitment of Jesus himself. Born into "a social milieu characterized by poverty," he proclaimed a message of good news for the impoverished. He spoke of "a kingdom of justice and liberation, to be established [for] the poor, the oppressed, and the marginalized of history."[17] And his words he backed with deeds. He chose to live and identify with those whom the rich oppressed and despised. He confronted and denounced the agents of injustice around him, whether leaders among his own people or representatives of Roman dominion.[18]

Jesus' contemporaries saw all this as having dangerous political significance, as being a threat to established social structures. It is not that Jesus sought to advance Jewish national interests against the interests of the Roman Empire. In fact, this was a goal he rejected. He did, however, call for universal peace and justice, and his message offended the guardians of oppression and injustice. Because of this, he underwent a political trial and suffered execution.[19]

The evidence, then, does not support the claim some make that the work of Jesus was a strictly "religious" matter and that he was not interested in changing the basic structure of the social order. Gutierrez acknowledges, however, that his work was not strictly political in significance. It is sin, "the breach of friendship with God and other men," that gives rise to oppressive social structures. It is sin from which the gift of Christ redeems us.[20]

Moreover, the kingdom Christ announced is not merely the establishing of a just society. That is part of it, to be sure, but also involved is "the promise and hope of complete communion of all men with God." These points together show why the "social transformation" wrought by the gospel is "permanent and essential." For the gospel "goes to the very root of human existence: the relationship with God in solidarity with other men."[21]

Gutierrez's concern to justify liberation theology by appeal to the Bible—and finally to Christ—illustrates one of his central methodological convictions. To be a Christian, he says, is to affirm that a Jew named Jesus "loved the poor," confronted "the great and powerful" on their behalf, and "was put to death as a subversive." It is to affirm further that this Jesus is the Christ, the Messiah in whom we meet God himself.[22]

This means that Christians are to make his "messianic practice" their own.[23] It means that for Christian faith, Christ is "the principle, the point of departure, of the interpretation of Scripture." He is indeed the "foundation of all theological discourse."[24] If this is so, we may ask how it meshes with the stress Gutierrez puts on solidarity with the plight and praxis of the poor. For in his view, this, too, has central methodological significance.

Consider first that according to Gutierrez, solidarity with the poor involves not merely acts of generosity, but participation in their struggle to change society. More precisely, it involves participation in socialist revolution, its conflict, and even its violence.[25] Such solidarity is the "necessary precondition" of fruitful theological reflection.

Now note the two ways in which this point about solidarity with the poor and the point about Christ as the foundation of theology are brought together. One connection is implicit in what we have already set forth: Christ himself identified with the poor. The other connection is in the idea that he *continues to reveal himself* through the poor.

Among the forerunners of liberation theology was the sixteenth-century missionary, Bartolome de Las Casas. In the name of the gospel, de Las Casas denounced colonization and called for social justice. One of his greatest insights, according to Gutierrez, was the idea that Christ speaks to us from among the poor. He once wrote that in the Indies he had seen "Jesus Christ, our God, scourged and afflicted and crucified, not once, but millions of times."[26]

In thus identifying the poor with Christ, he suggests, says Gutierrez, what is "deepest and most profound" in his theology: that "Christ calls us, summons us, challenges us, from within the mass of the oppressed." Indeed, these oppressed ones are today "historical agents" of the "new understanding of the faith" that has appeared in the theology of liberation.[27] And it is in view of the truth Las Casas taught that this fact accords with the idea of Christ as the point of departure for theological reflection.

Liberation theology ponders the revolutionary struggle of the poor in light of faith. To do this, Gutierrez tells us, "is really to examine the meaning of Christianity itself and the mission of the church in the world."[28] We have been learning about the meaning of Christianity according to the liberation point of view. What we have seen manifests itself in the corresponding account of church and society. That account also reflects, says Gutierrez, the wisdom of Vatican II and it is with this that we will begin to look at it more closely.

The church, said the council in its "Dogmatic Constitution on the Church," is a "visible sacrament" of salvation, a sign of Christ on earth. It is the means by which God meets humanity and brings us into unity with himself and with one another. In this (though not in all its texts) the council broke sharply with the "ecclesiocentric consciousness" of the Middle Ages. In the Middle Ages, being for or against Christ *meant* being for or against the church.

Now, says Gutierrez, the church understands that it is not the single locus of Christ's presence. For in being a sacrament it is precisely a sign of the work of Christ in *all* the world. Furthermore, it knows that to be an effective sign it must not exist for itself, but for others, serving as Christ served. And if it attains to a full understanding of the metaphor, Gutierrez suggests, the church will know also that to show full awareness that it is a *sign* of Christ's *wider* work, it must learn from the world as well as teach the world.[29]

In laying down this interpretation of Vatican II's doctrine of the church, Gutierrez is not claiming full conciliar endorsement of the theology of liberation. He is saying, though, that the main themes of this theology cohere with the council's basic outlook. The church should be a sign of salvation, and this means serving others as Christ did. Therefore, service of the poor and plundered and prophetic denunciation of those who do the plundering should especially mark the church's presence in the world. And if Christ is at work in all humanity and not the church alone, then it is plausible to suppose that he can speak through the revolutionary praxis of the poor. He can thus enlighten believers about the deeper implications of their faith.

Once so enlightened, true believers will seek nothing less than to be a church *of* the poor and *for* the poor. In the past, Christianity has been nearly synonymous with Western culture, the white race, the dominant classes. But in truth it must "build the church from

below, from the poor, from the exploited classes, from the margi-
nated races and despised cultures."[30] Otherwise, the church cannot
be a true sign.

More is required, however. The church of the poor must also
identify and cooperate with the revolutionary struggle of the poor.
Addressing the Latin-American situation in particular, Gutierrez tells
us that the church must adopt a praxis of subversion, a praxis that
will topple the present capitalist social order[31] and open the way to
"an authentic community of brothers and sisters."[32]

Short of this, the church's evangelism will neither gain a hearing nor accomplish its true objective. "Only a break with the unjust
order and a frank commitment to a new society," Gutierrez writes,
"can make the message of love which the Christian community
bears credible to Latin Americans."[33] In any case, the message
would not otherwise be truly preached. For the God who liberates
his people in history can be proclaimed only with *works*—deeds of
solidarity with the poor that undermine the "system of oppression"
and point toward a "classless society."[34]

The announcement of the gospel should result in "conscientization." That is, it should politicize its hearers, awaken them to the fact
of oppression, and produce commitment to change. This can happen
only when the announcement occurs within the very kind of commitment it is meant to evoke.[35]

Without liberation praxis, evangelism is deficient. *With* liberation praxis, it is dangerous. History is a realm of conflict, according to
Gutierrez.[36] When the church breaks with the prevailing social order
and attempts to politicize the lowly ones who are its victims, it can
expect the conflict to touch its own. It can expect, on the one hand,
to face calumny, torture, or martyrdom. Many have already
experienced these and others still do in Latin America.[37] It can expect, on the other hand, that occasion may arise when it must itself
employ "just violence" against the oppressor.[38]

To use terms drawn from Niebuhr, for Gutierrez, loyalty to
Christ engenders conflict with the surrounding culture. We have
seen, too, that the authority of Christ overrides other cultural authorities. Liberation theology's loyalty to the revolution of the poor
might appear to contradict this, but it affirms that these poor in fact
embody the present will of Christ. We have seen, finally, that the

proper business of the Christian community is to break with the surrounding cultural life in order to transform it.

We noted earlier the claim that liberation theology is compatible with the basic perspective of Vatican II. Gutierrez also shows that its main themes have received explicit support from the increasingly vocal clergy and hierarchy of Latin America.[39] Liberation theology is, indeed, an unsettling interpretation of the Christian gospel. But how can Gutierrez justify his claim that solidarity with the poor—and specifically the socialist revolutionary praxis of the poor—is the necessary precondition of fruitful theological reflection?

Gutierrez says this is where Christ reveals himself today. We may agree that in some sense he has told the truth. Surely the existence of the poor represents a massive challenge to bourgeois Christianity. Surely Christ does speak to us today through their pain and struggles. However, not all the poor practice socialist revolution. Why should we accept this segment of the poor as the present normative disclosure of Christ? If there are any Christian reasons for doing so, they will surely grow out of the original telling of the Jesus story.

But if one compares the revolutionary praxis of the poor and the original story of Jesus, it is the story that has the greater authority. And if the story has the greater authority, then our identification with socialist revolution must be contingent upon what the story says. Then we cannot claim, in any *logical* sense, that solidarity with socialist revolution is the necessary precondition of fruitful theology. It *may* be necessary, but that will depend.

Still, there is a point here that seems well taken. In any interpretation of a tradition we certainly reflect our standpoint. So we must take up a Christian standpoint to give a Christian interpretation of the Christian tradition. And although it may seem rudimentary to say this, it is important to do so. Christians have not always understood how misleading a theology may be which comes from persons who are comfortable with privilege. Gutierrez understands this well enough to challenge us.

We may say, too, that Gutierrez himself knows the kind of question I have raised.[40] He remarks in one place that the gospel continually challenges our attempts to embody it.[41] In another he even says that the Christian hope keeps us "from any idolatry toward unavoidably ambiguous human achievement, from any absolutizing of revolution."[42] What remains open to question, however, is whether this is a point to which he himself gives serious enough attention.

ROSEMARY RADFORD RUETHER

We meet now a writer whose works display throughout the overarching theme of deliverance from alienation through transcendence. In several books published from 1967 to the present, Rosemary Radford Ruether has spelled out the implications of this theme for the church's understanding of its mission in the world. In doing so she has drawn upon the prophetic, messianic, and apocalyptic elements of the Judeo-Christian heritage.

A provocative Christian social doctrine has come out of this. Her 1967 volume, *The Church Against Itself*,[43] took up the theme of constant renewal under God as a fundamental trait of the church. Succeeding volumes further explored this theme. They used it as a basis for calling the church to reconsider its relationship to poverty, oppression (especially the oppression of women), anti-Semitism, and the environmental crisis.

In expounding Ruether's developed social doctrine we will focus once again upon the questions central to this essay. Namely, how are we to regard the authority of Christ in a pluralistic world? And how in light of this are we to understand the role of the church within the cultural life of which it is a part?

Ruether's central theme involves analysis both of basic human problems and also of how we may overcome them. In looking at the first of these we notice, besides her account of the disorder in our existence, a strongly positive attitude to earthly existence, to our being bound up with this created world.

Her attitude to the created world is basic and will remain prominent as we move on to consider what she says about the human encounter with transcendence. In connection with this latter, we will meet with her ideas concerning the authority of Christ and the cultural task of the church.

The one word that best summarizes Ruether's analysis of the human plight is *alienation*. In suggesting an experience of brokenness, estrangement, and disunity, it identifies the fundamental problem which all our longing for salvation addresses.

We will begin by explaining what Ruether takes to be a characteristic and destructive feature of our culture: a mind-body dualism. Then we will consider briefly various aspects of the alienation to which she says this pernicious dualism leads.

According to Ruether, modern technological society still reflects the tension typical of ancient Greece between the mind and the body. The tendency remains, she says, to divide reality in two—the one part mental and the other bodily or thinglike. It is still the case that what we associate with mind we take to be superior, and what we associate with body we take to be inferior. In the terms of Descartes, who maintained the mind-body dichotomy in slightly different language, what is not mind or associated with mind, is simply object. As a reality outside the thinking subject, its status is that of a thing to be used.[44]

It is this "dualistic" and "hierarchical"[45] view of reality, says Ruether, that generates alienation. This alienation is an estrangement from self, from our fellow human beings, and even from the earth and sky.[46] Our heritage of dualism has led us to look askance at our bodies. Thus we fear and defame things sensual. We even imagine our salvation to reside in the final separation of the soul from the body. In being thus alienated from our bodies, we are alienated from our very selves, for to these bodies, Ruether believes, we are inextricably linked.

It is not only our bodies from which this dualism separates us. For it encourages in general a subject-object (or I-it) way of thinking. Whatever I—or indeed *we*, whether tribe or tongue, race or sex—associate with mind as opposed to body becomes a *thing*, an object outside and inferior to the community of thinking persons. Men associate themselves with the mind and associate women with the body. Whites do the same with blacks. In each case, and in others like it, the dualistic way of seeing reduces some to the status of inferior objects and engenders thereby divisions among people. We are thus alienated from one another.

Even our dealings with nature do not escape this. Nature is body, not mind. It is the object of human knowledge and human use. Under the influence of mind-body dualism, we come to treat it without respect. We thoughtlessly deface the landscape, pollute the air and water, and abuse the animals. This thinking estranges us even from our home of earth and sky.

All of this is epitomized, Ruether tells us, in the alienation of the sexes fostered by a pervasive symbolism. This symbolism sees man as a thinking, independent spirit, and woman as a bodily, sensual object, subservient to man.[47]

Because this wreaks havoc on the quality of human life, all of it must be overturned. In place of the "aberrant spirituality" of dualism we must give ourselves over to a "more deeply integral vision"—one that sees all things in their unity and interconnectedness. We must rebel against "this world," it is true. But this means rebellion against misguided values. It does not mean *flight from* the body, but a *return to* the body. We must return to what Ruether calls a "true body-self in community with our fellow persons and creation."

This return means we will neither exploit nor abandon what God has made. All creation—male and female, human and non-human—will enter into "harmonious and mutually supportive, rather than antagonistic, relations." We will aspire, in the imagery of Scripture, to "that 'good land' of messianic blessedness which makes all things whole."[48]

What leads us to this good land? What heals the brokenness in human relationships, the alienation? The answer, in a phrase, is "encounter with God."[49] In her book, *The Radical Kingdom*, Ruether expresses her certainty that no fixed nature imprisons human beings. Human consciousness can change and human community can be transformed. Indeed, the struggle for change and transformation—for a new being and a new order—gives to human life its distinctiveness.[50]

God's role in all of this is indispensable. In his meeting of men and women, God draws the human family out of the past toward a transformed future. As a God of grace, he provides a context of assurance within which to cope with the need for change. As a God of judgment, he provides a constant challenge to present wisdom and achievement. He shatters the tendency of us all to make a god of ourselves and our culture. Through human voices he beckons us never to stop, always to move on. Even those who speak for him give no final message. God's Word transcends every expression of it, never ceasing to call its hearers onward to new possibilities of existence.[51]

But God does not merely dissuade us from stopping. Rather, he establishes the direction of the journey. Our proper goal, as Ruether puts it, is to be delivered from alienation into a land of messianic blessedness. Ruether reflects the Judeo-Christian heritage in seeing God's Word as a constant summons to human transformation. She reflects it, too, in suggesting where his Word is leading us.

The messianic hope of the Hebrew prophets, she tells us, was a this-worldly hope, a confidence in the coming of a just and peaceful harmony on earth.[52] Later apocalyptic thought envisioned a heavenly world beyond space and time. Nevertheless, it preserved the prophetic concern with earthly history.

Although Ruether at times links apocalyptic thought with attitudes of otherworldliness,[53] she repeatedly suggests that it is at bottom consistent with Hebrew prophetism.[54] Although apocalypticism looks to the overthrow of the present evil age, this happens precisely in order to renew this world. "The apocalyptic view of redemption," she writes,

> is basically social and outer-directed. One does not look inward to the salvation of some personal essence; one looks outward at history and society, at injustice, oppression, and cruel and irrational destruction. It is this historical realm that is to be grappled with and radically reversed.[55]

Ruether's studies convince her, in other words, that the messianic hope remains alive as a *historical* and *social* hope. Even with the development in the Judeo-Christian tradition of the idea of heaven and life after death, the messianic concern for transformed human politics, for community on earth instead of alienation remains prominent. It is an integral part, indeed, of the apocalyptic outlook.

We have by now noted Ruether's analysis of basic human problems and traced the outline of what in her view would overcome these problems. Obviously, for her the human voices through whom God has spoken decisively are the voices preserved in the Scripture of the Judeo-Christian tradition. Among all of these, however, the one key voice, she says, is that of Jesus Christ. Thus we come directly to the question, central in these pages, of the authority of Christ.

In a 1981 volume entitled *To Change the World: Christology and Cultural Criticism,* Ruether claims that the center of Christian theology is "not an idea, but a person"—namely, Jesus of Nazareth.[56] And even though the Bible itself seems to sanction evil patterns of behavior and thought, it contains "revelatory paradigms by which to construct a redeeming vision of an alternative humanity and world."

Then she says, "The teachings and liberating praxis of Jesus prove to be a focal point for this critical and transforming vision." They illuminate our situation even today. Jesus does not recede into the past as a mere historical figure. Rather, he continues to show us true "messianic humanity." We glimpse in his life the pattern of human relationships that will one day arrive in fullness.[57]

In setting out to interpret Jesus, Ruether acknowledges the "hermeneutical circle" that encompasses all such interpretation. Even though the results of historical study do put limits on what one can truthfully say of Jesus, the perspective of the interpreter inevitably affects the judgments made about him.

Ruether admits that the questions she takes to be "most pressing and inescapable for our times" have shaped her own perspective. These are

> the questions of political commitment in the light of poverty and oppression, the question of anti-Judaism and religious intolerance, the question of justice for the female half of the human race, and the question of human survival in the face of chronic environmental abuse.[58]

Historical inquiry, she then argues, shows that Jesus' idea of the kingdom of God was in fact "primarily in the prophetic tradition." It represented the fulfillment of God's will on the earth, the satisfaction of basic human needs, and the establishment of peace and justice in the world.[59] His message was social and political. In it he was enlisting his hearers in a movement to vanquish historical evil.

What made his message original was not the repudiation of the prophetic heritage in a spiritualizing of the kingdom. It was rather his summons to a style of leadership and a form of community "based on service to others, even unto death." It was his critique of the lust for domination, prestige, power, and wealth, that he believed to be the fundamental root of injustice and oppression.[60]

As the key voice in the heritage, Jesus is crucial. What we say of him is the "pivot," Ruether says, of constructive Christian thought.[61] It is likewise the standard of authentic Christian life. We show that we embody truly the ideas of Christianity by following the "liberating praxis" of Jesus. As much as possible, we put ourselves "in the place where he put himself, as ones who make themselves last and servant of all."[62]

There are two ways, however, in which Ruether relativizes the authority of Jesus. One is to say that although Jesus is *our* Christ, the Messiah of the Christian tradition, this does not mean that he negates or displaces the symbols of communal liberation on which other faiths are based.

In Ruether's writings the usual context of this idea is the problem of Christian anti-Semitism. For her, Christianity's "anti-Semitic heritage" is no accident but the direct issue of "Christian theological anti-Judaism."[63] She repudiates this anti-Judaism in several ways, but returns often to this basic point: Christianity is not the only pathway to salvation. Not until we forsake "imperialist" attitudes and embrace "existing human pluralism," can Jesus' name "cease to be a name that creates alienation of Jew from Christian, Christian from non-Christian."[64]

Even, however, as the key voice of the *Christian* tradition, Jesus' word is not the final word. This is the second respect in which Ruether relativizes his authority. The cloud of past witnesses—and she apparently includes Jesus in this group—does rescue us in its guiding function from sheer "normless subjectivism." Yet in all Christian tradition there is no "absolute point of reference" for establishing our values or answering our questions.[65] Jesus himself pointed beyond himself to the Holy Spirit, whose function precisely is to surprise and radically recreate.[66] And it is the Holy Spirit alone whose word is final. It is in "present encounter" with this Spirit that we meet the absolute point of reference, the final authority.[67]

Ruether further illuminates all of this with her remarks on the "paradox of 'tradition.'" Tradition, she tells us, is true continuity with the gospel "only when tradition is free to be discontinuous with itself."[68] The authority of past witnesses functions properly only when it is a "handmaiden and not a dictator." To be true it must aid in the hearing of the Word without defining its exact content. The paradox is that while tradition assures continuity, true continuity means openness to discontinuity. In one passage Ruether says that we must be ready to break with tradition in such a way as to find "a new and more profound continuity."[69] By this she seems to say that the tradition calls for change, but not *any* change. The check on allowable discontinuity is this: it must grow out of what the church has believed before, and not deny it altogether.

Ruether does not, to my knowledge, deal with how these ideas about tradition might bear fruit in the resolving of theological disputes. Her chief concern is to argue for constant openness to transformation. The effect, certainly, is similar to that of her remarks on the Holy Spirit. Neither Jesus nor anyone else *in history* has final authority over Christian existence. This is a point she makes late as well as early in her scholarly career.[70]

We now move to consider the role of the church within the cultural life of which it is part. This is a central question—arguably *the* central question—in Ruether's writings. Her answer, broadly put, is this: the church's role is to mediate the reality of God to the world.

Ruether's view of God develops largely through reflections whose predominant theme is the church. It is therefore natural that her ideas about the church should resemble strikingly the ideas we have just been considering. God, we saw, shatters our idolatrous worship of present wisdom and achievement, calling us ever forward to new possibilities of existence. The church mediates the reality of God by itself having an "iconoclastic function"[71] in society. Despite their capacity for revolutionary change, human beings often contentedly accept what is, without thought of their need for renewal. It is the business of the church, in word and life, to question this, to break conventional images, to jar people loose from the grip of the customary.

In one chapter of *Liberation Theology*, Ruether discusses the Catholic religious order as a paradigm for a deeper understanding of the larger church. Monasticism first arose, she says, as a reaction against the "domestication" of the church under Constantine. In the early years, being a Christian meant leaving the "mainstream of society" and entering a "new community of personal rebirth, risk, and commitment." In the Constantinian era, however, being a Christian became part of ordinary good citizenship. It no longer signaled a passion for social and political rebirth. The monastic communities sprang up to fill the role played earlier by ordinary Christian congregations. In effect, they became communities of dissent from the status quo.[72]

Ruether proposes that the ideals of the religious orders and the early congregations represent in fact the "normative form" of the whole Chrisian community. What we should be considering, she tells us, is the idea of the "convergence of the religious order and the local congregation."[73] The truly Christian community lives by unordinary standards. It exists, she writes, "on the transcendent edge between the dominant society and some 'new world' which is about to be born."[74]

The ethos of iconoclasm must affect the church's self-evaluation as surely as its evaluation of surrounding culture. In order to mediate convincingly the reality of its image-breaking God, the church must be, in the phrase of the Ruether book title, *The Church Against Itself*. It must constantly repent of itself, constantly fight its own sin, constantly open itself to the new. It must itself embody the openness before God to which it invites society.[75]

We saw before that in Ruether's view, God not only challenges our uncritical acceptance of the customary; he also points us in the right direction. The church in like manner goes beyond questioning present forms of life to suggesting new ones. It is not only an image-breaking but an image-making entity. From the messianic vision of the Judeo-Christian heritage it finds the portrait of a new humanity: communal, nonexploitive, earth-embracing.[76] In the midst of society it tries to embody this new humanity. It lives at variance with the dominant way of life both to judge that way of life and also to transform it. It is, in short, a redeeming counterculture, a community whose way and words pull humanity toward renewal.[77]

Nothing of what the church says or stands for is final, of course. What we met before in Ruether's discussion of the Holy Spirit and of the paradox of tradition applies here as well. The church's message to society is itself constantly renewed under the impact of the "decisive moment" of encounter with the Spirit.[78] This idea is familiar by now and is reminiscent of the existentialist theologian, Rudolph Bultmann, whom Ruether admires. It brings to a close our exposition of her writings. At the same time it suggests the main question with which these writings leave us.

We have not in these pages dealt adequately with all of Ruether's concerns, most obviously, perhaps, her concern with the gospel and sexism.[79] From the standpoint of the issues pivotal to our overall project, however, what we've seen so far has been sufficient:

—The human predicament is alienation rooted in the dualism of mind and body.

—We are saved through encounter with God.

—We learn God's way in the Judeo-Christian tradition, especially in the voice of Jesus.

—God's *final* word, nevertheless, has yet to be spoken.

—The church's proper business is to transform society by its iconoclastic life and message.

A crucial question remains, however. What has happened in this account to the authority of Jesus Christ? What does it mean for Jesus to be the key voice to which the church attends, but not the final voice? Can the Spirit authorize thought and action contrary to the thought and action of the Nazarene? And if so, to what degree, and in what way?

When Ruether argues for the liberation of women from oppression at the hands of a male elite, she invokes the Jesus story in her support.[80] Sometimes she exhibits sympathy for the use of violence in a just cause, as she does in discussions of Reinhold Niebuhr and of South American liberation theology. When she does so, she does not invoke the Jesus story, nor even consider the New Testament's account of Jesus' own attitude to political violence.[81] His attitude appears to have been resolutely negative.[82] Her selective ignoring of Jesus certainly suggests that however important the authority of Christ is for Ruether's exposition, it remains nevertheless a highly ambiguous authority.

That this is so seems consistent with Ruether's overall account, according to which God is "the imageless one"[83] whose Word is a constant challenge and surprise. But how, we may well wonder, does this relate to the apparently opposite claim of the New Testament that affirms Jesus Christ as the very *image* of the invisible Father?[84] On its face, at least, this represents a biblical challenge to a central element of Ruether's interpretation, raising again the questions which will occupy us to the end of the study.

JOHANNES BAPTIST METZ

Nineteenth-century liberal assurances that the kingdom of God was emerging progressively within history fell under withering criticism from two sources. The first was from biblical scholarship, which awakened a sense of the New Testament's apocalyptic character. The second was from neoorthodoxy, which awakened a sense of the persistence and depth of human evil. Even with the passing of liberal optimism, however, liberal concern for *this* world as the locus of the kingdom of God continued to be influential, as our survey of recent theological writings has already shown.

Johannes Baptist Metz, a Catholic professor at Münster, exhibits this concern himself, but he also positions himself in an interesting relationship to both these factors in liberalism's decline. How he does this is an important and provocative part of his entire understanding.

What does it mean to be *in* culture *as* loyalists to Jesus Christ? For Metz it means above all, *political* engagement. To follow Christ truly is to seek a new world, a human culture politically transformed. It means to let the story of Jesus Christ guide all effort to that end. In filling out this claim Metz repudiates the bourgeois or middle-class religion from which his own "political theology" departs. He develops a view of the world as open to renewal and sets forth an understanding of the church—its accountability to Christ and its responsibility to society.

Metz says that bourgeois culture and religion are the consequence of the Enlightenment. In his *Faith in History and Society*, first published in 1977, and in English translation in 1980,[85] he attempts a "theological analysis" of the "crisis caused by the Enlightenment."[86] The "most important" element of this crisis is what he calls "privatization."[87] This tendency is nourished by the market economy and the ethos of personal freedom. It is the tendency for the individual to abstract his own interests from the public interest—

from the needs and concerns of the community. Related to, and exacerbating this, are the disparagement of tradition and authority and the corresponding veneration of reason.

These elements of the Enlightenment heritage also detach the individual from society. Now, for example, it is immature to depend for moral understanding upon the communal tradition and the guidance of those who mediate it. This compromises the autonomy of the individual. It is better to choose for oneself.

The Enlightenment envisioned the education of the entire human race in the use of the intellect so all people would be free from ideological domination. The peasant classes, however, were virtually illiterate at the time education was intensifying and the encyclopedias were being written. The paradoxical effect was thus the making, Metz tells us, of "a new elite or a new aristocracy": the middle class.[88] Its concerns were (and remain) autonomy, property, stability, and success. Another concern was and is free competition in a marketplace dominated by the principle of exchange, of always getting something in return.

These concerns do not fit well the practice of compassion on behalf of those not among the elite, those who are the least among the brethren.[89] It is just such a practice, however, to which Jesus invites his followers. The conflict this suggests raises the question of religion and takes us to Metz's account of how the Enlightenment understood it.

Enlightenment critics said religion was ideology. Voltaire, for instance, claimed it was the self-serving tool of the priestly class. These critics said also that its ideas were based on untenable tradition and authority. Yet there was a kind of religion the Enlightenment did affirm: natural religion, the religion of reason. Scholars thought this to be justifiable by reference to reason alone, without reliance on traditional claims concerning revelation.

Since it was middle-class reason that determined the contents of this religion, however, it came to reflect the middle-class ethos. It was as though specially prepared, Metz writes, "for the domestic use of the propertied middle-class citizen." He says further that

> it is above all a religion of inner feeling. It does not protest . . . or oppose in any way the definitions of reality, meaning, or truth . . . ac-

cepted by the middle-class society of exchange and success. It gives greater height or depth to what applies even without it.[90]

Metz remarks appreciatively that this was a point well noted by the neoorthodox or "dialectical" theologians, Karl Barth and Dietrich Bonhoeffer. Though in important respects he is highly critical of dialectical theology, he stands with it in rejecting the bourgeois colors of liberal Enlightenment religion.[91] The message of Jesus is *not*, he says, compatible with the present dominant social values. Yet the view that it *is* compatible with them presents a temptation to which the church is always in danger of succumbing. The church must face up, he says in *Followers of Christ*, to the danger of "creeping adaptation to the predominant expectations of society." It must beware the threat that the "religion of the cross" may become a mere "religion of well-being."[92]

These words are themselves reminiscent of the prophetic fervor of dialectical theology. The theme they evoke—what it means for the church to be *truly* Christian—will soon occupy us at greater length. But first we will consider certain propositions about the world that are central to Metz. Together they form the center of Metz's claim that loyalty to Christ demands commitment to the political conversion of the world. With these propositions we will see an important difference between Metz and the dialectical theologians.

A key work here is Metz's *Theology of the World*, published in the late 1960s. In it he offers "a theological interpretation of the secular world today."[93] Several themes intertwine, but for our purposes two closely related affirmations are especially important. One is that human beings shape the world. The Greeks, Metz reminds us, saw the world as "divinized." They believed that nature had a kind of godlike sovereignty over human life. It was unconquerable and uncontrollable.[94] Though this view remained influential into the Christian era, our ideas now are changing. No longer do we see ourselves as dominated by nature. We now believe, instead, that out of nature we form a world of our own imagining. Now we see ourselves as master builders, creating what Metz calls "the world of man, a *hominized* world."[95] Rather than being an "imposed fate," the world in this view comes into being through human freedom.[96]

This transition, Metz declares, has emerged *through* Christianity. The idea of a transcendent Creator—one who, as the author of 1 Timothy says, "dwells in unapproachable light"—divests nature of divine features. Now, being less awesome, it is more malleable. More than this, Metz goes on, according to the gospel the world exists precisely "for the sake of human freedom." It is meant to be in our hands. It is meant to be our responsibility.[97]

With this we have in fact adumbrated the second claim that is of interest to us here. According to Metz, the world Christianity envisages is an historical world. We are to understand it "as history."[98] Although for the Greeks the world is an uncompromising nature, indifferent to human strivings, for the biblical people it is hospitable to these strivings. God is *before* the world. His promises assure us that we do not seek a new city in vain. It will not come to us ready-made, but neither will it elude us inevitably. Our world is the framework of a story, a movement in a direction, a movement toward a promised ending.[99]

Secular versions of this new understanding—Marxism, for example—may speak of human responsibility for "the evolution of this world according to the laws of immanent progress." However, this masks what is really the case, Metz suggests, about "purely secular belief in the future." This is a painful, oppressive anxiety over where our freedom may actually take us. Without faith in the promises of God, without assurance that Jesus Christ *is* our future, we feel threatened by what lies ahead. Only with this faith and this assurance can we accept the "precariousness" of our freedom and at the same time look forward in confidence.[100]

We see in the Bible a striking antithesis. It says that the world is God's good creation, a place whose foundation and goal is Christ. It also says, however, that the world is the sphere of darkness, the dwelling place of evil powers. Any account of the world faithful to Scripture must deal with this antithesis.

Metz's own treatment of it develops in part through critical analysis of rival views. Neoorthodox writers attempt, he says, to

> fix this antithesis as a paradoxical unity, that is, to see the world in such a way that it is always and constantly both creation and potential disaster, promise and crisis, sign-post and darkness, and so on.[101]

Against this, Metz replies that the gospel does not envisage salvation *and* damnation, light *and* darkness for the world. It speaks of salvation *or* damnation, of light *or* darkness. The promise of the gospel is that God is indeed making the world new.

Another side of neoorthodoxy, represented by the existentialist thought exemplified by Bultmann, fails also to affirm the historical future. Its overriding concern is with the present moment of decision. "The present alone dominates," says Metz. "There is no real future!" Scripture, however, considers the world an "*historical* world." It is a world moving "toward the future of God ... promised to us in the resurrection of Jesus."[102]

Hope, indeed, is *central* to the scriptural vision, says Metz. Theologies, therefore, that neglect the idea of a coming new world not only neglect an important department of Christian doctrine, they neglect what is basic to all doctrine. Eschatology, he declares, should determine and shape every theological statement.[103]

Eschatology does shape the interpretation Metz gives to Scripture's dual claim that the world is good and also evil. The dialectical unity of these two is not the point. It is, rather, the potential of a world now evil to become a new world, a transformed world. Instead of explaining the antithesis paradoxically, in other words, Metz explains it historically, or better, eschatalogically. In light of the future of God, the present age stands condemned and the world is evil. But in that same light the present age stands open to renewal and the world is good.[104]

Both the critique of middle-class culture and the treatment so far of Metz's interpretation of the world illuminate this claim. It remains for us to clarify how Metz's outlook differs from that of nineteenth-century liberalism. Again, eschatology is pivotal, and in particular, apocalypticism.

We remarked earlier how biblical scholarship, by making the New Testament's apocalyptic tone familiar, helped undermine the liberal doctrine of steady evolution toward the fulfillment of God's purposes on earth. Metz resembles the liberals in seeing *this* world as the locus of divine concern. The liberals tended also, however, to look with favor on the cultural life of their time. They saw it, indeed, as a proper stage in the upward ascent of history.

As such optimism is foreign to the apocalyptic outlook,

however, it is foreign also to Metz. We have noticed already his repudiation of the present social values. Still, he hopes for the future. We are able to see how when we consider his reflections on apocalyptic symbolism. [105]

Metz does not deal with this explicitly in *Theology of the World*. He does in two later books, *Faith in History and Society* and *Followers of Christ*. In those books he attempts to distinguish evolutionary and apocalyptic consciousness. Today's evolutionary consciousness is loosed, as Metz apparently sees it, from the dogma of progress. It treats time as a continuum stretching foward without purpose and without end. Time for it is an "empty infinity" in which "everyone and everything is enclosed without grace." The signs of this outlook are easy, he says, to discern. They are, "on the one hand, widespread apathy, and, on the other, unreflecting hatred; on the one hand, fatalism and, on the other, fanaticism." They are the responses to which the "myth" of a bleak, relentless evolution leads. [106]

By contrast, apocalyptic consciousness fosters hope. It is not, though, a hope based on belief in the tidy, upward ascent of culture, and here is the difference between Metz and classic liberalism. The apocalyptic outlook brings in the ideas of interruption, discontinuity, and surprise. What lies ahead is God, the second coming of Christ, the transfiguration of all things. However, the way to this future is not a smooth way. It is marked by catastrophe, by radical upheaval. [107]

Metz's exposition suffers somewhat from unclarity and the lack of enlightening examples. Still, it conveys again the idea that it is worthwhile to seek a better world. And it adds to this the idea that renewal may involve abrupt transitions. For example, apocalyptic time is not orderly and predictable, but broken, startling, revolutionary. Finally, the exposition conveys the idea that the biblical hope means urgency and daring, a refusal to adapt to the status quo. It communicates a "feeling for the closeness of our deadlines," a readiness here and now to follow Christ. [108]

These remarks on the apocalyptic element in Metz's thought complete our treatment of his developed theology of the world. We will turn next to his account of the church.

Again, our question is, What does it mean to be *in* culture *as* loyalists to Christ? Metz's basic claim, we said, is that it means seeking the political conversion of the world. It is this, he would say, to which the church is called. We may clarify the claim in two steps. We will first consider Metz's understanding of the church's accountability to Christ. We will then look in more detail at his view of how it functions in the cultural life around it.

Following Christ is quite simply *the* key, Metz believes, to the authenticity of the church. The elaboration of this theme occurs mainly in his later writings, where we find constant emphasis upon it. Christian faith, he says, is not true faith unless it is "enacted . . . in the messianic praxis of discipleship,"[109] in the faithful "imitation" of its Lord.[110]

Metz agrees with the commonplace assertion that a "crisis of identity" now besets the church. The cause of this crisis, though, is not the content of the Christian message, but the denial by the church of its "practical meaning."[111] Thus the "basic imperative" of the church—that it "more decisively turn itself into a church that follows Christ"—is also the clue to resolving its present difficulties. "The way out of the crisis," he says simply, "is the way of following and imitating Christ."[112]

This means that the knowledge necessary to authentic Christian life is "practical knowledge."[113] And this we gain, Metz tells us, by remembering. We must remember especially the stories that narrate the beginnings of the larger Christian story still unfolding. From the start, he writes, Christianity has not been "primarily a community interpreting and arguing, but a community remembering and narrating." It has told the story of "the passion, death, and resurrection of Jesus," and it has told it "with a practical intention."[114]

Christians, he says further, are those who remember how Jesus inaugurated God's kingdom. He confessed himself as the one who was on the side of the oppressed and rejected, and proclaimed "the kingdom of God as the liberating power of unconditional love."[115]

To Metz this fact is deeply significant for how we do theology. Indeed, according to him "narrative memory" should have "cognitive primacy" in the church's effort to understand its faith. A theology that proceeds without relying on narrative memory contributes to "the extinction of the identifiable content of Christian salvation."[116]

By taking shape under the impact of the original stories, however, theology can break through the "magic circle of the prevailing consciousness" and mobilize a "dangerous tradition." This tradition is dangerous because it challenges the dominant structures of society.[117] Only such a theology can identify successfully what true Christianity is. Only such a theology can build up the "practical conformity to Christ" basic to an authentic Christian witness in the world.[118]

The church is accountable to Christ *for the sake of* the world.[119] The narrative and practical Christianity Metz recommends involves renunciation of many of the world's values. It does not, however, involve giving up on the world's future. As he says in *Theology of the World*, the Christian despises the present order because of the hope that it can be overcome. This hope provides an "initiative" for "changing the world toward the kingdom of God."[120] True Christianity, he says in *Faith in History and Society*, "introduces the remembered freedom of Jesus into modern society." It introduces this remembered story into its basic outlook or "consciousness" and into its way of life or "praxis."[121]

How does it do this? One way is through social criticism. A theology sensitive to the memory of Christ and the promise of God for the future will be a "political theology." It will make the public aware of the conflict between the message of Jesus and current social reality. The church is to bear a political witness of this kind, announcing a salvation that liberates and transforms the social world. Within the culture around it, Metz writes, it is to function "as an *institution of social criticism.*"[122]

Not merely, however, is it to *speak* in judgment. It is also, in its members' way of life, to *be* a social pioneer. Metz develops this idea by expounding three images of the church. According to one, the church is a paternalistic institution, a "church looking after the people."[123] The bourgeois image of the church, on the other hand, criticizes the idea of church authority connected with the paternalistic model. It does so, however, from the standpoint of bourgeois ideals.

A third, or "post-bourgeois," image is that of the church as "basic community." Here the people overcome excessive dependence on the pope and the bishops and take responsibility themselves for enhancing the church's faithfulness to its mission. Such a church is developing already in the third world, though it "scarcely exists" in Metz's own German Catholicism.[124] It is like the bourgeois church in criticizing forms of ecclesiastical authority that make people dependent. It is unlike it, however, in seeking to renew the church, not on the basis of modern values, but on the basis of the gospel.

It does not see the human person as "an essentially dominating kind of being" or accept the ethos of constant struggle for advantage over others.[125] Instead, the basic community church seeks a new humanity nourished by the values of the one who called himself the bread of life. The basic communities that make up such a church become "the bearers of anthropological revolution." They are the "heralds of a new political culture" characterized by the "non-dominating human virtues" of compassion, sympathy, love, peace, and solidarity.[126] Metz declares, "Living differently: this was always a characteristic mark of Christians." When the church *does* live by its "authentic message," it does the "political and moral pioneer work" that can contribute to nothing less than "the conversion of bourgeois hearts.[127]

A final way in which the church may change the world, adumbrated in Metz's writings but not developed at length, is that of "revolutionary force."[128] Although the love expounded in the Sermon on the Mount requires Christians to accept injustice against themselves, it does not permit acceptance of injustice against others. Since "love operates socially as the unconditional commitment to justice and freedom for others," one cannot successfully defend the "principle of unconditional nonviolence."[129]

Such a principle may disguise mere cowardice. Thus

> the face of love is not marked by it unequivocally; love is able—for moments only and never as something sought after but always as something forced upon it—to take on the ominous face of violence as the expression of desperation.[130]

Metz is unclear about the circumstances that would justify revolutionary violence. He once remarks that where "a social *status quo* is so full of injustice that it might equal that created by a [violent] revolutionary movement," love cannot rule such a movement out.[131] This is a puzzling statement. Is it a misstatement? Or does Metz mean that one cannot rule out revolutionary force in the name of love except when it may make matters *worse*? Equally puzzling—in light of his belief that narrative memory should have cognitive primacy in theology—is Metz's failure here to discuss Jesus' own relationship to revolutionary violence.

We have seen variations of this criticism all along. Instead of pressing it now, we will notice how the three writers we have considered here resemble one another. We will then look at how Metz's particular contribution moves us in the direction of figures we will meet in the following pages.

All speak passionately about the gospel and justice, calling the church to work at political and social transformation aimed especially at the redress of wrongs against the poor and oppressed. All of them sense a sharp contrast between the values of a truly faithful church and those of dominant Western culture. In stressing this, they show their awareness of how easy it is for Christianity to be domesticated by the world around it. Finally, all of them give strong, if not unambiguous, witness to the authority of Christ.

It is precisely here, however, that Metz in differing from the others builds a bridge for us to the next chapter. For he makes an explicit attack upon the idea of autonomous reason in morality, saying in effect that such a thing does not exist. To preserve its special identity, the church must give the memory of the Jesus story "cognitive primacy" in attempting to understand its faith and task. Only if the church does this can it hope to break through "the magic circle of prevailing consciousness" to challenge the dominant structures of society.[132]

If this emphasis on memory and story is not a glaring difference from what the others say, it is still a substantive one. Among the writers we meet next, all of whom emphasize the primacy of Scripture, two agree unmistakably with Metz's points about memory and story. Yet they draw conclusions from these points more radical in their way than his own.

CHAPTER • FIVE

The Bible as Benchmark: Hauerwas, Bloesch, and Yoder

INTRODUCTION

The Anabaptist vision central to our thesis stresses the authority of the Bible. In a chapter that ends our discussion of representative figures in Christian ethics since 1962, it is fitting, therefore, to consider three writers who themselves stress the Bible. All of them, indeed, define their distinctive contribution to current discussion in the special seriousness with which they take this book.

The first is Stanley Hauerwas, a leader among the "narrative theologians" who today are focusing attention upon the crucial role of stories in Christian life and thought. The second is Donald Bloesch, an evangelical Protestant who exhibits that movement's typical concern for biblical authority. The third is John Howard Yoder, a Mennonite distinguished for his provocative interpretation of the Anabaptist heritage.

We will finish the chapter with this Anabaptist account and thus be in a position to take up again the proposition that the true Niebuhrian way is the Anabaptist way. We will then assess that proposition both in the light of what Niebuhr himself has said and also of what representative writers since him have had to say.

STANLEY HAUERWAS

The first part of this chapter, and not only the third, deals with a writer who identifies with Anabaptism. Stanley Hauerwas is a member, in fact, of a Methodist congregation near Duke, the Methodist university where he teaches. His denominational commitment has by his own account, however, been vague at times. For years he was on the faculty at Notre Dame, where he worshiped with and was "sustained morally and financially" by Roman Catholics. Yet he wrote during this time that to him the Anabaptists, or Mennonites, exemplify the "most nearly faithful form of Christian witness." He also remarked with a touch of whimsy that his "ecclesial preference is to be a high-church Mennonite."[1]

While at Notre Dame he allowed that the ambiguity in all of this could be "deeply irresponsible," but said that he has tried nevertheless to be honest and faithful to his "office" as theologian. This office calls him, he said, to think and write not just for the church that does exist, but for the church that should exist and could exist if its members were "more courageous and faithful."[2] His published attempts to fulfill this office reveal both Catholic and Methodist influence and also—unmistakably—the influence of Anabaptism. What he says will at many points remind us of views held by the sixteenth-century Anabaptists we studied earlier. As we will later notice, moreover, there is striking similarity between his ideas and those of Mennonite John Howard Yoder.

What Hauerwas says will also remind us of Niebuhr. In graduate school he was a student of Niebuhr's distinguished pupil, James Gustafson. His concerns certainly reflect this academic heritage. In the four books we will examine here,[3] Hauerwas sets forth three broad claims.

One is that morality is not fundamentally about discrete acts and decisions, but about character. Here he exhibits an interest in the moral self reminiscent of Niebuhr's.

The second broad claim is that character takes shape under the impact of the narratives with which human agents identify. We need not belabor that Niebuhr was similarly concerned with the impact of narratives.

The third broad claim is that the story of the God of Jesus Christ determines true Christian morality and so produces a Christian community whose morality is distinct from other moralities. On this point Niebuhr's position was ambiguous, as we saw in chapter two, but the question behind it is certainly his own.

The first two of the broad claims we have noted constitute a critique of what Hauerwas calls the "standard account" of moral rationality. They summarize his understanding of morality in general. The last is the basis for his own constructive interpretation of Christian ethics.

We will begin with his general account. Here the first step is to summarize the view of morality he takes to have been dominant in Western thought since Kant and the Enlightenment. In this view, Hauerwas tells us, morality is basically a procedure for resolving questions about right and wrong. It is a method—ideally an "objective" method—for deciding in a quandary which action is the right action.

According to this standard view, the proper aim of moral reflection is to free all moral judgment from the individual's own interests and dispositions and from his own tradition and community. The moral ideal is the individual who in deciding how to act depends upon his own rationality without relying on the stories in his own history or the beliefs of his own people. These are contingent matters, compromising the "objectivity" true morality requires. The challenge of moral growth is precisely to overcome our reliance upon them. We can thus attain a universal point of view bearing no marks of our particular history. Only through such a morality can we overcome differences of historical background and thus resolve our moral disagreements.[4]

Now this account, though standard in liberal culture, has two things wrong with it, according to Hauerwas. One is that it focuses on actions and decisions instead of on the qualities of moral individuals themselves. It fails, he says, to "deal adequately with the formation of the moral self . . . the virtues and character we think important for moral agents to acquire."[5] Hauerwas elaborates at length on this objection in his first book, the 1975 study of *Character and the Christian Life*.

His basic point is that when questions of right and wrong arise, it is *persons* who decide and *persons* who act. What we *are* determines how we interpret and how we respond to the events in our lives. We cannot, therefore, give an adequate account of morality unless we treat the *being* of the moral self as prior to its doing.[6] It is matters such as character, virtue, and vision, says Hauerwas, that are truly basic in morality.

Let us consider these terms. All three are fundamental for Hauerwas and they are all closely related to one another. Vision, he says, drawing upon essays by Iris Murdoch, is how we see the world. It is the perspective from which we view things. The vision we have defines for us our place and purpose in the human enterprise. It determines what features of the world we will notice and what features we will fail to notice. It governs the choices that will confront us and those that will not. The moral challenge presented by the idea of vision is that of gaining a perspective adequate to the reality around us—that of seeing clearly, without illusion or fantasy.[7]

Hauerwas illustrates these points in his essay on Albert Speer, Hitler's architect and minister of armaments. The eyes with which he saw the world, Hauerwas reminds us, were those of a man preoccupied with the advance of his own career as an architect. The perspective this gave him, however, was inadequate to Nazi reality. He did not *see* the true significance of his work for Hitler. Even as minister of armaments, he held on to the illusion that he was above all an architect.[8]

It is our moral task to see clearly. Learning how to do so does not come, however, just by looking. It requires the trait of humility and the skill to recognize our shortcomings and step back from our self-deceptions.[9] With this we come to virtue, the second of the three terms we are considering here. Again, for Hauerwas our acts and decisions depend on what sort of persons we are. For that reason the formation of the self is the basic issue of morality. In light of this, it is clear why virtue is important in his account. For this idea focuses attention upon traits and skills, upon the abiding qualities of the moral self.

Not just any trait or skill, however, is a virtue, but only those formed deliberately on the basis of reasons rooted in the life of the moral agent and of his community.[10] Virtues, Hauerwas tells us, are interests, commitments, and abilities we have trained ourselves through "practical intelligence" to embody.[11] In acquiring them we determine what kind of moral agents we will be. They shape our sense of right and wrong and they are what enable us "to act one way rather than another."[12]

We may put this last point in different words by saying that in gaining virtues we determine character. By the term *character*

Hauerwas means the kind of person someone is—the total design or pattern of the moral self.[13] In having character we have a certain orientation, a certain moral direction. We have a consistency gained through repeated actualizing of particular intentions and projects.[14] Character is the total result of the self's moral history, open always to refinement, yet determining to a large extent what the self will be and do in the future.[15] Character, to recall Hauerwas's basic objection to the standard account, is what governs acts and decisions. For this reason, attending to character and the forming of character is to him the fundamental concern of morality. Resolving moral dilemmas is not by any means unimportant, but it is *persons* who do this, and what kind of persons we should be is the basic issue.[16]

We noticed before that character, virtue, and vision are closely related. The exposition so far shows that virtues affect vision. It shows, too, that virtues contribute to character which in turn affects vision. But it is also the case that vision affects character. For as Hauerwas suggests, how we see shapes what we decide.[17] Vision in this way molds the further history of the self and thus affects the further development of character.[18] We may say, indeed, that vision on the one hand and virtue and character on the other have a continuous reciprocal effect upon one another. All this implies the gradual formation of the moral self over time. And with this we come to the second main objection Hauerwas has to the conventional, modern understanding of morality.

This objection, prominent in his writings by 1977, faults the modern understanding for being self-deceptively ahistorical. According to the Kantian tradition, the aim of moral reflection is to emancipate the self from reliance in its decision-making upon the traditions and stories of a particular community. The self is to be independent in morality. It is to achieve a universal point of view undistorted by the contingent past.

Hauerwas says, however, that all this is pretentious and self-deluding.[19] We are historical beings who live in historical communities. Each of us grows up hearing stories that shape the ethos of our community and in turn the individuals who live within it.

All communities, in fact, depend upon narrative for their form and substance.[20] This is true even in the liberal, scientific culture that has produced the standard account of morality. For this account itself is rooted in a narrative—a narrative born, says Hauerwas, of the Enlightenment.

> The plot was given in capsule by Auguste Comte: First came religion in the form of stories, then philosophy in the form of metaphysical analysis, and then science with its exact methods. The story he tells in outline is set within another elaborated by Hegel, to show how each of these ages supplanted the other as a refinement in the progressive development of reason.[21]

In his next remark, Hauerwas spells out the contradiction. "So stories are prescientific," he writes, "according to the story legitimizing the age which calls itself scientific."[22] The age which upholds a narrative-free form of rationality relies, in fact, upon a narrative.

In communities with stories, then, the self emerges. Through our engagement with the ways and stories of a people, we take our shape as persons. We learn the skills and gain the interests that make us what we are. We become involved in a way of life. We gain a character and learn to see the world in a particular way.[23] It is not possible to detach the self we each become—with all our thoughts and skills and commitments—from the acts we perform.

Hauerwas quotes the remark of Dewey that "the key to a correct theory of morality is the recognition of the essential unity of the self and its acts."[24] We must acknowledge this unity—this fact that what we are determines what we decide and do. As soon as we do, we must also acknowledge that the community and stories we have lived with determine what moral reasons count with us—what we recognize as good or bad.[25] This is why attempts to establish the independence of morality from religion are bound to fail. For religious faith involves beliefs and practices and these affect our vision and thus our sense of what our obligations are.[26]

We saw that the standard account of morality itself has a story. It claims, however, to uphold an impartial rationality—to offer moral reasons not based on a particular tradition but on a universal point of view. Against this, Hauerwas objects that our account of moral rationality must square with the facts about our existence as historical beings. When it does we will acknowledge that moral criteria are never independent of the stories told and lived out in a community.

They are not the criteria an impartial spectator would give, nor could they be. They are grounded, in words Hauerwas quotes from Stuart Hampshire, "in the coherence of a single way of life, distinguished by the characteristic virtues and vices recognized within it."[27] Despite all efforts to deny it, they reflect the particular, contingent histories of those who invoke them. In morals there is no impartial rationality, only a rationality rooted in narrative.[28]

This explains why moral disagreements seem difficult or even impossible to resolve. For in any moral argument, final appeal can only be to the shared commitments and values of the people to which we belong. This appeal is to "the wisdom of the community's experience as it is found in our inherited language, practices, and institutions."[29] The reasons for moral judgments can derive from more than a merely private point of view. They need not be purely subjective reasons. Beyond this, however, there is no universal point of view—only the point of view of an historical community.

This is ethical relativism, and Hauerwas admits, indeed, to being a kind of relativist.[30] He says, however, that we can allow the truth in relativism without falling into "vicious relativism." There are, of course, limits on our ability to achieve moral agreement through argument. We need not accept the radical claim, however, that differences of background rule out making judgments on other traditions or attempting to change the minds of those who belong to them.[31]

He does not develop this point in detail, though what he does say is suggestive. He first lays it down as a plausible assumption that all human groups have at least something in common. Our "common historical nature," he says, makes it likely that this is so. Deep and intractable differences may remain, but the commonality means at least that where diverse ways of life come together, a "real confrontation" can occur.[32]

It is thus possible for the persons involved to make "rational comparisons" between the outlook they now hold and the alternative being presented to them. They can then adopt the alternative without "extensive self-deception, paranoia, or other such things."[33] A "real confrontation," in other words, is one in which a "real option" presents itself—a real possibility of understanding and of change.[34]

What cannot happen, Hauerwas tells us, is that deep differences of belief and practice be defeated purely by argument. Only confrontation with another way of life can jar human beings into considering a shift in outlook. We can imagine a society, he says to illustrate his point, in which no aspect of its own tradition calls slavery into question.[35]

The assumptions of such a society will not be "susceptible to argument," he continues, unless it is confronted by "an alternative society" in which slavery is absent. Only then can a real option exist. Thus, when alternative societies have real confrontations, human minds may change despite the truth in relativism.

These thoughts appear in an essay on "The Church in a Divided World" in the 1981 volume, *A Community of Character*. They furnish an apt transition from the question of morality in general to that of Christian morality in particular.

We may summarize what Hauerwas believes on this latter point by saying that the church is to be an alternative society formed by the Jesus story and pledged to serve the world by confronting it with the truth it could embody but does not.

Hauerwas's thoughts about relativism and moral transformation are not, however, the only ones reflected in what he says about the Christian morality. Even though much of his account—especially his interpretation of the church—is concentrated in the book published in 1981, everything we have been considering touches on what we are now going to consider. We will keep this in mind and limit ourselves to the particular concerns of our study. We may thus treat this second part of the exposition more briefly than the first.

Hauerwas argues that the Christian ethic is an ethic of virtue and character, concerned first with the formation of the self. The Christian tradition, with its interest in sanctification, understands that the project of becoming the right kind of person is more basic than the project of coping with moral dilemmas.[36] He argues, too, that one gains the kind of character Christian morality upholds through association with the Christian community—through participation in its rituals and practices and through attention to the story that makes it what it is.[37]

This brings us to Hauerwas's next broad claim. Not only is the Christian ethic an ethic of character; it is also an ethic rooted in a narrative, and in particular the narrative of Jesus Christ. This story forms the true Christian community and through the community forms the true Christian individual.[38] Scripture contains and illuminates the story and is therefore the highest written authority in the community. It preserves the memories upon which Christian identity depends.[39]

It is through the Jesus story that we come to know God, his lordship, his kingdom. Jesus teaches us the truth about the kingdom of God. That truth, says Hauerwas, "turns out to be the cross." In his whole mission Jesus appeared powerless, accepting suffering, refusing violence as a means to secure the kingdom. His powerlessness was in fact "the power of truth against the violence of falsehood."[40] It was a means of social transformation.[41] Hauerwas illuminates all of this in a passage from *Vision and Virtue* worth quoting at length. He writes,

> Jesus did not come with new political alternatives in the sense that Caesar or those that opposed Caesar would understand. He came proclaiming a new kingdom where men would share in the very life of God. He came not to the rich and the powerful, but to the poor, the weak, the dying, and the sinner. Through such as these the nature of his kingdom is revealed as the freedom to feed the poor and forgive the sinner. God, therefore, refused to establish himself through the violent power of this world with its many deceptions; his rule can be established only through the gentleness that comes from genuinely being weak and not just from taking the form of the weak.[42]

The point is that it would strike against the kingdom's ethos of love and forgiveness to use the methods of self-concern and animosity. Only the kind of weakness manifested in the Jesus story can lure us from our "pretentious attempt to make our lives meaningful through power and violence."[43] The cross of Christ was, in a phrase, "a social ethic." It is the business of disciples to "become the continuation of that ethic in the world, until all are brought within his kingdom."[44]

With this we come to the third broad claim in Hauerwas's view of Christian morality. It concerns the mission of the church and its relation to the surrounding cultural life. Here again, what is basic is remembering the story that defines the church—and remembering, too, that it distinguishes the church from the world.[45] The story gives to Christian life a distinctive shape. The church must have "an appropriate sense of separateness" from the society around it.[46] This does not mean withdrawal from, or rejection of, society. It only means serving society on the church's own terms, keeping faithful to its own distinctive way of life. Jesus defines this way, a way whose "hallmark" is the church's refusal "to secure itself by violence."[47]

The church's most important political task is to be truly itself. Its most important political question is what kind of community it must be to be faithful to the story that defines it.[48] The idea is that in being truly itself the church can provide to the world around it a "contrast model" of social life. It can be an "alternative polity," inducing the world to a reconsideration of its values. In the language introduced before, the task of Christians is to form the sort of community "that can become a real option and provide a real confrontation for others."[49]

It is by attending first to this—the challenge of witnessing to the truth of God—that the church transforms society. It may not be effective as the world judges effectiveness, but neither should it try to be.[50] It must sustain itself not by its effectiveness in the short run, but by its trust in the promise of God that its life "will not be without effect" and by the hope that one day all will be "brought within his kingdom."[51]

We considered first the general view of morality that serves as theoretical backing for what Hauerwas affirms specifically of the Christian morality. We will now sum up this latter view in the Niebuhrian terms we earlier suggested for characterizing the problem of Christ and culture. This will not only round out the exposition but will also keep before us the exact questions we are here exploring.

In chapter two we said the problem of Christ and culture exists because the church affirms Christ's authority in a situation of cultural pluralism. On these matters Hauerwas is unmistakable. A way of life is Christian only if it is defined by the Jesus story. No way of life whatever reflects a universal point of view. We inhabit a morally divided world. This is so because our outlooks mirror the variety of histories and communities from which we all emerge. One question this raises for Christians, we said in the same chapter, is how to understand Christ's authority in relation to other cultural authorities.

The question is complex, but in Hauerwas this much, at least, is clear: Christ's moral authority is final for Christians. In being loyal to it, the Christian community will find itself deeply at odds with other moral authorities in the surrounding culture.

The community does not, however, for this reason reject the surrounding culture altogether. We noted that the second main question is how the church should relate to the cultural life around it. According to Hauerwas, the church should serve it, and should do so precisely by confronting it with a distinctively Christian way of life. The church is to serve society precisely by being itself an alternative model of social life, drawing the world by example toward transformation into the kingdom of God.

All this is intriguing in light of our overall thesis, first because it is reminiscent of Niebuhr, and second because it is reminiscent of Anabaptism. Both these points will come out when in the next chapter I exploit Hauerwas's insights in my own account. It will also come out that important objections may be raised against Hauerwas. I postpone consideration of them here, however, and say only that we have met an ally of the position I will attempt to defend. We will now consider an American evangelical whose similarities with Hauerwas are striking, but never more striking than the differences.

DONALD BLOESCH

I said the writers in this chapter define their contribution to Christian ethics in terms of the special seriousness with which they take the Bible. This is true, certainly, of Donald Bloesch, a professor at the theological seminary of the University of Dubuque. The evangelical Christianity he represents intends to show at all times a high regard for Scripture—even, one might say, a militant regard. For as he himself remarks, "Evangelical theology aims not only to be faithful to Scripture, but also to expose the unfaithfulness of the Christian community to Scripture."[52]

Bloesch is interesting to us for another reason, too. He writes as a "socially concerned evangelical" for whom the gospel, as he often says, is "a stick of dynamite in the social structure."[53] He thus belongs to the growing community of evangelicals who, since the appearance in 1947 of Carl F. H. Henry's *The Uneasy Conscience of Modern Fundamentalism,* have tried to reestablish the connection between evangelical Christianity and what Henry called "the Christian social imperative."[54]

In setting out the details of his social doctrine, however, Bloesch reveals an outlook that at important points differs sharply from that of either Hauerwas or John Howard Yoder. That all three hold similar convictions about the place and importance of Scripture[55] makes the contrast among them an attractive and worthy object for further inquiry.

By first situating Bloesch's account more precisely in today's theological context, then marking down its central features, and finally posing some questions, I intend here to establish a basis for later assessment of the contrast. The assessment proper will occur in the final chapter in light not only of the differences themselves but also of the larger argument put forth in the essay as a whole.

In working out the implications of scriptural authority for Christian social doctrine, Bloesch picks out and repudiates two main misconceptions. One of these, illustrated in conservative, "privatistic" evangelicalism, divorces the gospel from matters political and economic. Under its impact the characteristic response to social controversy is silence, and to social injustice, acquiescence.

But in truth, says Bloesch, the gospel "has tremendous social and political repercussions." Failure to see and act upon this is a way of "burying the gospel."[56] Invoking H. Richard Niebuhr, he says the true church seeks the conversion, not only of individuals, but also of social structures.[57]

The other misconception is typical of the "avant-garde" theology of today, especially in liberation and political theology. It interprets the gospel in exclusively social terms. Here, according to Bloesch, the matter of personal salvation from sin and death receives little or no attention as concern centers on liberation from political-economic injustice and oppression. Not only does this view lose the sense of a supernatural world to come; it also denies the need to convert unbelievers through kerygmatic proclamation. According to its "syncretistic or univeralistic" outlook, the church's missionary task is simply to help all people—whatever their religion—to be agents of love and justice in the world.[58]

But in these "well-meaning" efforts to make Christian faith credible and this-worldly, the avant-garde theologians have "only succeeded," Bloesch contends, "in emptying the faith of its biblical content."[59]

We have now a rough sense of how Bloesch sees himself in relation to evangelical Christianity on the one hand and liberal, social Christianity on the other. These are the two currents in contemporary theology with which he concerns himself in his writings. The one he identifies with, even though he criticizes its impulse to social and political passivity. The other he reproves, though he does appreciate, he says, its "sensitivity to social injustice." His relation to these currents is more complex than this, of course,[60] but since our special interest is social doctrine, what we have said is adequate. Knowing, then, his basic theological orientation, let us now attend in more detail to his constructive position concerning the questions of Christ and culture we are here exploring.

If the Bible is basic for true theology, its witness to Christ is what makes it so. In Bloesch's evangelical perspective, the Holy Spirit so led the scriptural writers that "what was actually written had the very sanction of God himself."[61] Though the book has a "fallible element" and "bears the marks of historical conditioning," it is "not mistaken in what it purports to teach, namely, God's will and purpose for the world."[62]

Still, the Bible is not *in itself* final. It "points beyond itself to the absolute authority," who is God "as we find him in Jesus Christ."[63] Thus the Old Testament, though it anticipates the gospel, does not present it in "final or definitive form." It is Christ who brings us the "final and complete" revelation of God's will and purpose.[64] The Bible's authority is actually "eroded" when a "narrow biblicism" overlooks this point and appeals to Scripture "without focusing attention on its center and divine content, Jesus Christ."[65]

This means that Christ must be the criterion of the church's activity in society. The church must decide how to relate to the cultural life around it by reference to him. Bloesch appeals to Christ, indeed, to support his central claim, namely, that the church's fundamental mission in society is a spiritual mission, not a political one. The Old Testament, he says, did lean toward a purely political conception of salvation, but the New Testament was different.

It is true that in remarks at Nazareth noted in Luke 4, Jesus quoted from Isaiah 61:1-2 and 58:6, where the writer clearly had political-social deliverance in mind. But Jesus "was definitely not thinking of political liberation." Bloesch argues that Luke 7:22 makes this clear. Here Jesus responds to a question from two of John the Baptist's disciples. "Go," he says, "and tell John what you have seen and heard: the blind receive their sight, the lame walk, lepers are cleansed, and the deaf hear, the dead are raised up, the poor have good news preached to them."

Bloesch interprets this to mean that "Jesus came to offer deliverance from the power of sin and death rather than from political and economic bondage." He then proceeds in the following paragraphs to cite further evidence from the Gospels that this is so: Jesus refused to be the political Messiah the Jews expected; he called his followers to a ministry of proclamation, not the building of a new social order.[66]

The interpretations of Jesus we have met so far are strikingly different from this one. These differences raise questions to which we will want to attend to in time, but our task now is to understand Bloesch. As we proceed with this task, one thing will be clear: by his interpretation of Jesus Bloesch does *not* mean to support what he calls "individualistic, privatistic religion."[67]

Consider first the idea of spiritual mission. It refers, in Bloesch's picture, to the "mandate" all Christians have "to prepare [people] for life with God in eternity."[68] The church, we have said, should consider this its primary task. It is a task that consists in helping sinners to have faith in God and thus enter into a salvation that endures beyond this world in an eternal, heavenly world. It is accomplished through a prophetic and evangelistic ministry—the condemnation of sin and the announcement of the divine grace revealed in Jesus Christ.[69] The reason *this* is basic, and not social and political action, has to do with the root cause of human suffering. Our plight is due more, Bloesch believes, to our fearful, unconverted hearts than to our social and political institutions. Sin is what produces oppressive social environments. It is not, at bottom, the other way around.[70]

Among other things, this is a claim about *how* the church should deal with social and political evil. It is not the expression of indifference to such evil. Although the church's primary concern is the conversion of individuals, in just this work it helps (though indirectly) to build "a more just society." The church, Bloesch explains, is the creator of regenerated persons, and regenerated persons "are moved to create a new social order."[71]

This is not all, however, for social and political concern belongs to the very process of making new persons. Part of what this involves, according to Bloesch, is precisely the exposure of social forms of sin. In fulfilling its spiritual mandate, the church must preach the law of God in its "social dimensions." It must condemn not only adultery, murder, and the like, but also "social maladies," such as environmental pollution, nuclear warfare, discrimination, and exploitation.[72]

Bloesch's concerns thus reach beyond those of a purely privatistic religion. Still, the basic remedy for social evils is the conversion of individuals. According to Bloesch, persons with transformed values, after all, are the ones who are able to build a better world. And this latter—the actual construction of a better society—is itself a part of Christian obligation.

The church has a "cultural mandate"—the adjective no doubt reflects his appreciation of H. Richard Niebuhr—in addition to the spiritual one. The embrace of the gospel requires us to accept this mandate. It requires us to become involved in "political programs for social change."[73] Even though this is not our distinctively Christian calling, it belongs nevertheless to our "wider mission" in the world. Social justice (if not morality) *can* be legislated. True Christians, "working as a transforming leaven in the secular stations of life," will do all they can to help establish just laws and institutions in the world.[74]

Here we must emphasize a distinction Bloesch draws between what the church as institution can do and what individual Christians can do. As a public organization, the church's business is, in his language, "spiritual" rather than "cultural." However, it may offer "prophetic criticism" regarding social questions as its spiritual mandate requires. This apparently means (his expositon here is not clear) that the church may speak such criticism not only through its individual members, but also in public, official pronouncements.

The institutional church, however, must not go beyond this and use its corporate power to facilitate the fulfillment of what it recommends. The establishment through "social action" of new policies and institutions is the cultural mandate of the church. This is to come, according to Bloesch, through individual Christians. It is they in their role as citizens who must effect the concrete measures necessary to "redress social wrongs and abuses."[75] Thus the institutional church retains the special role of "critic and moral monitor of the world," preaching a gospel whose implications are always "politically revolutionary." It will always be a spur against the flank of the established social order.[76]

Bloesch does not mean to deny that Christians may band together corporately in efforts to establish just laws and institutions. Ideally, however, they will do so as "concerned citizens" in conjuncton perhaps with other persons, and not as an official church body. It is true, he admits, that the distinction between the spiritual and cultural mandates of the church "may become hazy." The line between prophetic criticism of society and social action in support of specific solutions may not always be easy to draw. "Yet the church best maintains its identity and integrity when it holds fast to the principle that the two mandates are not the same, even though the distinctions may not always be clear in actual practice."[77]

All this concern with the social and political relevance of the gospel implies a certain confidence in the prospects for change in the world. Bloesch does not believe, though, that heaven is in the "continuum" of history. It is not a utopian goal attainable on earth.[78] For him the kingdom of God is eschatological—something to be finally established in a future that is beyond history.[79] Still, it does touch our world, if only in earthly, broken signs. Though in its fullness it lies beyond history, we can still be "instruments" in its advance "within history."[80] Both in the life of the church and in the social and political structures outside the church, the kingdom can be present—though imperfectly present—today.[81]

For this world and its history, then, Bloesch has hope, but it is a limited hope. Our final deliverance takes us to a heavenly city, not an earthly one and saves us not only from social and political evil but also from the powers of sin, death, and the devil.[82] But now notice this: In the support of God's kingdom and fulfillment of earthly hopes, both the church and the social and political structures outside the church play a part. Ideally, the church is actually allied with the state. Both struggle against the kingdom of darkness.[83]

This is an important part of Bloesch's account of church and society. In it his most important mentor is Calvin. Both Luther and Calvin saw a fundamental dichotomy between holiness and sin, the kingdom of God and the kingdom of Satan. Both said the state as well as the church participate in fulfilling the divine purposes. Calvin, however, saw the role of the state in a more positive light than Luther did—and so does Bloesch. For him the state is not a mere "dyke against sin," as Luther said. It is a means, ideally, of helping to build up a "holy commonwealth" that is a sign on earth (though a "broken sign") of the coming kingdom.[84]

The state has a special responsibility under God, and so does the church. They are "two modes of the divine rule," each distinct from the other and each indispensable. The special responsibilities of church and state complement each other,[85] although "this ideal can be approximated where the state is infused with Christian values." The church proclaims the law and gospel, seeking conversions to God. The state preserves order (as Luther said) and in addition establishes and serves the cause of justice. The church bears the sword of God's Word. The state bears the sword of physical force. The church concentrates on spiritual need and the "spiritual righteousness" given in the new birth by the Holy Spirit. The state concentrates on temporal and material need and the "civil righteousness" that preserves our world from chaos.[86]

For the individual Christian, all of this means "dual citizenship" and a two-track moral responsibility. Christians belong both to God's kingdom and to the secular state. They must work, therefore, both to make people "disciples" of Christ (their primary task) and to establish social justice.

What complicates things, however, is the difference between the laws of the kingdom and the laws of the state. They "are not and cannot be the same," says Bloesch. Jesus forbade his disciples to resist the one who is evil, but this command cannot apply to the secular realm. "For then society would be threatened with chaos. How we act as an ambassador of Christ," Bloesch continues, "will often be different from how we act as a responsible citizen of the state." A Christian judge fulfilling his or her responsibility in the public domain may send a transgressor of the civil law to prison. But as a Christian in "the personal or private sphere of life," this judge may in love bring the prisoner "a cup of cold water" and thus fulfill the "obligations" as a member of the kingdom.[87]

In developing these ideas Bloesch invokes both Luther and Reinhold Niebuhr. Both understood, he says, that one cannot govern society by the radical ideal of love. Christians must be willing to compromise this ideal and to resort to force, if necessary, in order to fulfill their social and political obligations.[88] It is proper to do this when the welfare of others is at stake. For themselves, Christians must meet evil with a self-sacrificing spirit and a refusal to strike back. In this they help, paradoxically enough, to *defeat* the forces of evil. But where the helpless and downtrodden depend upon them, the requirement changes. Now, for the sake of others, they must be prepared to lay aside the principle of nonretaliation.[89]

Under certain conditions, even revolutionary violence may be permissible for the Christian. Bloesch is in fact not clear about this. He says in one place that Jesus preached a revolution of the heart that would result in "freedom to enter into the struggle for a just society . . . without resort to violence."[90] Yet he says, too, that though Christians can never be committed wholeheartedly to a violent revolution, they may nonetheless find themselves caught up in one that humanly intolerable oppression has made "inevitable." These remarks show a reserve which clearly puts distance between Bloesch and that "theology of revolution" which, he says, "upholds violence as a Christian way of life." They do not, however, add up to an unmistakable No to violent revolution.

Even if Bloesch is unclear about revolution, this much, at least, is certain. He rejects absolute or "doctrinaire" pacifism and favors a "pragmatic pacifism" that, in allowing the use of force, shows greater respect for "the realities of the human situation." He suggests, moreover, that this is compatible with Christian Scripture. Although Jesus prohibited the violent defense of his own kingdom, he "did not disarm the centurion." In this he was like John the Baptist who himself did not disarm soldiers who came to hear him preach. These are points, Bloesch claims, that make it an "open question" whether even the New Testament itself supports "absolute pacifism."[91]

Mention of revolution reminds us that the state does not always fulfill its mandate to preserve order and establish justice. In light of this, we will make a final point about Bloesch's view of church and state. It is that the church must keep a certain critical distance from the state. It must be a "conscience" to the state—a "goad" reminding it of its pretensions and shortcomings and urging it to a truer fulfillment of its task. If the state should not listen and become actually demonic, denying basic human freedoms to its citizens, then—though only as a "last resort"—the church must defy it and refuse to obey its laws.[92]

This last shows that for all his concern to connect the gospel and the secular world, Bloesch remains aware that the way of the church and the way of the world are not necessarily the same. He says, indeed, that the church is truly the church when it is an "alien force"—a "colony of heaven" in the world.[93] Today, accommodation to the spirit of the times threatens the integrity of Christian witness. The proper response to this is a return to the "way of confrontation," where the church "calls the culture to repentance." The church is to redeem the world, not make common cause with it. It is to transform culture (he quotes H. Richard Niebuhr) and Christianize the social structures.[94] When it capitulates to dominant values, it fails to do this. Indeed, it contributes instead "to the vacuity and dissolution of the surrounding culture."[95]

This concern to keep a sharp distinction between church and world appears strikingly in two books Bloesch has written on the rise of ascetic, communal life within contemporary evangelicalism.[96] One of these books appeared in 1964, and the other—a kind of update— ten years later. These books admiringly describe and evaluate "evangelical communities" whose existence, he says, is both a challenge to the church today and a sign of its renewal.[97] Bloesch defines the evangelical community as "a group of persons who are concerned with the renewal of evangelical Christianity and who seek to contribute toward this renewal by living the common life under a common discipline."[98]

Examples of such communities include Koinonia Farm in the state of Georgia, the Ecumenical Sisterhood of Mary in West Germany, and the Iona Community off the northwest coast of Scotland. Such communities tend toward certain common traits, Bloesch tells us. These include an emphasis on sanctification and discipleship (as well as divine forgiveness) and a belief in the idea of Christ as pattern and example. They include a determination to overcome barriers of class, race, family, and property and a commitment to disavow the world's sin and identify with its needs. They also include a refusal of "the use and threat of violence."[99]

In their "radical" or "exceptional" witness to Christ, these communities are symbols of the coming kingdom. They are symbols of the day when violence and narrow loyalties, injustice, and class distinctions will all be "superseded."[100]

Bloesch says that the role of evangelical communities is to bear a witness not only to the world but also to the church. Local congregations often lose sight of the difference between the values of the gospel and those of surrounding culture. Radical communities "serve as beacons or signposts that remind the church of its basic purpose and that point the church toward its final goal."[101]

He suggests also, however, that not all Christians are called to such radical witness. The religious community is not to be the "rule" for all the church, even though it is a sign of what the church should be.[102]

It is puzzling, however, why this should be the case. Bloesch's point reminds us of monasticism and of Thomas Aquinas. It is surely incompatible with this approving remark published in a later work about the Reformation: "To counteract the view that costly discipleship is intended only for the religious elite, Luther and Calvin sounded the universal call to discipleship."[103] Here Bloesch says what writers sympathetic with the Anabaptist heritage, including Hauerwas and Yoder, would urge him to keep in mind at every point. For it is an idea fortified by Scripture, and such writers are like Bloesch in wanting to ally themselves unmistakably with what Scripture teaches.

Bloesch presents us, however, with an inconsistency. He affirms the point about discipleship, yet also contradicts it. From the standpoint of the other writers in this chapter, his account contains further objectionable features. Some of these we will consider in detail in the final chapter when we also look at objections to what Hauerwas and Yoder have to say.

But it is important to mark some of the questions now because Bloesch's exposition represents a special challenge to the argument of this entire study. As an evangelical, he claims, like the defenders of Anabaptism, to uphold Scripture as the benchmark of Christian existence. Yet his conclusions about Christian social doctrine differ substantially from theirs.

Consider the idea that Christ's mission was fundamentally spiritual, not political. This goes against what Hauerwas has said and it goes against what we will notice Yoder saying in a moment. Does the Jesus story back up Bloesch's claim, or doesn't it? We will want to find out.

Or consider the idea of two-track moral responsibility, where the Christian acts differently as ambassador of Christ than one does as citizen of the state, or the idea that the New Testament does not give clear support to absolute pacifism. These ideas, too, challenge Anabaptist ways of thinking. We will come back to them, but not before turning to the final segment of our exploration into the current theological context of our discussion.

JOHN HOWARD YODER

To this point we have considered no writer who belongs to a religious community linked directly with the sixteenth-century Anabaptists. We turn finally, however, to someone who does—the Mennonite theologian John Howard Yoder.

Yoder was a longtime teacher at his denomination's seminary in Indiana and is now on the faculty of the University of Notre Dame. He offers an interpretation of his Anabaptist heritage whose centerpiece is a single basic claim. It is that the man Jesus, in his actions and teachings and cross and resurrection, provides the normative pattern for Christian existence—a pattern socially and politically relevant today.

This one basic claim ramifies into several, equally striking companion claims: that the church must be a community of nonresistant love, that it must be willing to accept the role of outsider in society, that precisely in this role it must exercise political responsibility. Yoder says further that a community thus committed to the gospel ideal will by its word and example have a transformative impact upon the surrounding culture.

Despite the language of this last summarizing sentence, Yoder has so far shown little positive feeling for the writings of H. Richard Niebuhr. In chapter two we noted that in a largely unsympathetic critique of Niebuhr's well-known book, he charged him with treating Christ and culture as though they were entirely separate from each other. In the same essay he attacked his doctrine of the Trinity for relativizing Christ's authority.

Yoder elsewhere advances these same criticisms. Nowhere, to my knowledge, does he bring out positive connections between Niebuhr's thought and his own.[104] We will see, in the last chapter, how these connections can be made. For now, however, we may concentrate on what Yoder himself believes.

Among the writings we consider here, Yoder's earliest deals with the relation of church and state.[105] Later writings, with their focus on the authority of Jesus and on the political significance of the church, build on this initial discussion. Our primary interest, however, is not the evolvement of Yoder's thought, but his mature position, viewed in light of the problem of Christ and culture as we have come to understand it. I will attempt here, therefore, to set forth a summary that is compatible with his most recent statements, beginning with the question of Jesus, his authority and his political significance.

Let us begin with Jesus. Yoder tells us that he is *the* criterion of Christian social and political responsibility. In becoming flesh God did not give his general approval to human ideas of morality. He did not ratify conclusions we may reach apart from this revelation of himself. Instead, God gave us through Jesus "a new, formative definition" of what it is to be human in society—a new standard to live up to.[106]

There is a marked difference, therefore, between a social ethic shaped by the story of Jesus and one that is not. The full implications of this are often unacknowledged, however, even though they are crucially important for the Christian community today. Can Jesus truly be our pattern, or must we somehow diminish his authority to make the Christian way compatible with what other sources of ethical wisdom decree?[107] To this Yoder replies unmistakably: No, we must not diminish Christ's authority. Confessing that he is Lord makes a difference, and it is a difference we are bound by our faith to embrace. The temptation is great to do otherwise and so avoid the risks of following the crucified one. But that does not change the fact: true Christian faith lives the Jesus story.[108]

If we attend to this story, says Yoder, we will find a moral vision that is at the same time a distinctive political strategy. He allows that this goes against much conventional opinion. It is commonplace to suppose that because of his rural background or apocalyptic outlook or purpose of atonement for sin, Jesus has no immediate relevance for the questions of social ethics.[109]

But in truth, Jesus was a "model of radical political action." Yoder tells us that recent New Testament studies document this point.[110] This, indeed, is what he means to establish in *The Politics of Jesus*, his most influential book. Here he adds the "focusing effect" of a persistent question about Jesus' political outlook to the results of recent biblical scholarship. His purpose is to state the results of this scholarship so arrestingly that Christian ethicists will be compelled to take note of it.[111]

We will consider now one part of Yoder's undertaking in this book, his attempt to show that Jesus was himself concerned about political questions. To do this, he relies largely upon Luke, a writer often thought to have played down any threat Christianity may have posed to the established social order. But throughout Luke's Gospel—starting with the birth announcement—Luke shows Jesus as "an agent of radical social change."[112] He is one who will put down the mighty from their thrones and exalt those of low degree. He is the one who will fill the hungry and send the rich empty away.

Jesus himself, according to Luke, puts the outlines of his mission in expressly social terms. In a statement at the synagogue in Nazareth he invokes the vision of Isaiah 61. The coming of the Messiah is good news for the poor and the captive, good news for the blind, the oppressed, and the victims of inequity.[113] Jesus says the vision of the prophet is fulfilled as he stands before his hearers.

What this means we cannot know exactly, Yoder tells us. This much is clear: The subject here is an event, and the event brings a "visible socio-political economic restructuring of relations among the people of God." It is brought about, Yoder continues, through divine intervention "in the person of Jesus as the one Anointed and endued with the Spirit."[114]

But another thing is equally clear: the event is not to be understood in a nationalistic sense. The remarks of Jesus that follow the reading of the passage from Isaiah undercut "racial egoism" and suggest that the new age will embrace all mankind.[115]

In Yoder's view Luke brings out both of these facts about Jesus—that his mission is political and his vision is universal—as the account continues. Jesus names twelve persons to be key leaders in a community of disciples he gathers about him. He takes the message outlined at Nazareth to a wider public—one that includes non-Jews as well as Jews. He spells out in his sermon on the plain a social ethic guided by the boundless love of God.

At the feeding of the multitude he does, it is true, refuse overtures aimed at making him the leader of a messianic insurrection,[116] but in so doing he by no means withdraws from society. He confides to his disciples that he expects his mission to be controversial and to bring him suffering and death. Indeed, they themselves must be prepared for crucifixion.

Now he sets his face toward Jerusalem. On the way, as Luke finds it important to remark, someone tells him that Pilate has massacred a group of Galileans—what we would expect to be mentioned in the account of a political figure. Later, someone tells him that Herod is out to kill him. This is understandable, Yoder suggests, only if he was seen as a threat to Herod's government.[117]

Once again Jesus reminds the people that the community he is calling into being must be willing to bear the "hostility" (as Yoder puts it) of the surrounding society.[118] Its way of life involves the cross and differs sharply from other ways. When the disciples, not fully comprehending, quarrel with one another about who will rank highest in his coming kingdom, Jesus reprimands them for failing to see that its trademark is service, not privilege.

Never, though, does he reprimand them for thinking he will set up a "new social order." We would expect this if his interests were purely "spiritual," as some say, but it does not happen. The disciples have misunderstood what the new order will be like, that is all. Writes Yoder: "The alternative to how the kings of the earth rule is not 'spirituality' but servanthood."[119]

Jesus rides into Jerusalem amid politically charged exclamations from a company of hopeful followers. In the temple he asserts his authority in a (nonviolent) clash with the exploiting merchants,[120] and then establishes an influential, daily teaching presence there. Encounters with the religious leaders during this period all underscore his "rejection of the status quo," including a "repudiation of the Roman occupation." This latter is clear from the question about payment of taxes to Caesar, which, had Jesus felt otherwise, could hardly have been considered a serious trap by those who questioned him.[121]

These encounters lead in the end to the prospect of imminent arrest. Having eaten the Passover supper, Jesus reminds his disciples of their call to be servants, not lords. He then goes in their company to the Mount of Olives. There he prays the Father to "take this cup" from him. He is struggling, Yoder suggests, with the temptation of messianic violence. For in rebuking Peter's attempt a few moments later to defend him with the sword, Jesus uses the same language as in his prayer. "Shall I not drink the cup which the Father has given me?" he asked.[122] As it had been before, it was tempting to attempt a Zealot-like crusade, but again Jesus rejects the temptation.

In the trials that follow his arrest, Jesus says nothing to undermine the impression that he is a threat to the Jewish and Roman authorities. Of this Yoder writes:

> That the threat was not one of *armed*, violent revolt, and that it nonetheless bothered them to the point of their resorting to illegal procedures to counter it, is a proof of the political relevance of nonviolent tactics, not a proof that Pilate and Caiaphas were exceptionally dull or dishonorable men.[123]

When Jesus is finally executed, it is in part because Pilate considers him a danger to the Roman Empire. What is also true, Yoder insists that in suffering this punishment, Jesus both exemplifies and establishes his kingdom.[124] Moreover, he marks out the pattern for his disciples. We may ask whether a regime whose values include the nonviolent acceptance of suffering is really believable, really deserving of our loyalty. But no longer, Yoder tells us, can we do this in the name of Christian theology. For this fact we cannot avoid: Jesus calls us precisely to an "ethic marked by the cross." Jesus calls us to a way of life which renounces any recourse to violence. Yet this way of life threatens the dominant society so much that it brings risk of punishment upon the persons who adopt it.[125]

Before we consider what a church that took all of this seriously would be like, we must clarify two points. One has to do with Jesus as the norm of Christian life in society. This is a point made not only in the Gospels, Yoder says, but throughout the New Testament. In remarks buttressed with many quotations from Scripture, he shows that the first Christians were expected to live as Christ lived. They were to imitate the Father in forgiveness, in compassion, and in self-giving ministry to others. They were to endure the hostility of the world, value servanthood over dominion, and bear innocent suffering without complaint. Furthermore, they were to regard all of this—even the death that could come with it—as the way to victory over evil.

What the New Testament does not present, however, is a "*general* concept of living like Jesus." Its writers do not appeal to just any feature of his life as backing for what they say. They never cite his example in order to support celibacy, for instance, or rural life. There is one point at which imitation holds. That is

> at the point of the concrete social meaning of the cross in its relation to enmity and power. Servanthood replaces dominion, forgiveness absorbs hostility. Thus—and only thus—are we bound by New Testament thought to "be like Jesus."[126]

The other point concerns the political relevance of all of this. As Yoder points out, the authorities did regard Jesus as a politically dangerous figure and they did take steps to nullify his impact. But in the face of this, Jesus refused the Zealot-like response his disciples were hoping for and persevered in the boundless love of the Father. He had said not to resist the evil one—to love and pray even for the enemy. Now he embodied these ideals himself. For those who were counting on him, it was hard, surely, to look on with hope. It was hard to believe that his forgiving acceptance of unjust execution was a step toward sociopolitical renewal.

But it was that, as Yoder says through all his writings. The cross changed history. Christ's weakness was a kind of power.[127] That this should be so goes against conventional expectation, it is true, but surprise is a mark of the gospel: after the cross comes the resurrection. As Yoder says, having faith means, in part, having confidence in the power of the resurrection. We must believe that God will attain his ends in ways that are wondrous and beyond prediction.[128]

We may grant these points, however, and still wish to know better how the changes really happen. How is it that the strategy of Jesus can alter history? How is it that those who today adopt his cross as a model can be effective agents of social and political transformation?[129] These matters are important. We can better understand them in the context of what Yoder says about the church and its relation to surrounding culture, and so we may turn to that topic now.

The church is the community which confesses Jesus Christ as Lord. This confession marks it off from the rest of society.[130] Yoder not only asserts these points; he says that the mainstream of Christian social doctrine takes neither of them seriously—or seriously enough. It has long been commonplace to interpret Jesus' lordship in a way which denies that his life and teaching are the norm of social ethics. Instead of showing how the Christian way differs from other ways, theologians typically have tried to fit it into the framework of some "wider wisdom."[131]

But Jesus himself, if not these theologians, believed that his true followers would embrace a distinctive morality. This morality is the one set forth in his teaching and life and cross.[132] For this reason his true followers today must attend to these things. In social ethics we are faithful to the gospel, Yoder says, only "if we are telling the story of Jesus."[133]

Narrative is the key, in fact, to the church's self-understanding. In orienting itself today the church must look to the story of its founder. It must adopt his cause as its own.[134] In doing so, and thus keeping the memory of Jesus constantly alive, it will cultivate an "alternative consciousness"—a way of thinking that goes against the "commonplaces" of the age.[135]

The temptation to deny this has always been strong. One reason is our tendency to defend the dominant social system. Another, Yoder claims, is the "risk and uncertainty" that go with loyalty to Christ. We may argue that it is "provincialism" we wish to overcome in linking up with the wider wisdom. More important than our fear of provincialism, however, is our concern to avoid the costliness of the Christian way.[136]

The clearest test of our loyalty to Christ comes at the point of violence and war. We may be tempted, of course, to abandon Jesus on other issues, but on this one the temptation is especially pressing.[137] Here risk and costliness loom large. Here the story of our faith and the reality of our politics contradict each other and we think it necessary, as Yoder says of certain modern ethicists, to "leave the story behind."[138] But the story, as we have seen, is what makes our ethics the ethics of the gospel. And the story calls us to nonresistance. As God loves boundlessly, embracing even sinners, so must we. As Jesus refused violence as a means of overcoming evil, so must we.[139]

In *The Original Revolution* Yoder writes: "Christ is *agape*; self-giving, nonresistant love." He says further that the cross—"the un-complaining and forgiving death of the innocent at the hands of the guilty"—reveals what this love is. It shows *how* God deals with the evil in our world. Then he says, remarkably, that true Christian love "seeks neither effectiveness nor justice, and is willing to suffer any loss or seeming defeat for the sake of obedience."[140] In language equally strong, he says that such love is required, not merely of a prophetic few, but of every Christian. Each of us must obey the call to

> absolute nonresistance in discipleship and to abandonment of all loyalties which counter that obedience, including the desire to be effective immediately or to make oneself responsible for civil justice.[141]

This is not legalism, he says. It is "solidarity with Christ": the true disciple lives in this world as Jesus did.[142] And neither, he says, is nonresistance compliance with evil. It is a kind of patience, to be sure, but it is not resignation and it is not complicity. Although it excludes "retaliation in kind," it "does not exclude other kinds of opposition to evil" such as nonviolent resistance.[143] The Christian task is not the merely negative one of avoiding wrong; it is the positive one of being a "reconciling presence" among people. From this perspective, Yoder tells us, the believer might well "justify firm nonviolent restraint, but certainly never killing."[144]

Yoder knows well that the Old Testament record does not always accord well with this vision.[145] From the beginning, however, there is a readiness to accept the *difference* between the people of God and the surrounding society. Abraham, with his bold break from the civilization of Chaldea, is for Yoder a fine symbol of this.[146] He is a reminder that faithfulness may mean laying aside the way of life that is dominant around us. So if today the call to nonresistance puts us at odds with our world, it should be no surprise, and surely no basis for refusing the call. God has always asked for courageous dissent.

As Abraham symbolizes such dissent, the emperor Constantine symbolizes the loss of it—the failure of the church to live the story of its faith. In the century between the Edict of Milan and the appearance of Augustine's *City of God*, Christianity underwent a momentous and (to Yoder) unhappy transition. The church began to bless the present order and receive support from it. Instead of preaching ethics and judgment like the prophets, it began to see Christ as patron of the empire and to view the empire's leader as God's chosen instrument. Now the whole society was Christian and all its people considered able (regardless of personal confession) to live by Christian standards.

But all this demanded modification of those standards so they would suit the requirements of the empire and fit the needs of persons with "only a moderate level of devotion." Among these modifications was a change in the church's attitude to violence and war.[147]

The transition Constantine symbolizes meant further that God was now identified with some to the exclusion of others—the barbarians. It thus "opened the door," as Yoder writes, "to the concept that one nation or people or government can represent God's cause in opposition to other peoples who, being evil, need to be brought into submission." This eventually led to the church's complicity in nationalism, with which we today have become familiar.

This, says Yoder, exploiting the conventional epithet against his own tradition, is the "real sectarianism." The true "un-Christian divisiveness," he explains, "was the formation of churches bound to the state and identified with the nation."[148] How, he wants us to ask, can we ever have thought it justified to identify God's cause with a particular human power structure? For this undermines the church's vision of catholicity just as it enfeebles the church's power of prophetic criticism. Hence it is pernicious..[149]

For Yoder, then, the Constantinian transition was simply a disaster. But if it did lead to wrong relations between church and state, what relations would be right? In 1964—eight years before *The*

Politics of Jesus appeared—Yoder published his book on this topic, *The Christian Witness to the State.*

He takes for granted in the book that God's cause is not to be identified with some particular power structure. An important question remains, however. How should the church relate to the state in its role as enforcer of justice and keeper of order? This is the question he confronts in the book. He suggests several arguments in answer to it. One of them is this: for the Christian Jesus is the ethical norm. The state relies on violent force to preserve justice and order, but this violates Jesus' ideal of nonresistance. Therefore, the Christian cannot participate fully in this work of the state.[150] Yoder's further arguments respond to two dilemmas this creates for the church, first, how to value what the state does and, second, how to bear witness to the state.

Regarding the first dilemma, Yoder says that though the state resorts to evil, it is still an agent of divine providence to which the Christian must be subject. God uses the state to preserve those conditions necessary for human society and for the work of the church. God does not for that reason, however, endorse the *means* the state employs, nor does God absolve Christians of their duty to follow Jesus. Being *subject to* the state, therefore, does not necessarily mean *obeying* the state. It means consent to the state's sovereignty and refusal to rebel, but it allows disobedience when this is required by faithfulness to Jesus and accompanied by a willingness to accept the lawful punishment.[151]

This contrasts sharply, as Yoder points out, with both Reformed and "extreme" Lutheran positions. The Reformed position holds that the Christian must obey a just state, but may disobey, or even rebel against, one that is unjust. According to the extreme Lutheran position, on the other hand, the state is instituted by God and thus embodies his will. It therefore deserves our total obedience.

Against both of these, Yoder says that Christians must never refuse to be subject to the state nor ever, on the other hand, fully agree with what it stands for. Because the state uses force as its ultimate authority, Christians will always find themselves in tension with it. They should not be surprised, therefore, if their submission turns out to be a "suffering submission."[152] Among the key scriptural passages for all of this are Matthew 5 to 7, Romans 12 and 13, and

Revelation 13. His conclusions, Yoder says, conform to the pattern these passages suggest.[153]

We now turn to the second dilemma: How, if Christians do not participate fully in the social order, can they witness to it "in a relevant way"?[154] How, despite being alien from that order, can they have a constructive influence upon it?

Yoder gives a twofold answer. He says that in its social critique the church must always look at "available, or at least conceivable, alternatives."[155] He means by this that the church must press political leaders toward the divine morality without offending in such a way that they dismiss the Christian witness altogether. Thus the church may refrain, for example, from calling the state to nonresistance. This would seem absurdly unrealistic. It can, however, demand decent treatment of war prisoners or call for an end to capital punishment.[156]

The point here is not that one morality exists for the state and another, more rigorous, one for Christians. "God's only ultimate will is what He has revealed in Christ."[157] It is, rather, that our social critique must set forth the highest standard it believes is possible for our political leaders to understand and consider. This is not, of course, a fixed standard, but one that moves up or down with the level of comprehension of those addressed. Progress in society occurs when heads of state under Christian influence grow in comprehension and the chasm narrows between state policy and the one true will of God.[158]

There is a second way in which the church can bear a constructive witness, and that is by what we may call transformative example. A truly faithful church upholds the divine standard in its own life and so serves the larger society.[159] Writes Yoder:

> The church is herself a society. Her very existence, the fraternal relations of her members, their ways of dealing with their differences and their needs are, or rather should be, a demonstration of what love means in social relations.[160]

The church, in other words, is a "model society." As an example of how it has indeed affected the wider world, Yoder cites the "Christian community's experience of the equal dignity of every member." He suggests that this is what "laid the groundwork for modern conceptions of the rights of man." But it is not only through its internal life that the church shows the outside world a better way; this also happens through its service to nonmembers. Schools and hospitals, for example, began as "services rendered by the church." Only later did they become the concern of secular governments as well.

What all this suggests is the ideal of "constant inventive vision" on behalf of society. Part of the church's ministry, in other words, is that of pioneering new ways of meeting social needs.

The example of the organized community is not all, however. There is also the example of individual Christians living the way of discipleship on their jobs and in their neighborhoods. This, too, Yoder says finally, has tranformative impact, sharpening sensibilities, altering outlooks.[161]

According to Yoder, the church must be willing to accept the role of outsider in society. Now we see how precisely in that role it can change society. A critic might grant this, however, and still ask, "But couldn't the church be even more effective if its members would enter the political process and gain the power necessary to help manage society?" To this, Yoder would reply that it is fine to gain political power—so long as exercising it does not compromise the ideals of discipleship.[162] He would say, too, that although this places limits on Christian involvement with established political structures—more limits under some governments than others—it does not foredoom the church to impotence. A minority living out its vision, despite every pressure to do otherwise, can modify a whole society. The movements of Gandhi and Martin Luther King, for instance, demonstrated this.[163]

It is wrong in any case, however, to suppose we can ever really control how society goes. Even if we rely upon the threat of violence to steer it in a preferred direction, we cannot be sure to succeed. Our predictions and calculations fail because human social systems change constantly with variation in the awareness and intentions of individuals. So it is not as clear as we might think that being in a position of control enhances social effectiveness.

It is clearer than we might think, on the other hand, that an ethic whose means always conforms with its ends is wise. Having such an ethic is how, indeed, to be truly responsible. For the kind of "calculus" that will employ means incompatible with the "projected ends" simply overlooks the limits of our ability to control events.[164]

True Christianity avoids this mistake. Its end is a community of forgiving love and its means is the same as its end. It may not always be clear, Yoder allows, just how the means will produce the end. But in faith the Christian believes it will happen. After the cross came the resurrection, and this shows that temporary defeat is better than complicity with evil. Even if our faithfulness should be ineffective in the short run, that does not make it so in the long run.[165] Faithfulness is finally more effective than compromise. It is the way, indeed, to the victory of the Lamb.[166]

How shall we express all this in the Niebuhrian language we developed earlier? Yoder does acknowledge, of course, the authority of Christ. In all his writings he emphasizes the cultural opposition to the Christian way. Of the scope of Christ's authority he asserts that it is supreme at one point—that of the concrete social meaning of the cross. For the church this means, he says, a participation in surrounding culture marked by (and thus limited by) the ethic of forgiving, nonresistant love represented by that cross.

But this limitation in no sense means withdrawal from cultural tasks. It rather defines the proper Christian way of transforming all our human life into the shape of God's kingdom. In short, it shows us precisely how to be *in* culture *as* loyalists to the cause of Christ.

What shall we say in criticism of this account? We will say nothing here, but pass directly to the final chapter. There I will attempt to set forth a vision heavily indebted to Yoder's own. That attempt will itself involve constant responding to objections and potential objections against what this man has had to say.

CHAPTER • SIX

The Social Ethics
of the Cross:
The Radical Vision After Niebuhr

INTRODUCTION

Yoder argues a position rooted in the story and ethos of the
Anabaptists—Reformation radicals who sought full solidarity with
Christ in the midst of a hostile world. I intend now to suggest a view
of Christ and culture that grows in large part out of what he has said.
I will rely also upon what H. Richard Niebuhr has said. For a main
element of what I am claiming in these pages is that despite the
usual opinion, his writings point to and indeed buttress the radical
vision.

Niebuhr says that Christ is the transformer of culture. I will say
that Anabaptism knows the true manner of his transforming work. I
will say, too, that Niebuhr's own theology backs up the Anabaptist
point of view.[1]

The other theologians we have considered will themselves
figure in the argument. In marking out the present context for discussion of Christ and culture, I am seeking the means, first, for filling
out my own proposal in more detail, and second, for testing it against
the wisdom of others. These means are now at hand and may be put
to service. I will be attempting in what follows to defend the radical
vision, but more than that, I want to refine it. In doing so, I will so-
licit Niebuhr's help as well as that of those who have written after
Niebuhr. The result of all of this will be the "constructive elaboration
of the thesis" promised at the end of chapter one.

In chapter two we looked at Niebuhr's account of the problem

of Christ and culture. Basing our conclusions on his entire theological achievement, we said that the factors which give rise to the
problem are two: Christ's authority and cultural pluralism. For
Christians, Christ is the point (in Niebuhr's metaphor) at which God
and the proper human response to God come precisely into focus.[2]
His story—his words, deeds, and destiny—is what guides and shapes
genuine Christian existence. But there are other stories than his,
which nourish other ways of life. This fact marks out the Christian
way as a particular alternative always challenged by the rival alternatives with which it coexists.

We saw that the problem engendered by all of this has two
main features. One involves questions about the proper relation of
Christ's authority to other cultural authorities. These other authorities can include, for example, rival religions, family, nation,
philosophy, science, and the arts. At least some of these other authorities normally impinge on Christian lives. How then should we
regard them, since they too can affect how we think and live? Is the
story of Jesus Christ supremely authoritative over them? If so, is its
authority supreme in all respects? If not in all respects, in which?
What would make proposed answers to such questions adequate and
justifiable?

Other questions, we said, make up a second main feature of the
problem of Christ and culture. They concern the relation of the
church to the cultural life surrounding it. Should Christ's followers
seek purity by attempting to disconnect themselves as much as possible from the society around them? Or should they try to integrate
themselves into all its structures and institutions? Or do both of these
questions oversimplify? Is not the real issue that of how, or in what
respects, to be separate and how or in what respects to be integrated?
This latter, we suggested, *is* the real issue. The question Niebuhr's
achievement requires us to face is this: What precisely is it to be *in*
culture *as* loyalists to the cause of Christ?

We have before us the Niebuhrian conception of the problem
of Christ and culture developed earlier. It will be the lens we look
through in setting forth a radical Protestant perspective on the problem. This vision will define the church's place and purpose in light of
the Anabaptist understanding.

We will deal with the two broad features of the problem in

order, taking special care to connect the radical heritage and the deepest insights of Niebuhr himself. This will involve, first, an attempt to interpret and defend a radical understanding of the authority of Christ. It will involve next an attempt to interpret and defend a radical perspective on Christian social doctrine, focusing to begin on three radical social virtues and then on the question of the church's relation to the surrounding culture. At the end of the chapter we will recapitulate the main points.

THE AUTHORITY OF CHRIST

All the writers we have consulted agree that Jesus Christ is God's Word to humanity. All of them grant his authority—his power and right to shape us in belief, conduct, and attitude. They all say that he is the criterion of authentic Christian life. Not all of them, however, stress the narrative quality of our existence and so not all of them tell us with equal urgency to remember, to focus our attention on the Jesus story. We saw that Metz tells us this, and Hauerwas and Yoder, too.

Niebuhr provides backing for what these writers say with his reminder that we cannot help but have commitments rooted in history and his insistence that attending to a shared story is a central part of moral responsibility. He provides more backing for their ideas with his suggestion that the narration of events connected with Jesus is what gives Christians their special identity.[3]

Moreover, this emphasis on remembering the Jesus story was characteristic, too, of the Anabaptists. Solidarity with Christ required discipleship, obedience. These in turn required a knowledge of the Christian Bible, and especially of the story which is its centerpiece.

Those who stress the telling of the story thus agree at this point both with the wisdom of Niebuhr and with the legacy of Anabaptism. They direct us, by consequence, to one important way of characterizing the radical vision: it is a narrative vision. Here the authority of Christ touches us through the story told of him in Scripture, and that story is where ethical reflection begins and ends. It is the key to right method in going about our investigations.

We may acknowledge that biblical scholarship has shown that interpreting the story is a highly complex task. It requires, certainly, the cooperative effort of the whole community of faith. Even then, no doubt, complete agreement on the facts and meaning will remain elusive. But from the radical point of view we must persist in this activity despite the difficulties. We must always let the story (or our best reading of it) raise questions for us. We must always let the story guide our answers. This is where true God and true humanity come sharply into focus. It is thus the very measure of our thinking.

This means that the radical vision parts company with what Hauerwas calls the "standard account" of morality. It cannot uphold the autonomous individual as the ethical ideal. It cannot speak of a universal point of view bearing no marks of a particular history. It cannot subordinate questions of character to the task of resolving moral dilemmas. For if the radical vision is a narrative vision, then the fundamental moral task is that of forming skills, interests, and dispositions congruent with the alternate story of our lives. This is true, first, because the total pattern of the moral self is what determines how we deal with moral dilemmas. It is true, second, because we are historical beings, unavoidably shaped by the traditions and narratives of the particular communities to which we belong.

These points fit nicely with Niebuhr's own ideas of moral responsibility. He, too, is concerned with the moral self. He, too, affirms our rootedness in history. But if we now say that the radical vision is a Christocentric vision, it may appear that we have departed from Niebuhr.

The sixteenth-century Anabaptists did, indeed, conceive of Christian life as solidarity with Christ. It meant solidarity with the Jesus of the Bible story now exalted as our Lord and Liberator, now embodied in the church, now ready to effect apocalyptic transformation. Yoder, their spiritual descendant, speaks himself of solidarity with Christ and makes the Jesus story central to his outlook.

Niebuhr says, however, that we distort radical monotheism if Jesus Christ becomes "the absolute center of confidence and loyalty."[4] He finds fault with a form of piety which he calls "Unitarianism of the Son." He warns against a devotion so focused upon Jesus as to blur our vision of the one God who is Father and Spirit as well as Son.[5]

The proper Anabaptist response to this is that solidarity with Christ cannot be other than solidarity with the *God* of Jesus Christ. No doubt we can distort radical monotheism by centering our faith upon someone regarded only as a man, upon Mary's son rather than the God who became incarnate in him. But christocentricity, rightly understood, does not do this. It does not in any way oppose or obscure theocentricity. It does not even suggest that our knowledge of God is limited to what we find in the Jesus story. What it does say is that in Christ God reveals his way and will, and gives us the definitive criterion for how we speak and live our faith in him.

Niebuhr himself makes a claim similar to this one with his metaphor of Christ as "focusing point" and his idea (expressed in the same year as the remarks about "Unitarianism of the Son") that for Christians moral responsibility means being answerable to "*God-in-Christ* and *Christ-in-God.*"[6] The idea is that we know what God is like through Jesus Christ. This concept appears in Niebuhr's writings to the end of his life.[7]

We must grant, it is true, a certain ambiguity in his thinking. Not only does he warn us away from exclusive attention to Jesus Christ; he also speaks of a knowledge of God and God's will that comes to us through nature. And although he nowhere disputes the idea that Jesus was committed to nonviolence, he criticizes those who insist that Christians must embody this trait today.[8] Still, Niebuhr's overall position, affirmed despite the ambiguity and with great vigor at the close of his career, lifts up the Christ as the one by whom we know God and the proper human response to God. The direction in which this takes us, I suggest, is toward the high Christology exemplified in Anabaptist solidarity with Christ.

I conclude that a carefully expressed Christocentrism, though not compatible with Niebuhr's every utterance, nevertheless fits his general perspective. We have met, however, two other explicit challenges to this element of the radical vision. One is John Macquarrie's claim that we are more likely to secure moral bonds between ourselves and non-Christians if we depart from a "Christocentric position" and base our ethics instead upon "the common humanity" we all share.[9]

This challenge reflects the conviction that there is a "natural law" given with our existence and that the obedience of Christian faith is continuous with this law. We may reply by acknowledging that a Christian ethic unrelated to common human aspiration would neither appeal to anyone nor challenge anyone. It would thus have no power to transform society. In any case, moreover, it would be logically impossible to have a Christian ethic entirely unrelated to common moral sensibility. For wherever there is human *community*, there must logically also be at least some sense of truth and justice. It must be the case, in other words, that at least some moral concepts common to all human communities have taken root.[10]

From this, however, it by no means follows that we should abandon Christocentrism. Even if we do have a perspective on what is universal, our perspectives all differ as a function of our particular histories. This is a point Niebuhr stresses and any investigation of the real moral differences that divide our world bears it out.

In another attempt to affirm the natural law, that of Bernard Haering, we saw how the moral differences in our world are too marked to permit denial of the substantial conflict between the Christian morality and other moralities. Thus Macquarrie's objection to Christocentrism seems mistaken in part because it underestimates the moral discord in our world. Furthermore, it asks us to play down the distinctiveness of our particular history as Christians, and thus invites accommodation with the dominant ethos of the surrounding culture.

Another challenge to the Christocentrism of the radical vision comes from Rosemary Radford Ruether. She claims that in all Christian tradition there is no "absolute point of reference" for determining morality. Even Jesus pointed beyond himself to the Holy Spirit. Today, she says, it is through "present encounter" with this Spirit that we meet the absolute point of reference, the final authority.[11] The Spirit's function is to surprise and recreate, and we must expect our encounter with the Spirit to take us beyond past understanding. Ruether allows that new understanding must in some sense grow out of Christian tradition. On the other hand, she does not allow that Jesus or anyone else *in history* can have final authority.

We may from the radical standpoint agree that the Holy Spirit will guide us toward better understanding. But the biblical passage that affirms this idea does not stop with it. "When the Spirit of truth comes, he will guide you into all the truth," says John's Gospel. The evangelist says more, however, for next we find these words from Jesus: "He will glorify me, for he will take what is mine and declare it to you."[12] This suggests that we properly evaluate spiritual insights by testing them against the Jesus story.

In his essay on the Trinity, Niebuhr backs this up. The Spirit "is not confined to the historic Jesus but lives in the community he founded and leads," Niebuhr tells us. He does not tell us, however, that for this reason Jesus lacks final authority. Instead, he speaks of the need for "criteria by . . . which to determine what is and what is not divine spirit," and he then quotes approvingly this remark by Paul about the Spirit: "Any one who does not have the Spirit of Christ does not belong to him."[13]

On biblical grounds, then, the radical vision can withstand Ruether's challenge to its Christocentrism, and Niebuhr himself is a witness to this fact. The Spirit does advance our understanding, but not in the sense of mitigating Christ's ultimate authority. Yoder says well what Anabaptist solidarity with Christ implies. The Spirit's true function in the church is "to make present for hitherto unforeseen times and places and questions the meaning of the call of Jesus."[14]

This remark, in directing our attention to the *call* of Jesus, suggests still another question about the radical perspective. It is one thing to affirm solidarity with Christ, but another to specify its exact significance. Yet this latter is something we must do in order to deal adequately with the problem of Christ and culture. For we may say that Christ's authority is ultimate in relation to other cultural authorities and still ask whether we are to adopt *all* his ways of thinking and living.

Gilkey raised this issue for us by noting that we always interpret our experience of God within a particular context. He further warned that an insular Christianity, cut off from its own cultural surroundings, will be empty and ineffective. We saw that according to him Christianity must always forge a "synthesis" with the surrounding culture, opposing it only in its "false religion dimensions."[15] We cannot, in other words, appeal to the story told in Scripture for a full-blown science or even politics, sociology, or economics. At such points we must learn from authorities broadly respected in our time and place or risk complete irrelevance to our time and place.

Gilkey thus says there are legitimate boundaries to the authority of Christ. Only in rebuking "religious idolatries" and their attendant distortions of value, norm, and fundamental outlook are we bound as Christians to appeal to it.[16] That Christ's authority touches all of life does not, Gilkey would say, make us captive to his entire worldview.

Earlier, in our exposition of his views, we suggested that Gilkey fails to present adequate safeguards against undue alliance with the surrounding cultural life. Yet even though aversion to insularity and embrace of synthesis can easily become aversion to nonconformity and embrace of compromise, we must allow that Gilkey has a point. Sheer, undiscriminating hostility to broadly accepted knowledge and institutions would no doubt diminish Christian credibility. The Bible does not in any case require such an attitude.

Yoder, defending Anabaptist Christocentrism, points out that the New Testament nowhere asks us to adopt *all* Christ's ways of thinking and living. Invoking copious biblical support, he says that it does not present a "*general* concept of living like Jesus," but urges conformity with him at one point. The crucial point of conformity is that of "the concrete social meaning of the cross in its relation to enmity and power. Servanthood," he goes on, "replaces dominion, forgiveness absorbs hostility. Thus—and only thus—are we bound by New Testament thought to 'be like Jesus.' "[17]

We must emphasize that the cross is an expression of radical devotion to God and that such devotion is also part of what it is to be like Jesus. But Yoder himself brings this out. He argues his point carefully and persuasively.

Notice now this important difference between him and Gilkey. It is that he takes greater pains than Gilkey does to let the Bible narrative of Christ define the precise significance of his religious authority. This difference reflects the radical heritage with its characteristic focus upon the Jesus story. It reminds us, too, of Niebuhr's own view of morality, his emphasis on human historicity, his interpretation of moral responsibility, and his idea of narrative as the key to the church's identity. Moreover, it allows acceptance of the point about the boundaries of Christ's authority while providing adequate protection against compromise of the Christian witness. The church may indeed be Christocentric without being insular, and the justification for saying so is in the Bible itself.

Yoder's point does not imply, of course, that in learning the significance of Christ's authority we may narrow our interest to his trial and execution or even to the gospel account of his entire public life. We need to learn the concrete social meaning of the cross. What *does* the cross say about God and society, about the norms and interests of Christian life, about the church's role in the wider culture? In order to learn this, we must consider the whole context—the story that lies behind the cross and the story that issues from it. This means first that we must attend to the Bible. It means also that we must attend to the long history of the church and to our own special circumstances today. Some of this we have done and some we will do again.

Let us now consider what we have accomplished to this point. We have established the narrative quality of the radical vision and shown that the idea of the Jesus story as the measure of our moral thinking finds support from Niebuhr as well as from the Anabaptist heritage. We have met several challenges to Anabaptist christocentrism and have shown the precise focus of Christ's authority. We will now turn to the social doctrine that issues from all of this.

THREE VIRTUES:
THE SELF AND THE COMMUNITY
IN RADICAL PERSPECTIVE

The radical vision upholds Christ as the model of the self and of the Christian community. Sixteenth-century Anabaptist Hans Denck wrote that the Holy Spirit "equips and arms the elect with the mind and thoughts of Christ."[18] Yoder says that through Jesus God has given us "a new, formative definition" of what it is to be human in society.[19]

Since our special concern here is social ethics, we will now consider three social virtues[20] implied by the Anabaptist idea of solidarity with Christ. The ones I have chosen are especially important in defining the radical vision. They have also figured prominently in our discussion so far and require clarification and defense in light of it. The first of these virtues is political engagement. The second is universal loyalty, and the third is nonviolence.

1) *Political engagement.* No writer we have met denies that the gospel has political implications. Each opposes individualistic interpretations of Christian faith and each upholds the task of social transformation as a genuinely Christian task.

The American evangelical, Donald Bloesch, differs from the others, however, in holding that the church's *basic* mission is "spiritual," not political. The backing for this, he says, is Jesus himself. Even in the often-quoted sermon at Nazareth, he concentrated upon matters spiritual. He offered deliverance from sin and death, not from political and economic bondage. And since Jesus is the "final and complete" revelation of God's will and purpose, the church must concentrate upon the same things. It must seek conversions and prepare individuals for life with God in eternity. The church does have an obligation, Bloesch tells us, to build a better society, but this is not the fundamental obligation. Unconverted hearts, not oppressive social environments, lie at the root of human suffering.

Like other writers in our survey, Bloesch assumes that we constantly form the world out of our own imagining and freedom. The world is not sheer fate and so we are not self-deceived when we seek change in its politics and social life. Among these writers he is alone, however, in denying—and denying sharply—that Jesus himself focused on this kind of change.[21] Certainly Yoder thinks that Jesus did focus on it, and this, according to him, is why the radical vision must itself do the same.

We cannot lightly pass over this difference between the two writers because they both claim to represent strict faithfulness to Scripture in a setting of widespread unfaithfulness to it. From Yoder's standpoint, therefore, Bloesch's view is a challenge to which we must pay attention.

What arguments support the proposition that Jesus was concerned primarily with the salvation of individuals? One of them turns upon an interpretation of Luke 7:22. There the evangelist has Jesus replying as follows to a question from John the Baptist: "Go and tell John what you have seen and heard. The blind receive their sight, the lame walk, lepers are cleansed, and the deaf hear, the dead are raised up, the poor have good news preached to them."[22] This answer shows, according to Bloesch, that Jesus did not have political liberation in mind even in the Nazareth sermon.

In fact, however, there is no justification for saying this. Luke 7:22 consists largely of phrases from Isaiah 35:5-6 and 61:1, this latter belonging to the very passage Jesus quoted in Nazareth. Bloesch admits that Isaiah 61:1 concerns sociopolitical deliverance. Yet he argues, in effect, that Jesus gave it a new "spiritual" interpretation.

When, however, the remark by Jesus given as evidence for this is in part a quotation from the same passage in Isaiah, Bloesch has surely failed to make his case. He has given us no reason at all to reject the more natural interpretation, namely, that in both the sermon at Nazareth[23] and in the reply to John's question, Jesus was explaining his purpose in the (sociopolitical) terms of Old Testament prophecy.

Bloesch says further that Jesus refused to be the political Messiah the Jews expected. This point is true but it does not follow from it that Jesus' interests were spiritual instead of political. He might have rejected conventional expectations and still held out his own distinctive political vision. We have seen that this is exactly what Yoder argues at length. His arguments would have to be refuted in order to establish Bloesch's claim.

But there is more. In a work on the Gospel of Luke published after *The Politics of Jesus*, Richard Cassidy has pressed a thesis similar to Yoder's. The Gospel of Luke, he says, presents Jesus as critical of the political establishment and committed to "a new social order . . . based on service and humility" and opposed to "the use of violence against persons."[24]

All of this casts doubt upon Bloesch's idea that Jesus' refusal to be the expected political Messiah shows that he was primarily interested in the salvation of individuals. It casts doubt, too, upon a third point of Bloesch's argument, namely, that Jesus called his followers to a ministry of proclamation, not the building of a new social order. Here again Cassidy lends support to Yoder's own position. Both writers simply deny that Jesus substituted "spirituality" for the prophetic goal of social transformation.

None of this means that the radical vision must interpret the gospel in exclusively social terms.[25] Bloesch follows the New Testament, certainly, in saying that it is important to address individuals with the message of the gospel. No doubt he is also correct in saying that this task itself contributes to a more just society. Yoder expresses the same idea with his remark that because transformed individuals behave differently, "the preaching of the gospel to individuals is the surest way to change society."[26]

The point, then, is not to reject Bloesch's concern but to go beyond it. We must acknowledge frankly that addressing individuals is itself a political act and deny altogether that personal conversions matter more than social changes. These interests must be kept to-gether, as they are in Scripture.[27]

From all this I conclude that if we make the Jesus story our cri-terion, we must regard political engagement as a fundamental virtue. That is, we must accept social transformation as a basic, not a secondary, Christian task and we must train ourselves in the skills and interests appropriate to this task. The radical heritage points toward such a conclusion. The Anabaptist witness addressed social and political structures as well as individuals. It spoke judgment upon rulers and institutions while upholding an alternative form of social life as a way of changing the world. This was a form of political engagement. Anabaptists believed that the Bible requires such en-gagement, and I am saying they were right.

2) *Universal loyalty.* Here I borrow a term from Niebuhr to name a second social virtue required by the radical point of view. The term denotes the consent to all of being that must flow from true faith in the one God who is Maker of all. When our loyalty is universal, we exclude no part of his creation from that loyalty.

As a paradigm of failure to embody this virtue, Niebuhr cites nationalism. Here we narrow our allegiance to a single nation, and so value part instead of all. Our loyalty is limited. Indifference toward some whom God has made is consistent with such nationalistic loyalty and perhaps even demanded by it.

Universal loyalty is different. We deny worth to no part of God's creation, and must therefore disavow in-group/out-group dis-tinctions. Universal loyalty requires what Haering calls "cohu-manity." This is the trait of being with and for all others, seeing oneself as bound to the entire human family. Niebuhr tells us that Jesus was like this—uniquely devoted to God and so able to love men and women with the perfection, he says, of the divine *agape*.

Yoder notes what in view of this should be no surprise, namely, that Jesus specifically rejected nationalism. Yoder supports this point by invoking Jesus' remarks at Nazareth and his refusal to lead a na-tionalist liberation movement. We may add that Jesus' question at the temple in Jerusalem also supports it. "Is it not written," he said, quoting Isaiah, " 'My house shall be called a house of prayer for all the nations'?"[28]

The Anabaptists themselves repudiated the close link between church and state that had to their day been a hallmark of Catholic and Protestant Christianity. It was incompatible, they believed, with allegiance to Christ. In Yoder's writings this element of the Anabaptist heritage becomes precisely an aversion to nationalism. Identifying God with some part of his creation opens the door, he says, to the pernicious idea that one group can represent God *against* another and seek to bring it into submission. To him, when churches identify with nations they no longer bear witness to Christ.

All this supports the connection I am suggesting between the Anabaptist way and the virtue of universal loyalty. But consider now a potential objection.

We saw that a principal feature of the Anabaptist ethos is community—the sharing of Christian life in solidarity with one another. The love of the community, we noted, expresses itself in mutual aid, mutual forgiveness, and discipline. This may remind us, however, of a criticism such as the one Jack Sanders, in his *Ethics in the New Testament*, directs against the Johannine writings. These writings advance an ethic of love for those *in* the community, he says. They urge a connection with the wider world only in the sense of inviting it to adopt the community's beliefs. To him this is an in-group/outgroup mentality and he dismisses it as the "moral bankruptcy of the Johannine ethics."[29]

I leave to others the direct interpretation of the New Testament writer, though what I say now will perhaps contribute indirectly to it. Suppose Sanders made a similar charge against the Anabaptist ethos? How might the defenders of this ethos reply?

There are several ways. One is to say that although the Anabaptist heritage distinguishes the church from the world and upholds the Johannine virtue of communal solidarity, it does not thereby *exclude* anyone from the sphere of concern. True Christians, said one Anabaptist pastor, "help and aid" the needy person, "whether or not he is a member of their church."[30] According to Anabaptist understanding, even persons disciplined to the point of expulsion from the church stay within the orbit of solicitude. The point of discipline is not to limit Christian love, but to express that love and to strengthen Christian witness.

This leads to a second response. It is true that Christians are to love one another, but the goal of their life together is not advantage for a few, but salvation for all. In the Anabaptist picture, Christians preserve an identity over against the surrounding cultural life, but they do so with the purpose of being a light for men and women everywhere, showing the way to a better life. They are evangelists, inviting all who will to join them in their task.[31] They treat no one as an enemy who does not. They meet opposition—even violent opposition—with patience and forgiveness.

There is one more thing. The Anabaptist idea of community implies that each Christian will belong to a particular fellowship limited enough in size to sustain a certain degree of intimacy. For as we saw, part of the meaning of shared life is mutual aid, forgiveness, and discipline. These, especially the latter two, presuppose closeness and familiarity. This does have the effect, we must grant, of focusing our attention upon a few, and one may indeed wonder whether such a focus accords with universal loyalty.

We may reply that such focusing of attention cannot in any case be avoided under the conditions of this world. No individual can distribute himself or herself equally among all people. Each must share affection and time and goods with some among the billions in our world or have, in effect, nothing whatever to share. This means that the virtue of universal loyalty cannot be interpreted to disallow special communities within the wider community that embraces all human beings. The point is that universal loyalty requires every special community to serve the wider community. This is a criterion well met in the Anabaptist understanding of shared life within the church.

A common theme in what we have read so far is that of Christian responsibility toward the poor and the oppressed. The argument is that solidarity with Christ requires special regard for society's victims. Jesus fills the hungry and exalts those of low degree. Gutierrez said, indeed, that the true witnesses of Christ join forces with the oppressed. They struggle with them, even fight with them, against the systems of injustice in our world. According to him, the true witness is a revolutionary; more precisely, a socialist revolutionary.

The gospel indisputably demands special concern for the victims of injustice. Just for this reason the radical vision must itself agree with writers who emphasize this concern. We saw that Yoder himself exhibits such agreement. But on the view I am proposing we must understand all this from the standpoint of universal loyalty. This virtue requires concern for the oppressed, and requires it emphatically. At the same time it requires concern for the oppressor— what the gospel calls love for the enemy. One group may dominate another, but both belong to God's creation. Universal loyalty no more allows violence and ill will against a social class than against a nation. Such loyalty will certainly oppose the oppressor and seek political transformation. It will not, however, resort to the weapons that destroy.

The radical vision, then, cannot follow Gutierrez into violent revolution. But with this point we come to another distinctive social virtue of the radical tradition, the last of the three we shall consider here.

3) *Nonviolence*. This is the virtue of seeking personal, social, and political goals without recourse to the killing and maiming of persons. It means commitment to a frame of mind, a course of action, and it means having skills appropriate to this commitment. From the radical point of view, it is a defining feature of the Christian way of life.

Because the radical point of view defers to the Jesus story, we must know whether the story upholds this virtue. Several writers we have met say that it does. According to Haering, Jesus sought liberation by "nonviolent means." Macquarrie denies that Jesus was a violent revolutionary, saying he was too radical to use "weapons of the existing order" and thus entrap himself or his disciples in "the circle of violence." In the previous chapter we saw that Hauerwas and Yoder draw similar conclusions.

Donald Bloesch, on the other hand, raises doubts. In defending a "pragmatic pacifism" that allows the use of force—perhaps even revolutionary force—he notes that Jesus did not disarm the centurion who requested healing for his ailing servant. To Bloesch this suggests that his own pragmatic view may in fact be compatible with the New Testament. The incident certainly invites us, he would say, to doubt whether disciples are enjoined from violence absolutely.

This is not a forceful argument, as Bloesch himself seems well aware. It raises questions but certainly does not resolve them. For someone who strongly affirms the authority of Scripture and the "absolute authority" of Christ, however, it is better than no argument at all. Recently, however, Stephen Charles Mott has made a more impressive case for doubting that Jesus embraced the virtue of nonviolence as I have defined it. In his *Biblical Ethics and Social Change*, he presents arguments Bloesch could fasten upon. For just this reason we must confront them here. Bloesch substantially agrees with the radical view of the authority of Christ. But if one could show that this authority does not call for the virtue of nonviolence, then the radical vision would at just this point require substantial amendment.

Let us consider, then, what Mott says. The first part of his book sets forth a theology of social involvement. The second explores different pathways to justice, with one chapter focusing upon the question with which we are now concerned. Mott agrees that in working out a Christian social ethic we must look to the teaching and example of Jesus. But although most Christian theologians—even those who do not endorse nonviolence themselves—believe that in the Gospels Jesus himself is committed to it, Mott denies this. It is true, he allows, that according to the New Testament account, Jesus prohibited retaliation or the protection of one's own property. But it is wrong to read that account as prohibiting the use of violence in defending *others*.

Consider Matthew 5:38-42. There we find the classic statement that we should not resist the evil one, nor in other ways evince a "self-protective consciousness."[32] Mott tells us that these verses concern *bilateral* relationships, not *multilateral* ones. That is, they define a person's duty only in a situation involving one other person. They say nothing about that duty when the situation involves a third party. Thus they do not even apply to the question of whether we may resist (or violently resist) an injustice done to others. The effect of this is that we may not appeal to these verses in support of a political nonviolence such as Yoder espouses.[33]

Mott tells us, in the second place, that the historical Jesus never really repudiated the so-called Zealot option. We have seen already how this idea—that Jesus was tempted by but did not support a contemporary resistance movement—is pivotal in Yoder's account of Christian social doctrine. The trouble, according to Mott, is that contrary to the usual opinion, the Zealot party did not even exist at the time of Jesus. He cites recent studies of Josephus which argue that the Zealots did not become a party until about A.D. 67. An uprising, led by Judas the Galilean more than sixty years before this, had been followed by a period of quiet. "The last flurry of insurrectionist activity," he writes,

> had been in the generation previous to that of Jesus' ministry and not even the beginning signs of the deterioration which led to the Roman War would occur until more than a decade after his crucifixion.[34]

It is therefore doubtful, he concludes, whether Jesus would have had to take a position vis-à-vis a Jewish resistance movement.

The New Testament does say, of course, that Jesus refused violence as a means of protecting himself. It says that he dealt with his enemies by dying for them and that he thereby provided a model for Christian conduct. Mott realizes these things but makes two points in response to them. First, when we are admonished, as in 1 Peter 2, to regard Christ's suffering as a pattern, the issue again concerns bilateral relationships, not multilateral ones. Second, when at his arrest and trial Jesus rejected the idea of violent resistance, he was doing so not because he embraced the principle of nonviolence, but because he believed that God *willed* his death for our salvation.

This latter point he supports with exegesis of Matthew 26:52-54, where Jesus responds to Peter's violent act against the high priest's servant. He also appeals to John 18:36-37, where Jesus reminds Pilate that his supporters do not fight in his defense. In both passages, Mott assures us, Jesus is opposing efforts to prevent his death, not upholding an ethical principle.

All these are arresting arguments, but none of them succeeds in confirming Mott's position. In reply to the claim about Matthew 5:38-42 we may invoke the context, and not only the chapter in Matthew itself, but also the wider context, including related materials in both the Old and the New Testaments.

Mott says these verses prohibit only personal self-protectiveness. But notice that Jesus is here addressing the disciples as a group. He is explaining how they can be God's witnesses in the world, how they can be a "light" showing the way to the Father in heaven.[35] In 1 Peter 2, with its similar point about undeserved suffering, we find a similar affirmation of purpose. You behave this way, all of you, so others, seeing your way of life, may turn to God.[36]

All this strikingly resembles the vision of Deutero-Isaiah, with which we know Jesus was acquainted. There the prophet repeatedly pictures the nation of Israel, or the faithful community within the nation, as effecting the conversion of the Gentiles through obedient, suffering witness for God. He even uses the metaphor we find Jesus using in the gospel; namely, that of the community as "light" in the world.[37] Thus the issue in Matthew 5 is the witness of a *community*, not merely of individuals abstracted from the community. Both the immediate context and the heritage out of which Jesus speaks point in this direction. As for the goal of such witness, it is nothing less than the transformation of the enemy, the persecutor. In reaching out to embrace all, the community brings salvation to all.[38]

Notice, however, that on Mott's view it would be perfectly legitimate for the community to organize itself for the use of violent force in protecting its own from persecution. But this is just what it cannot do and at the same time be in its communal witness a light to the world and an example of the Father's boundless love.

I conclude, therefore, that Matthew 5:38-42 is not merely about bilateral relationships, as Mott claims. To suppose that it merely concerns how single individuals should meet evil against themselves is to misread it. The text clearly means to define the proper response of the entire Christian community to violence and hostility.

But what of the claim about the Zealots? Even a defender of nonviolence such as Richard Cassidy accepts the recent research claiming that Judas the Galilean did not found the Zealot party. The point, however, is this: even if the Zealots became an organized party only a generation after Jesus, it seems certain that the *question* of violent insurrection was alive during his lifetime. Judas led a revolt during the turmoil after Herod's death in 4 B.C. and his son Menahem emerged, years later, as a rebel leader in the war of A.D. 66-70. This, together with the statement of Josephus that Judas's principles were seed from which the later strife and warfare grew, suggest continuity, at least, between the one uprising and the other.[39]

Furthermore, we must not overlook the community's memory of the Maccabean War against the Syrians. A high point of this rebellion had been the success of Judas Maccabeus in entering

Jerusalem and rededicating the desecrated temple in 165 B.C. Each December the Festival of Dedication (mentioned in John 10:22) memorialized the occasion. This, too, makes it likely that the option of insurrectionary violence belonged to Jewish consciousness in Jesus' day.[40] An episode at Jesus' trial certifies that this was so. At the request of the chief priests and their allies, Pilate released Barabbas from prison. According to Luke's trial narrative, this man had been thrown in prison for insurrection and murder.[41]

All this shows that Jesus could confront the option the Zealots later took up, even if the formal party did not yet exist. The relative paucity of insurrectionary violence during Jesus' lifetime is by no means evidence against his own opposition to it.

The Gospel of Matthew tells us that Jesus once rebuked his disciple Peter for taking up the sword on his behalf. The Gospel of John tells us that at his trial, Jesus told Pilate that his supporters would not fight for him.[42] According to Mott, however, neither remark has any relevance to the issue of violence. For in the Gospel accounts Jesus was simply opposing efforts which would forestall the death that he believed to be God's will.

But these are surely strained interpretations. Take first the episode in Matthew. Why not follow what seems the natural interpretation and see Jesus' response to Peter's act in light of Matthew 5:38 and its prohibition of resistance against the evil one?[43] Why not also see the rebuke in light of the commissioning speech of Matthew 10? There Jesus told the Twelve to expect persecution when they proclaimed the kingdom but to regard it as opportunity for bearing witness. He said further that they must be prepared even to be killed for their witness. All this is consistent with the vision of chapter 5. What is more, it prepares us for the episode of Peter's violence and Jesus' response. It serves as explanatory background for the episode. Why not acknowledge this? Why not see the evangelist as here driving home his point about the kind of witness and attitude toward our enemies for which Jesus stands?

There is nothing in Matthew's account to divert us from this. Jesus does suggest there is a divine intention behind what is happening,[44] but are we to suppose that the author believes that the bare fact of death is what God wills for Jesus? In light of his theme of public witness, is it not more likely that Matthew is portraying Jesus as believing that God wants him to bear the witness to which he has been called, even though it should lead to death? Why not see this whole episode, indeed, is an affirmation that the way of the cross—the way of love, the way of nonviolence—is *how* God achieves his purposes?[45]

It cannot, in any case, be true that Jesus' behavior here is no paradigm for us. Matthew makes it clear that disciples must be willing to share their teacher's lot, bear his cross, and walk in his footsteps.[46] And what can this mean, anyway, if it does not mean adopting the way of Jesus vis-à-vis the surrounding world?

Of the passage in John where Jesus tells Pilate his supporters would not fight in his defense, Mott writes: this is so "not because Jesus chooses nonviolence, but because he chooses death." The point is not that "violence is the wrong means," but that "it has the wrong end: to prevent Jesus' death."[47]

The text of the Gospel, however, does not support, nor even begin to support, this claim. Mott says Jesus' kingship was unique. His task differed from that of other kings in that (as he said himself) he came into the world "to bear witness to the truth."[48] This is certainly correct, but neither it nor anything else in the Gospel (nor even in Mott's own arguments) contradicts the idea that the truth includes the nonviolence of divine love. According to Mott, the truth to which Jesus witnesses is the truth about God and eternal life. It is through his death that he makes this witness most effectively.

But saying only this is not enough. A mere death says nothing of substance about God or eternal life. In order to illuminate, a death must occur in an illuminating context. It must heighten the truth in a way of life. If Jesus truly revealed God, therefore, he must have chosen, not death in itself, but a way of life that involved a willingness to die. And there is no reason to doubt that the statement about his servants expressed in part what this way of life is like. Nor is there reason to doubt that he expected his followers to share in this way of life. Whatever we say, it is certainly the case that John's Gospel is like Matthew's in calling those who follow Jesus to share his destiny and way of life.[49]

Despite Mott's wish to cast doubt upon Jesus' embrace of non-violence, he has not succeeded in doing so. Yet we may still ask whether the virtue of nonviolence supported by the scriptural narrative requires the *exceptionless* practice of nonviolence. Are we, in other words, to consider the prohibition of violence as an *absolute* prohibition?

Yoder says that killing is never justified for the Christian. Hauerwas upholds nonviolence without (in the writings we have looked at) addressing the question of exceptions. But Bloesch and others in our study do discuss this question and do allow exceptions. Haering is deeply hesitant about violence and admires those who reject it, upholding "the power of conscience to convince and to convert." Yet even Haering allows that in some circumstances violence is justifiable.

Must the radical vision deny this entirely? Must the virtue we are now considering show itself in exceptionless obedience to a rule? Does the Bible story actually require this?

Much of the hostility to the radical vision stems from the sense that its answer to these questions is Yes. To those who reject this vision, the difference between the radical approach and other approaches comes down in large part to the difference between legalism and a rejection of legalism. Fidelity to Christ seems deeper and more truly biblical when it acknowledges moral ambiguity, when it grants the need for exceptional practice in exceptional circumstances. In the New Testament we find Jesus making the law of the Sabbath subservient to the human good. We find Paul and Jesus (in Matthew) allowing exceptions to the prohibition of divorce.[50] It is natural in light of this to doubt whether nonviolence is *always* demanded. Why shouldn't the spirit of nonlegalism obtain here as well?

Similar questions can be raised in connection with other radical virtues. Yet nonviolence, perhaps because it belies so sharply our ordinary values—even ordinary church values—seems especially to call them forth. In any case, the challenge posed here is legitimate. But it is better to deal with it in connection with the question of the church's responsibility in the world. This is the context in which it is characteristically set forth, and the issues of nonviolence and responsiblity cannot at any rate be separated from one another.

So we will now turn to the task of working out a radical perspective on these matters. We have seen that a community shaped by the Jesus story must embrace, in addition to the virtue of nonviolence, the virtues of political engagement and universal loyalty. What now, in light of all this analysis, may we say about the proper relation of the Christian community to the cultural life around it?

THE CHURCH AND
THE SURROUNDING CULTURE

Because our earthly life comes from God and is the object of his loving interest, we must honor our bodily existence, regard the present world with hope, and embrace the task of transforming human culture. This affirmation must be a basic element of the radical vision after Niebuhr. It expresses Niebuhr's own convictions and it has been corroborated overwhelmingly in writings we have studied from the period since his death. It is clearly fundamental to an adequate understanding of the church's relation to surrounding cultural life.

A second basic element of the radical vision also reflects the broad consensus of recent Christian thinking. It is that the goal of the transformative process is a world whose form is Christ—a world, that is, whose people and structures embody the values revealed in Christ.

A third element, again attested broadly, is that the church must be an agent of social conversion. It must represent Christ in the midst of human culture, participating in cultural life, yet participating critically. It must always confront the dominant ethos with the higher ethos of the kingdom; it must always seek transformation.

These points of agreement among writers we have considered do not change the fact that the radical vision is distinctive. It is made so by its uncompromising view of Christ's authority, and the distinctive elements of the vision are what must especially concern us here.

In taking up these elements we will begin, however, with a metaphor common to all Christians, the metaphor of the church as the "body of Christ." Macquarrie, himself far from the radical tradition, thinks that of all the names for the church, this one is most appropriate. Without doubt it is wonderfully concise, signifying much about the church and its relation to surrounding culture.

First, this New Testament image tells us that the Head of the church is Christ. It tells us, too, that the church's strength resides in the union of its members with Christ and with one another. It also tells us that these members are to be Christ's agents, his hands and feet in the world, doing his work and advancing his goals.

These meanings leap out at us, but there is further richness here that bears remarking. For one thing, the metaphor reminds us of the image, common among Catholics since Vatican II, of the church as "sacrament of Christ." It suggests the idea (expressed by Haering, for example) of the church as a visible sign of grace—a tangible form of Christ's presence in the world today. In all of this it brings to mind as well the Anabaptist idea of "solidarity with Christ."

This phrase, we saw in chapter one, aptly summarizes the various strands of Anabaptist dissent from the magisterial Reformation. As such, it connotes belief that the Jesus of the Bible story is now the exalted Christ, Lord and Liberator of us all. He is tangibly present in the church, soon to effect the transformation of all things. It connotes further a reliance upon the grace of Christ, a loyalty to his ways, a willingness to share his life in the church.

The context of Paul's "body of Christ" metaphor shows that it includes *all* the motifs I have said belong to the Anabaptist idea of solidarity with Christ.[51] The biblical metaphor encapsulates, in fact, the vision expressed by the summarizing phrase. The distinctiveness of the radical point of view owes much, of course, to the radical sense of solidarity with Christ. But this is something, it turns out, to which *the common Christian heritage directs us.* So when we mark the characteristic features of radical understanding, we are bringing out the meaning implicit in what Christians everywhere acknowledge. For most of us, due substantially, no doubt, to the sheer inertia of conventional interpretation, this implicit meaning must be *made explicit.* But it is there, even if we have not recognized it, and evidence that this is so will continue to mount as our study proceeds. The New Testament faith, when deeply understood, points us *all* in the radical direction.

What is it, then, that distinguishes the vision of church and culture we are here considering? Two statements summarize the matter. One is that on the radical view, solidarity with Christ makes the church an *alternative society* in the midst of the surrounding culture. The other is that according to radical conviction, the church must be a *transformative example* in the midst of surrounding culture. Let us consider each of these in turn.

1) *The Church as Alternative Society.* Nothing is more certain than this: The radical vision sees a world sharply at odds with the gospel and calls the church to nonconformity. According to it, a people truly formed by the Jesus story is a people marked off from the rest of society. It dissents from customary ways and embodies a new possibility for the world to consider.

Of course, all the writers we have studied acknowledge the contrast between Christian and prevailing values. Ruether, sounding almost Anabaptist, even suggests the religious order as a paradigm for the whole church. Monasticism arose, says this Catholic writer, in reaction to the church's failure under Constantine to be a community over against the prevailing ethos. Now, to regain its true place, the church must give thought to the "convergence" of the religious order and the local congregation. It must be once again an image-breaking entity, pioneering a new humanity. All this is certainly intriguing. Yet in its *emphasis* upon separation from the world, the radical tradition remains distinctive.

This emphasis yields, on the one hand, a characteristic guardedness about participation in the institutions of the surrounding culture. Imitating Christ at the point of the concrete social meaning of the cross in no way means refusal to embrace the created world or to accept responsibility for taking care of it. It does, however, require that our involvements in this world reveal, not hide, our fundamental loyalty to Christ.

Just here, however, the church has often failed. In its involvements with the state it has failed conspicuously. Loyalty to Christ means nonviolence and concern for all of God's creation. In its rash partnership with government, however, the church has often disregarded both of these. It is doubtless true, as Gilkey says, that all societies have a religious undergirding, a network of shared symbols that give direction and meaning. What is also true is that since Constantine, the church has too easily supposed that its proper business is to shore up the religious undergirding of nations and empires. It has debased its own symbols in the service of self-interested, sword-brandishing societies whose ways defy the true meaning of the gospel.

On the radical view the corrective to all of this is unblushing recognition that the church cannot be fully integrated into the surrounding cultural life. We would all think it odd if someone claiming to be Christian tried to redeem human sexuality from within the brothel, as though this were a proper means of cultural transformation. The radical point is that we must be prepared to keep our distance from any number of social institutions, including some that are ordinarily considered honorable. Even if few of them resist the church's values as sharply as prostitution does, there are many from which we must at least withhold our *full* participation.

One of these is the state. By no means is it unambiguously evil. Government institutions deter crime and preserve order and so work for human good. Yet they embody beastly power, too, achieving their ends by a show of violence, mistreating outsiders, preying on dissenters. Against all this the church must bear a witness, and do so in part by withholding participation. Moral differences do exist from government to government, so how much participation we withold will depend in part on where we live. But so long as states flaunt their military might and secure themselves through warfare, those who embody the social virtues of the cross will remain apart. How far apart must be the constant object of reflection as the church's circumstances vary and its understanding deepens.

Being an alternative society is partly a refusal of certain practices dominant in the surrounding culture. It is a matter, in other words, of *selective* cultural involvement. Being an alternative society is also, however, the deliberate formation of a contrasting mode of life. This is the other side of separation from the world, the positive embodiment of Christ in the new community. According to the radical vision, the faithful share a common life, in need supporting one another, in failure disciplining and forgiving one another, in joy celebrating with one another. Sustained by the liberating power of the Spirit, they grow together in the way of Christ and so represent his kingdom in the world.

A natural objection to this, however, is that it may foster a self-regarding perfectionism in the church. Niebuhr has many admiring things to say about the radical understanding of Christian faith. For one thing, it is serious about the lordship of Christ. For another, it stimulates—unintentionally, Niebuhr thinks—"reformations in both church and culture." He goes on to say that the radical answer to the questions we are looking at still "needs to be given." He even says that the authority of Christ makes that answer "inevitable" in the church.[52]

But Niebuhr bridles at the thought of Christians turned in upon themselves, obsessed with developing their own life and their own holiness. In *Christ and Culture* and in his essay on "The Responsibility of the Church for Society," he says that radical movements—monasticism, for example, and the Protestant sects—tend to be like this. They are thus guilty, he tells us in the essay, of "isolationism," the "heresy opposite to worldliness." This heresy occurs when the church "seeks to respond to God but does so only for itself."[53]

The radical ideal (not always realized) in fact agrees with this concern. In the description in chapter one of Anabaptist solidarity with Christ, we saw the importance of witness. We saw how the church was to be a "lantern of righteousness" so that people everywhere might find the way to life and "all war and unrighteousness" might come to an end. After Niebuhr, the radical vision must certainly emphasize this part of its tradition. The alternative society Christians shape must reach beyond itself. Its contrasting mode of life must consist of love for those without as well as those within. It must respond to God not for it own sake but for the sake of all whom God has made. It must bring new life to all the world.

But how? This question takes us to a second distinctive element of radical understanding. In attempting to answer it, we will only be elaborating upon the striking image of the church to which just now we have returned.

2) *The Church as Transformative Example.* Anabaptist Peter Riedeman, in his *Account of Our Religion, Doctrine and Faith*, suggests the metaphor of the church as a "lantern of righteousness." In this body, he continues,

> the light of grace is borne and held before the whole world, that its darkness, unbelief and blindness be thereby seen and made light, and that men may also learn to see and know the way of life.[54]

This of course is a variation on the words of Christ, who called his disciples the "light of the world" and commanded them to summon all humanity to the praise of God by their good works. Yoder, the modern Anabaptist, expresses a similar idea by calling the church a "model society" whose "constant inventive vision"—constant pioneering, that is, of new ways to meet human need—sharpens sensibilities and alters outlooks in the surrounding culture. Hauerwas, himself sympathetic with Anabaptism, says that in its communal life the church must confront the world with a "real option" and so prompt it to a reconsideration of its values.

These ideas are a distinctive emphasis of radical consciousness, but they are not by any means unique to it. We have noticed several other writers saying similar things. Haering sees the church establishing "model communities" in society. Ruether says it must be a redeeming "counter-culture." Metz says its task is "political and moral pioneer work"; the many communities of the church are to be the "bearers of anthropological revolution," converting bourgeois hearts.

All of this reminds us, too, of an image from Niebuhr's writings. As we saw in chapter two, Niebuhr conceives the church as "social pioneer," responding ahead of others to the leading of "God-in-Christ and Christ-in-God." In functioning "as a world society, undivided by race, class, and national interests," it offers a "direct demonstration of the love of God and neighbor." Thus it realizes "the highest form of social responsiblity in the Church."[55]

We know the immense importance of social responsibility in Niebuhr's account of Christian ethics. These remarks remind us of his own agreement with the idea that we practice such responsibility when we participate faithfully in the life of an exemplary community. The evidence from other writers suggests, indeed, that this is a fairly common theme of recent Christian moral thought.

If we ask now what distinguishes the radical interpretation of the theme, we must underscore the sharp differences between the exemplary community and the wider society. In radical perspective, for example, nonviolence and universal loyalty are important social virtues. But the wider societies in which the churches live typically refuse these virtues. They brandish weapons and secure themselves at the expense of others, building up walls of hostility instead of tearing them down.

The temptation is strong to accommodate the Christian witness to this harsh reality. To radical eyes the church has usually done so, often with explicit denial that the ethic of Jesus holds good in sociopolitical contexts. Donald Bloesch offers us a striking example of such denial with his claim that obedience to all Christ's commands would bring "chaos" to society. "How we act as an ambassador of Christ," he says, "will often be different from how we act as a citizen of the state."

The radical vision, however, bridles at such moral dualism, upholding consistent solidarity with Christ as the proper Christian form of social responsibility. Niebuhr once tells us that to the church Christ is "the expected deliverer from evil." That is just the radical point! True faith envisions the transformation of all things through Christ and so esteems the way of the cross as socially and politically relevant today.

Here we may recall that one feature of Anabaptist solidarity with Christ is apocalyptic consciousness—a sense of the imminent end of the present age with its evil rulers and institutions. The apocalyptic element in the Christian heritage seems exotic, even alien, to modern understanding. Nevertheless, it is there, and not just among radical groups, but in the church's founding document, challenging us to spell out its meaning for today.

We noticed earlier an intriguing attempt by a contemporary Catholic, Johann Baptist Metz, to do just this, and what he says can be illuminating now. His interpretation actually brings together both prophetic and apocalyptic insights. He speaks on the one hand (like the ancient prophets) of the real possibility of transformation in this world. But he adds to this the apocalyptic sense of coming interruption, discontinuity, upheaval. Our advance to a new world is not smooth but difficult, not predictable but startling. Changes occur abruptly, necessitating constant uneasiness about the present order and constant readiness to meet new challenges. In true apocalyptic consciousness, all of these things—the discontent, the hope, the sense of urgency—join with willingness to follow Christ and so produce, Metz tells us, a revolutionary witness in the world.

The importance of this interpretation here is that it helps us clarify the relation between the apocalyptic element in the radical heritage and the church's responsibility for society. The "sharp differences" between church and world reflect the conviction that the values and purposes of Christ really will prevail in the end. Embodied in the church they really do transform society. Despite many setbacks and many trials, and against all conventional expectation, the new community midwives a new world.

Yoder, invoking the surprise of the resurrection, expresses ideas similar to these. In his forgiving acceptance of unjust execution, Jesus seemed powerless, but he was not. God used his cross to change our history. Today, having faith involves confidence that similar surprises will continue to occur until the day of final victory over evil. Yoder reminds us, too, however, that even if the radical hope for society envisages what conventional minds would not expect, it is by no means an irrational hope. This hope rests, it is true, upon faith that through the grace of God human beings may somehow be persuaded, rather than coerced, into a new pattern of existence. And no one thinks it obvious that this will happen. However, Yoder insists that no one should think it obvious that this will *not* happen.

For one thing, we easily overrate the coercive alternative to radical hope. Yoder observes that even though power backed by the threat of violent force may appear to offer us the possibility of "control" over the direction society takes, this is to a large degree delusory. Because of the unpredictability of the individuals who make up human social systems, these systems constantly surprise us. They surprise even those in a position of "control." This makes it far from certain that the calculated use of violent power will yield the results predicted by our analysis.[56]

This is a negative reason not to dismiss the radical hope. Yoder suggests, too, a positive reason to embrace it: the record of social movements such as those led by Gandhi and Martin Luther King. These movements held up before the world the exemplary witness of a few. What these few achieved, Yoder suggests, proves that such a witness can really modify surrounding culture.

Let us attend further to the idea of exemplary witness by a few. One way to grasp the significance of such witness is to imagine that we belong to a moral world much like the one we meet daily in the newspapers, the office, or the street. In this world we deal with those whom we consider a threat to our welfare by being constantly ready to take preemptive action—even violent action—against them. Realizing this, however, the others adopt plans to prevent our preemptive action from succeeding. We in turn must take further preventive measures, "outbidding" our opponents. This we do even though it is natural for them to reply with yet more belligerent gestures of their own.

As this process continues, neither party is willing to depart from it. The result is an ever higher level of conflict—and an ever lower level of morality! We may be committed to do only the least bad thing that is necessary in order to prevent something worse from happening, but the moral currency is still further and further debased. The process, if not interrupted, must lead in the end to disaster. This in fact is what we contemplate all the time in connection with the arms race. It is what we see regularly in reports of wars and revolutions around the world.

If we ask now what can stop such moral decay, the answer is that at least some people must resist it by limiting the preventive measures they will take against their enemies. Moreover, their policy must somehow have a persuasive effect upon others, so enough of these others will join with them to make enough of a difference. To improve morally upon a world that harbors villainy, at least some of us, in other words, must be ready to change it by transformative example. We must sometimes refuse to do the least bad thing that seems necessary to prevent an even worse effect. This may be costly to ourselves as well as others, but it is indispensable in resisting the decay and prompting reconsideration of moral values.[57]

For the radical vision, a central feature of exemplary witness is nonviolence. This virtue defines one important limit upon the preventive measures a disciple may take against those who threaten human welfare. But now we may return to the issue with which we ended our discussion of nonviolence and ask whether this limit is to be thought of as absolute. Is nonviolence *always* required? Or should the spirit of nonlegalism (reflected in the New Testament view of Sabbath-keeping and marital steadfastness) obtain here as well?

Yoder has written a short book in which he says that he could "justify firm nonviolent restraint, but certainly never killing."[58] His subject in the book is the "standard question" used to test the consistency of pacifist arguments against warfare. What would you do, it is asked, if a gun-bearing criminal threatened to kill your wife or your daughter?

Yoder deals with the question in several ways, one of which is to say that the policy of nonviolence urged by Jesus must determine even our response to criminal attack upon self or family. We assume too quickly, he tells us, that in this circumstance the only alternative to violent action is the victim's death. Other creative responses could effectively unnerve the attacker. These include a loving gesture, perhaps, or display of moral authority, nonlethal force, a ruse, or even simple undefensive harmlessness.[59] All of them leave open possibilities of reconciliation otherwise closed off by defensive killing. And even if they should fail, death is not, after all, the worst of fates. Martyrdom is an important theme in the Christian heritage. The tradition of the martyrs shows that a believer's innocent death can contribute much to eventual victory over evil in this world.

All this is both moving and illuminating. But it is in part mistaken, I believe. Yoder does not in fact show that someone with the biblical virtue of nonviolence could never, under any conditions, maim or kill another person. This virtue embodies a command of Jesus, a part of the new law given to disciples. But as noted earlier, the New Testament accords to human welfare a higher place than the letter of the law. The story that shapes the Christian virtues shows Jesus making the law of the Sabbath subservient to human good. It shows Paul and Jesus allowing exceptions to the prohibition of divorce.

The Old Testament itself, moreover, exhibits openness to exceptional practice for exceptional circumstances.[60] A vision which upholds what Scripture tells must take all of this seriously. It should not regard the law against violence differently from these other laws unless it can make a good case for doing so. I believe this has not been done so far.

Consider now a related theme in the biblical story. The purpose of faithful witness, including the witness of nonviolence, is to reduce suffering—to somehow establish under God the reign of justice in this world. Yoder once remarked in an early essay that true Christian love "seeks neither effectiveness nor justice, and is willing to suffer any loss or seeming defeat for the sake of obedience."[61] Even allowing, however, that the way of the cross is costly, Yoder is certainly wrong in saying this.

According to Matthew and Luke, Jesus himself ranked justice among the weightier matters of the law.[62] Both evangelists interpret his ministry through the vision of Deutero-Isaiah. The author of Matthew actually speaks of him as fulfilling the prophecy of a servant of God who will "faithfully bring forth justice."[63]

We cannot doubt, therefore, that these writers—both of whom call us to the love of enemy—regard such love as a form of effective action for the weak and the oppressed. Such action, after all, is what the Old Testament virtue of justice involves.[64] Christian love is not always effective in a direct, immediate way, but neither, we must insist, is it indifferent to the question of effectiveness.

Let us say that a berserk man (I once saw a report of such a thing on television) begins indiscriminately shooting children at play in a schoolyard. Can we imagine any scenario in which the radical disciple might himself resort to maiming or killing the man?

In reply we must first affirm that in such circumstances radical virtue would surely call for creative, nonviolent action. Does it require us, though, to deny altogether the possibility of recourse to violence? Given what we saw before about legalism in the Bible and what we have seen just now about the Bible's interest in effecting justice, I cannot believe that it does. Not even the disciple can repudiate violence absolutely.

The whole body of Yoder's writings, if not the remark I have just quoted, appears to agree that Christian love is in some sense effective. We saw in our exposition that to Yoder Jesus embodies a distinctive political strategy. His unjust execution is a form of power—a means of establishing the kingdom. Still, the thing to underscore from his viewpoint is that the kingdom comes through the nonviolent love of the cross. We must not, he insists, pay lip service to this while falling into step with the pattern of the surrounding culture.

But does a nonlegalistic account of the radical tradition inevitably push toward the cultural accommodation Yoder fears? Does it amount, in fact, to a failure of the "nonviolence test" often used in these pages to criticize what other writers have to say?

Let us recall three things about the interpretation given so far. One is that the radical vision is a narrative vision. The fundamental moral task is to form the virtues—the skills, interests, and dispositions—congruent with the story told in Scripture. The second grows out of the first. It is that the virtue of nonviolence means not only seeking our goals without killing or maiming persons; it means developing the skills appropriate to this commitment. The third is that the radical vision is apocalyptic; it is awake to massive defiance of the way of Jesus in surrounding culture and it is resolved to make a public witness against it.

In light of all this we may deny a legalistic understanding of nonviolence without dissolving either the differences between the radical community and the wider society or the differences between radical and nonradical Christian social doctrine. It still remains that the special calling of true disciples is to advertise in habit and demeanor the peaceableness of God's kingdom. And this still requires a focus upon certain dispositions and abilities.

True disciples nurture the spirit of forgiving love, and instead of learning the skills of violence, learn and practice the skills of nonviolence. In this world many are ready to retaliate. Legions devise and manufacture weapons and still more legions plan and train for bloodshed. Peacemakers, on the other hand, are few, and Christians are called to be among them. They are to bring the world up short by risking the way of Jesus, by refusing even to prepare themselves to do violence.

Radical disciples, therefore, do not keep guns at bedside, but dare to *plan* on responding without violence to anyone who threatens home or family. Nor do they train for sharpshooting in the police forces of this world, nor join its armies and march as symbols of lethal force and narrow loyalty. These things are incompatible with their distinctive virtues and their distinctive witness. Circumstances could arise, we may admit, when tenacity in nonviolence would lose all semblance of constructive witness, but the disciple who then attempted to maim or kill another would be committing an utterly strange act, difficult and thoroughly out of character.

We can hardly overemphasize, moreover, how bizarre the circumstances would have to be for this to happen. Consider the example of the berserk man shooting schoolchildren. In this world it is commonplace to give evil for evil and many are trained and ready to maim or kill. It is thus unlikely that someone prepared in the skills of discipleship would ever be crucial to putting a violent stop to the carnage.

The radical vision, then, need not be legalistic in order to be distinctive. Accounts of the Christian social ethic which do not bring out the kinds of points I have been making here are substantially different from the radical account. That because of this they are also inadequate, or inadequate in part, is one of the claims I am making in these pages. I wish now, however, to acknowledge the need in all of this for an appropriate humility. The issues we have considered, not least of all this last one, are difficult. We may agree that the special project of the church is reconciliation, that this project is to transform all of culture, and that it puts all who embrace it upon the road to Jerusalem and the cross. The difficulty of knowing exactly what this means in every aspect of our lives reminds us that the exemplary community must itself be ready always to reevaluate, to repent, and to learn from the Spirit of Christ who must continue to guide us toward the truth we never fully comprehend. Such readiness is itself a part, no doubt, of what it means to be a transformative example in the midst of the surrounding culture.

We began this section of the chapter by suggesting that the implicit meaning of what Christians everywhere acknowledge points us toward the radical vision. One part of this meaning, we then saw, is the idea of the church as alternative society. It participates selectively in the practices and institutions of surrounding culture while living out, for the sake of all the world, its own contrasting form of life. Now, having explored what it means and why it is important for the church to be a transformative example, we are ready to summarize the main conclusions of this study.

A RECAPITULATION

I have attempted in these pages to illuminate what Niebuhr called the problem of Christ and culture. As my central thesis I have set forth the claim that the Anabaptist way is the best way to embody Niebuhr's vision. It is through radical solidarity with Christ, I have said, that the church fulfills its transformative task in the world. In elaborating and defending the thesis, I have shown several main subtheses to be true as well. I wish now to mark these down and to comment on them briefly.

1) The question of Christ and culture does not concern *whether* the church should participate in cultural life, but *how* it should participate. We belong necessarily to culture, and this is true even when we keep our distance from the ethos prevalent around us. It is sense-

less, taking Niebuhr's definition of the term, to stigmatize anyone or any group as being *against* culture.

2) Moralities reflect stories. They grow out of shared histories, of which there are many in this world. Neutral standpoints are therefore necessarily elusive. We may expect genuine Christian morality to be distinctive, challenging and being challenged by the rival moralities with which it coexists.

3) Properly, Christian moral reflection takes the Christian narrative as its starting point and final criterion. The first Christians recited a story. To be authentically in their tradition, we must do the same. We interpret the story in a pluralistic world where we have to justify our beliefs, sometimes by adjusting them. But to remain Christian we must remain fundamentally at home with Scripture's story.

4) According to that story, Jesus Christ is the point in history where God and the proper human response to God come precisely into focus. Therefore the Christian community upholds Christ as the measure of its moral understanding; the Christian morality is Christocentric.

5) For a narrative vision, the basic moral task is the shaping of character. This includes the forming of appropriate virtues and appropriate skills, interests, and dispositions. Three virtues among those upheld by the Christian narrative have special importance in defining Christian social doctrine. They are political engagement, universal loyalty, and nonviolence.

6) The church serves the surrounding culture by being an alternative society and a transformative example. In this way it is, under God, an agent of social conversion, midwiving a world whose form is Christ.

7) The social doctrine articulated in this study and summarized in the points we have just been making, is a modern statement of the radical vision. It is a statement faithful to the Anabaptist heritage and viable in the world today.

8) H. Richard Niebuhr's thought, taken as a whole and with full awareness of its development, points in the radical direction. The case for this is not unambiguous, but it is clear enough that routine, uncritical appeals to his writings in defense of nonradical social doctrine should henceforth cease.

This last point recalls again the overall thesis of the study. I have offered many reasons for regarding it as true. Let me finally suggest another. Once in the early 1930s, Niebuhr was ruminating upon the dilemma Americans felt of not knowing what constructive thing to do about the current fighting between the Chinese and Japanese. He remarked that "radical Christianity" (his words) does something constructive even when it cannot intervene directly with what is going on. How? It does this, he said, simply by building "cells of those within each nation who . . . unite in a higher loyalty" than loyalty to nation or to class. It is in embracing this higher loyalty that they "prepare," as he said, "for the future."[65]

This remark is close, surely, to the spirit of the vision I have been describing. For what the radical heritage holds up before us is nothing less than the prospect of social change through the witness of small groups—cells of Christians, if you please, who by their solidarity with Christ remake the world.

Notes

CHAPTER ONE

1. Richard Niebuhr, *Christ and Culture* (New York: Harper and Row, 1951), pp. 116.

2. Ibid., p. 118.

3. Ibid., pp. 229, 231.

4. That the transformationist, or conversionist, theme is Niebuhr's own—not only in *Christ and Culture* but also in other works—is shown clearly, for example, in Paul Ramsey's essay on Niebuhr in his *Nine Modern Moralists* (Englewood Cliffs, N.J.: Prentice-Hall, Inc., 1962), pp. 149-179.

5. Klaus Deppermann, Werner O. Packull, and James M. Stayer, "From Monogenesis to Polygenesis: The Historical Discussion of Anabaptist Origins," *Mennonite Quarterly Review*, XLIX (April, 1975), pp. 83-121.

6. Donald Durnbaugh, *The Believers' Church* (Scottdale: Herald Press, 1985), p. 68.

7. Conrad Grebel's words, quoted in George H. Williams, *The Radical Reformation* (Philadelphia: Westminster, 1962), p. 96.

8. J. Denny Weaver, "Discipleship Redefined: Four Sixteenth Century Anabaptists," *Mennonite Quarterly Review*, LIV (October, 1980), pp. 255-279. The phrase itself he has borrowed from John Howard Yoder, who uses it in remarks about the Anabaptist Michael Sattler. See p. 257.

9. Hans Denck is a prominent Anabaptist whose discussion of the relation of Jesus and the Christ differs from what this summary suggests. The practical effect of his arguments, however, keep him well within the mainstream of Anabaptism. Cf. ibid., pp. 263-271. As backing for the summary I have given, see, for example, remarks of representative Anabaptist writers on the following pages of Walter Klaassen, ed., *Anabaptism in Outline: Selected Primary Sources* (Scottdale, Pa.: Herald Press, 1981). Pp. 24-25, 31, 196, 325, 343.

10. Note, for example, remarks of representative Anabaptist writers on the following pages of Klaassen's book: pp. 46, 66, 67, 106.

11. See, e.g., John H. Yoder, "The Prophetic Dissent of Anabaptists," and John C. Wenger, "The Biblicism of Anabaptists," in Guy F. Hershberger, ed., *The Recovery of the Anabaptist Vision* (Scottdale, Pa.: Herald Press, 1957).

12. Conrad Grebel, as quoted in Wenger, "The Biblicism of Anabaptists," pp. 171-172.

13. See Yoder, "The Prophetic Dissent of Anabaptists," pp. 95-96.

14. The Old Testament, said Hans Pfistermeyer, "has been fulfilled and explained by Christ. What Christ has explained and helped us to understand, I will adhere to, since it is the

will of the heavenly Father." Quoted in Klaassen, ed., *Anabaptism in Outline*, p. 149.

15. Bernhard Rothmann, quoted in Klaassen, p. 150.

16. The terms the Anabaptists used most often in their writings were *Nachfolge* (discipleship) and *Gehorsam* (obedience), says Robert Friedmann, in "The Doctrine of the Two Worlds," in Hershberger, ed., *The Recovery of the Anabaptist Vision*, p. 115.

17. Hans Denck and Peter Riedeman, for example. See Weaver, "Discipleship Redefined," p. 226, and Robert Friedmann, *The Theology of Anabaptism* (Scottdale, Pa.: Herald Press, 1973), p. 89. For a useful comparison of the Lutheran and Anabaptist perspectives on justification, see Hans J. Hillerbrand, "Anabaptism and the Reformation: Another Look," *Church History*, XXIX (1960), pp. 404-423.

18. Remarks of Balthasar Hubmaier and Bernhard Rothmann, quoted in Klaassen, ed., *Anabaptism in Outline*, pp. 102, 106.

19. See Friedmann, *Theology of Anabaptism*, p. 78, and Hillerbrand, "Anabaptism and the Reformation," p. 412.

20. Anabaptist writings reflect what Gustaf Aulèn calls the "classic view" of the atonement. For his famous typology of atonement doctrines, see *Christus Victor* (London: S.P.C.K., 1953).

21. See, for example, Riedeman's remarks in Klaassen, *Anabaptism in Outline*, pp. 29, 31, 67.

22. Quoted in Klaassen, *Anabaptism in Outline*, p. 86. See also the famous epigram of Dietrich Bonhoeffer: "Only he who believes is obedient, and only he who is obedient believes," in *The Cost of Discipleship* (New York: Macmillan, 1963), p. 69.

23. Quoted in Klaassen, *Anabaptism in Outline*, p. 35.

24. See Hillerbrand, "Anabaptism and the Reformation," p. 416.

25. See Walter Klaassen, *Anabaptism: Neither Catholic nor Protestant* (Waterloo, Ontario: Conrad Press, 1973), pp. 28-35.

26. The quote, from Denck's essay on God and evil, appears in Angel M. Mergal and George H. Williams, eds., *Spiritual and Anabaptist Writers* (Philadelphia: Westminster, 1957), p. 99. Weaver, in "Discipleship Redefined," says the Anabaptist account of discipleship and Christian freedom parallels the Pauline paradox of grace. Denck himself reflects this in the essay quoted here. He speaks of the "Christ whom no one may truly know unless he follow him with his life. And no one may follow him except as he already knows him:" Ibid., p. 108. Also in Weaver, p. 267.

27. See, e.g., J. Lawrence Burkholder, "The Anabaptist Vision of Discipleship," in Hershberger, ed., *The Recovery of the Anabaptist Vision*, p. 138.

28. The first two quoted phrases are from Peter Riedeman. The third is from Jacob Hutter, quoted in Klaassen, *Anabaptism in Outline*, pp. 112, 275.

29. Robert Friedmann, "The Doctrine of the Two Worlds," in Hershberger, ed., *Recovery*, pp. 105-118. In the cover letter of the 1527 Schleitheim Confession, Michael Sattler explained the document to his fellow Anabaptists. He said its points and articles make known that "we who have assembled in the Lord at Schleitheim . . . have been united to stand fast in the Lord as obedient children of God—sons and daughters, who have been and shall be separated from the world in all that we do and leave undone . . ." Quoted in John Yoder, *The Legacy of Michael Sattler* (Scottdale, Pa.: Herald Press, 1973), p. 35.

30. See, for instance, the Münster debacle. On this see George H. Williams, *The Radical Reformation*, pp. 362-368.

31. See Walter Klaassen, "The Anabaptist Critique of Constantinian Christendom," *Mennonite Quarterly Review*, LV (July, 1981), pp. 218-230.

32. Quoted in Klaassen, *Anabaptism in Outline*, p. 280.

33. See, e.g., articles four and six of the Schleitheim Confession, in Yoder, *The Legacy of Michael Sattler*, pp. 37-38.

34. Most Anabaptists (though not all) said, indeed, that no Christian could even be a magistrate. Some could imagine Christian service in government but doubted, given the attitudes of the world they knew, whether anyone so employed could (as Hans Denck put it) "keep Christ as a Lord and master." Quoted in Klaassen, *Anabaptism in Outline*, p. 250.

35. Anneken of Rotterdam, quoted in Burkholder, "The Anabaptist Vision of Discipleship," p. 146.

36. Quoted in Franklin Littell, *The Origins of Sectarian Protestantism* (New York: Macmillan, 1964), p. 134.

37. The first remark, by Hubmaier, is in Klaassen, *Anabaptism in Outline*, p. 194. The next two, by Grebel, are in Mergal and Williams, *Spiritual and Anabaptist Writers*, p. 76.

38. So said Hubmaier, as quoted in Durnbaugh, *The Believers' Church*, p. 269. Hutterite Anabaptists actually repudiated private property and practiced a kind of Christian communism. On this whole matter, see J. Winfield Fretz, "Brotherhood and the Economic Ethics of the Anabaptists," in Hershberger, ed., *Recovery*, pp. 196-199.

39. See, e.g., quotations in Klaassen, *Anabaptism in Outline*, pp. 219, 221.

40. Quoted in Klaassen, *Anabaptism in Outline*, p. 324.

41. Quoted in Klaassen, p. 343.

42. A few Anabaptists, notably those involved at Münster, embraced an eschatology of revolutionary violence. Most did not. Anabaptist hymns, to take one measure of popular piety, nowhere reflect the idea. See Friedmann, *The Theology of Anabaptism*, p. 107.

43. Littell, *The Origins of Sectarian Protestantism*, pp, 61-62.

44. Words of an unnamed Anabaptist at the 1538 Bern Colloquy, quoted in Klaassen, *Anabaptism in Outline*, p. 100.

45. Niebuhr does not speak directly of Anabaptists but of such sixteenth-century sects as now represented by the Mennonites. The Mennonites, of course, are the heirs of Anabaptism. See *Christ and Culture*, p. 56.

46. Ibid.

47. Origen, *Against Celsus*, 8.

48. Augustine was born forty-two years after Constantine became emperor and became a bishop by the year 396. See Ernst Troeltsch, *The Social Teachings of the Christian Churches* (New York: Harper and Row, 1960), ch. 1. See also Roland H. Bainton, *Christian Attitudes Toward War and Peace* (New York: Abingdon Press, 1960), p. 85.

49. Augustine, *City of God*, 15.1.

50. Ibid. 9.1.

51. Ibid. 5.15.

52. See Bainton, *Christian Attitudes Toward War and Peace*, pp. 95-100.

53. Augustine, *City of God*, 5.25; 1.21.

54. See, e.g., "The Schleitheim Confession of Faith," in Yoder, *The Legacy of Michael Sattler*, p. 35.

55. See, e.g., Augustine, *City of God*, 10.18, 25. The quotation is from Psalm 73:28, as given in Henry Bettenson's translation of *City of God* (New York: Penguin Books, 1972).

56. Ibid., 11.2.

57. Discipleship was a central motif in early Christian ethics. See, for example, Eric Osborn, *Ethical Patterns in Early Christian Thought* (New York: Cambridge University Press, 1976).

58. Reinhold Niebuhr, *An Interpretation of Christian Ethics* (London: SCM Press, 1936), p. 199.

59. Karl Barth, *Church Dogmatics*, trans. by G. W. Bromiley (13 vols; Edinburgh: T. and T. Clark, 1957-1969), II.2, p. 568.

60. Ibid., p. 569.

61. Ibid., III.4, pp. 397-470.

62. George Forel, ed., *Christian Social Teachings* (Garden City, N.Y.: Doubleday, 1966), pp. x, 184.

63. Guy F. Hershberger, *War, Peace and Nonresistance* (Scottdale, Pa.: Mennonite Publishing House, 1944), and *The Way of the Cross in Human Relations* (Scottdale, Pa.: Herald Press, 1958).

64. Martin E. Marty, "A Decade of Religious Books," *Christian Century*, Nov. 14, 1979, p. 1128.

65. John Howard Yoder, *The Politics of Jesus* (Grand Rapids: Eerdmans, 1972), p. 239.

66. Ibid., p. 101.

67. John Howard Yoder, *The Original Revolution* (Scottdale, Pa.: Herald Press, 1971), p. 138.

68. For an account of these developments, see, e.g., the relevant chapters of John Dillenberger and Claude Welch, *Protestant Christianity* (New York: Scribners, 1954).

69. Karl Barth, *The Epistle to the Romans*, trans. by Edwyn Hoskins, sixth ed. (New York: Oxford University Press, 1968), p. 330.

70. Ibid., p. 10.

71. Ernst Troeltsch, *The Social Teachings of the Christian Churches*, 2 vols. (New York: Harper and Row, 1960).

72. See, for instance, his *Violence: Reflections from a Christian Perspective* (London: SCM Press, 1970).

73. See his *Christ and Power* (Philadelphia: Fortress Press, 1977), *Victory over Violence* (London: SPCK, 1975), and *Was Jesus a Revolutionist?* (Philadelphia: Fortress Press, 1971).

74. Besides *Truthfulness and Tragedy* (Notre Dame: University of Notre Dame Press, 1977) and *Vision and Virtue* (Notre Dame: Fides Publishers, 1974), see his recent social ethics, *A Community of Character* (Notre Dame: University of Notre Dame Press, 1981).

75. For a recent bibliographical essay detailing these developments, see Allen Verhey, "The Use of Scripture in Ethics," *Religious Studies Review*, IV (January, 1978), 28-37.

76. Carl F. H. Henry, *Christian Personal Ethics* (Grand Rapids: Eerdmans, 1957), p. 327.

77. See Jack T. Sanders, *Ethics in the New Testament* (Philadelphia: Fortress Press, 1975).

78. Stanley Hauerwas, "The Moral Authority of Scripture: The Politics and Ethics of Remembering," *Interpretation*, XXXIV (October, 1980), pp. 356-370. The essay is reprinted in Hauerwas's *A Community of Character* (Notre Dame: University of Notre Dame Press, 1981).

79. See, e.g., James F. Childress, "Scripture and Christian Ethics," *Interpretation*, XXXIV (October, 1980), pp. 371-380.

80. I wish to acknowledge my indebtedness in this paragraph to an unpublished paper by my colleagues John Brunt and Gerald Winslow.

81. See Martin Heidegger, *Being and Time*, trans. by John Macquarrie and Edward Robinson (New York: Harper and Row, 1962), especially pp. 188-195.

82. See his *Truth and Method* (New York: Seabury, 1975) and *Philosophical Hermeneutics* (Berkeley: University of California Press, 1976).

83. Ludwig Wittgenstein, *Tractatus Logico-Philosophicus*, 4.5.

84. Ludwig Wittgenstein, *Philosophical Investigations*, par. 114.

85. Ibid., par. 23.

86. A view apparently held, for example, by William Frankena. In his study "Is Morality Logically Dependent on Religion?" he criticizes those who would ground all ethical principles on religious beliefs. He says they thus "introduce into the foundations of any morality whatsoever all the difficulties involved in the adjudication of religious controversies. . . ." He supposes, apparently, that these difficulties can be avoided. The essay is in Gene Outka and John P. Reeder, Jr., ed., *Religion and Morality* (Garden City, N.Y.: Doubleday, 1973). The quotation is on p. 313.

CHAPTER TWO

1. See H. Richard Niebuhr, *The Meaning of Revelation* (New York: Macmillan, 1941), p. 36.

2. So writes Libertus A. Hoedemaker, *The Theology of H. Richard Niebuhr* (Philadelphia: Pilgrim Press, 1970), p. xvii.

3. Failure to interpret the Christian ethos in this way regularly inspired censure from Troeltsch. For example, of "Early Catholicism" he remarks disapprovingly: "The idea of a Christian civilization, of a spirit which should penetrate, mold, and renew the common life,

was entirely absent." *The Social Teachings of the Christian Churches* (New York: Harper and Row, 1960), p. 126.

4. Richard Niebuhr, *Christ and Culture* (New York: Harper and Row, 1951), p. 10.

5. Ibid., p. 11, emphasis mine.

6. Ibid.

7. Ibid.

8. Ibid., p. 13.

9. Ibid., p. 14.

10. Ibid.

11. Ibid., p. 16.

12. Ibid., pp. 18-19.

13. Ibid., pp. 21-22.

14. Ibid., pp. 24-25.

15. Ibid., pp. 25-26

16. Ibid., pp. 27-28.

17. Ibid., p. 29.

18. Ibid., p. 32.

19. Ibid., p. 33.

20. Ibid., p. 39.

21. See above, p. 4.

22. See Yoder's privately circulated paper, "Christ and Culture: A Critique of H. Richard Niebuhr," pp. 6-12. This paper is available from the library of the Associated Mennonite Biblical Seminaries in Elkhart, Indiana.

23. See Niebuhr, *Christ and Culture*, pp. 12-13.

24. Ibid., p. 45

25. Ibid., p. 49.

26. Ibid., pp. 50-51.

27. Quoted, ibid., p. 50. Niebuhr refers to *The Didache* by the title *The Teaching of the Twelve Apostles.*

28. Ibid., p. 52.

29. Quoted, ibid., p. 54.

30. Ibid., pp. 49, 55.

31. Cf. Yoder, "Christ and Culture: A Critique of H. Richard Niebuhr," pp. 11-13, 18.

32. Niebuhr, *Christ and Culture*, p. 69.

33. Ibid., p. 72.

34. It is not entirely consistent, of course, for him to do so, since he has also called Tertullian anticultural.

35. Ibid., p. 45.

36. Ibid., pp. 64-65.

37. Ibid., p. 72.

38. Ibid.

39. Ibid., p. 72.

40. Ibid., p. 69, for example.

41. See, for example, the section heading, ibid., p. 83.

42. In order, St. John, Calvin, Edwards. Ibid., pp. 204, 218, 220.

43. Quoted, ibid., p. 228.

44. Ibid., p. 190

45. By *culture*, Niebuhr says that he means that total process and result of human activity "to which now the name *culture*, now the name *civilization*, is applied in common speech." Ibid., p. 32.

46. "His whole theology is a 'moral theology,'" writes Hoedemaker of Niebuhr. Hoedemaker, *The Theology of H. Richard Niebuhr*, p. 80. Though theology and ethics were inseparable for Niebuhr, he did distinguish them. According to James Gustafson, Niebuhr said often in his lectures on ethics that theology "is reflection on the action and nature of God. Ethics is reflection on the response of man to the action and nature of God." See p. 40 of Gus-

tafson's introductory essay in H. Richard Niebuhr, *The Responsible Self* (New York: Harper and Row, 1963). On this cf. John Godsey, *The Promise of Richard Niebuhr* (New York: J. B. Lippincott, 1970), p. 87, and Lonnie Kliever, *H. Richard Niebuhr* (Waco, Texas: Word Books,1977), p. 64.

47. In both of these, Niebuhr's viewpoint is Christian, as he would be eager to acknowledge. In *The Responsible Self* he describes "human moral life in general." In doing so, however, he emphasizes that he has a viewpoint: that of a Christian believer. See pp. 42-46.

48. H. Richard Niebuhr, "Reformation: Continuing Imperative," *Christian Century*, March 2, 1960, p. 249. This was part of a series: "How My Mind Has Changed."

49. Niebuhr, *The Meaning of Revelation*, pp. 5, 7, 12. On the point about our immersion in a particular society, see p. 15: "To be in history is to be in society, though in a particular society."

50. Niebuhr, *The Responsible Self*, p. 71.

51. Ibid., p. 96.

52. Niebuhr, *The Meaning of Revelation*, pp. 13-15.

53. This is clear from discussion in the book where Niebuhr presupposes that genuine communication can occur between one historical community and another. Ibid., p. 62. I am indebted for this point to Paul Ramsey, *Nine Modern Moralists* (Englewood Cliffs, N.J.: Prentice-Hall, Inc., 1962), p. 162.

54. Niebuhr discusses the theory of value in his chapter on "The Center of Value" in *Radical Monotheism and Western Culture*, Harper Torchbooks (New York: Harper and Row, 1970). This book was first published in 1960. The essay dates back to 1952.

55. Ibid., p. 118.

56. Ibid., p. 119.

57. Ibid., pp. 110-111.

58. See H. Richard Niebuhr, "The Ego-Alter Dialectic and the Conscience," *The Journal of Philosophy*, XLII (1945), pp. 353-354.

59. "The idea of responsibility, with the freedom and obligation it implies, has its place in the context of social relations." H. Richard Niebuhr, "The Responsibility of the Church for Society," in *The Gospel, the Church and the World*, ed. by Kenneth Scott Latourette (New York: Harper and Brothers, 1946), p. 114.

60. Niebuhr, *The Responsible Self*, p. 56.

61. Ibid., pp. 61, 97.

62. Ibid., p. 98.

63. Ibid., p. 96.

64. Niebuhr, "The Ego-Alter Dialectic and the Conscience," p. 354.

65. Niebuhr, *The Responsible Self*, p. 109. See also his account of the Christ image in Christian life, pp. 152-156.

66. Ibid., p. 112.

67. Ibid., pp. 102-103.

68. This phrase appears in the interpretation of Niebuhr given in C. Eric Mount, Jr., "Realism, Norm, Story, and Character: Issues in the Civil Religion Discussion," *Journal of Church and State*, XXII (1980), p. 52.

Another way in which Niebuhr suggests that moral life involves a shared way of life is with Josiah Royce's idea of loyalty. One becomes a moral self, he says, by committing oneself to a cause in which one is "associated with other loyalists to the same cause." *The Responsible Self*, p. 83.

69. Niebuhr, *The Responsible Self*, p. 97.

70. Niebuhr, *The Meaning of Revelation*, p. 101.

71. Ibid., p. 80.

72. Ibid., p. 69. See also p. 111.

73. Ibid., p. 32.

74. Ibid., pp. 16, 35.

75. Hans W. Frei, "The Theology of H. Richard Niebuhr," in *Faith and Ethics*, ed. by Paul Ramsey (New York: Harper & Row, 1957), p. 77.

76. H. Richard Niebuhr, "The Doctrine of the Trinity and the Unity of the Church," *Theology Today*, III (1946), pp. 371-384.

77. H. Richard Niebuhr, *Radical Monotheism*, pp. 59-60.

78. Niebuhr, *The Responsible Self*, p. 154.

79. Ibid., p. 156.

80. Niebuhr, *Radical Monotheism*, pp. 32-35.

81. Ibid., p. 48.

82. Ibid., pp. 40-42. See also Niebuhr, *The Responsible Self*, pp. 149-178.

83. See, e.g., *The Responsible Self*, pp. 152, 156.

84. See ibid., pp. 163-164.

85. See Niebuhr, "The Responsibility of the Church for Society," pp. 114-117, 119.

86. Ibid., p. 117

87. H. Richard Niebuhr, *The Social Sources of Denominationalism* (New York: World Publishing Company, 1972), p. 265. See also the rest of his chapter ten, "Ways to Unity." This book appeared in 1929.

88. Niebuhr, "The Responsibility of the Church for Society," pp. 130-132.

89. H. Richard Niebuhr, *The Purpose of the Church and Its Ministry* (New York: Harper and Row, 1956), p. 31.

90. Niebuhr, *Christ and Culture*, pp. 190, 208, 214, 218.

91. Niebuhr, *The Meaning of Revelation*, pp. 117-118.

92. Ibid., pp. 120-125.

93. Niebuhr, *The Meaning of Revelation*, p. 32. Italics mine.

94. Niebuhr, "The Ego-Alter Dialectic and the Conscience," pp. 352-359.

95. Niebuhr, *The Meaning of Revelation*, p. 80. Revelation, he says here, "conditions *all* our thinking." Italics mine. See also p. 101.

96. "Introduction to Biblical Ethics," in *Christian Ethics*, ed. by H. Richard Niebuhr and Waldo Beach (New York: Ronald Press, 1955), p. 31. Italics mine. The essay appears without byline, but was, it says on p. iv of the preface, Niebuhr's "special responsibility."

97. At least once in *Christ and Culture*, Niebuhr, despite what he says elsewhere in the book, speaks of the "Christ who gives the new law" (p. 13).

98. Niebuhr, *The Meaning of Revelation*, pp. 5-16, especially pp. 7, 15.

99. Alasdair MacIntyre, *A Short History of Ethics* (New York: The Macmillan Company, 1966), p. 95. A similar point appears in his *After Virtue* (Notre Dame: University of Notre Dame Press, 1981), pp. 178-180.

100. See above, pp. 67-68.

101. On why and how this is possible see the fruitful discussion in James W. McClendon, Jr., and James M. Smith, *Understanding Religious Convictions* (Notre Dame: University of Notre Dame Press, 1975).

102. See Niebuhr, *Christ and Culture*, p. 11.

103. Niebuhr, *Christ and Culture*, p. 29.

CHAPTER THREE

1. See, e.g., chap. 9 in Langdon Gilkey, *Maker of Heaven and Earth* (Garden City, New York: Doubleday, 1959).

2. See Ernst Troeltsch, *The Social Teachings of the Christian Churches* (New York: Harper and Row, 1960), especially pp. 331-344.

3. Langdon Gilkey, *How the Church Can Minister to the World Without Losing Itself* (New York: Harper and Row, 1964), pp. 15-18. Cited after this as *Church*.

4. Ibid., p. 19. Gilkey notes that this is much the same as the thesis in Will Herberg, *Protestant, Catholic, Jew* (Garden City, N.Y.: Doubleday, Anchor Books, 1960), pp. 85-86.

5. *Church.*, p. 19.

6. Ibid., p. 52. In this book the term *conservative* designates roughly the Fundamentalist-evangelical churches. The term *liberal* roughly applies to the churches in the tradi-

tion going back to the social gospel movement of the nineteenth and early twentieth centuries.

7. Ibid., p. 51. The concept of *relevance* is prominent in Reinhold Niebuhr's thought. See, e.g., chapter four of his *An Interpretation of Christian Ethics* (London: SCM Press, 1936).

8. The concern with the gospel's "relevance" to daily life, Gilkey writes, is "the most precious heritage we have received from liberalism." *Church*, p. 52.

9. See, e.g., Langdon Gilkey, *Society and the Sacred* (New York: Crossroad, 1981), p. 149. Cited after this as *Society and the Sacred*.

10. Langdon Gilkey, *Reaping the Whirlwind: A Christian Interpretation of History* (New York: Seabury Press, 1976), p. 41. See also p. 191. Cited after this as *Whirlwind*.

11. See *Society and the Sacred*, p. 21, and *Whirlwind*, p. 295.

12. *Society and the Sacred*, p. 20. Tillich's epigrammatic statement of this point is that "religion is the substance of culture and culture is the form of religion." It can be found in, e.g., *The Protestant Era* (Chicago: University of Chicago Press, 1957), p. 57, and *Systematic Theology* (3 vols.: Chicago: University of Chicago Press, 1951-63), III, pp. 158, 247.

13. *Society and the Sacred*, p. 44.

14. *Whirlwind*, p. 291.

15. See *Society and the Sacred*, pp. 24-25, and *Whirlwind*, pp. 290-291.

16. *Whirlwind*, p. 291.

17. Ibid.

18. *Church*, pp. 75-83.

19. See, e.g., *Whirlwind*, pp. 266-270.

20. Ibid., pp. 267-268.

21. *Society and the Sacred*, p. 165.

22. Ibid., p. 141.

23. This is reminiscent of his teacher, Paul Tillich, in *Christianity and the Encounter of the World Religions* (New York: Columbia University Press, 1963).

24. *Society and the Sacred*, p. 166.

25. Ibid., p. 142.

26. Ibid.

27. Ibid., p. 148.

28. Ibid., p. 147.

29. Ibid., p. 149.

30. Ibid., p. 148.

31. See ibid., p. 147.

32. The "secret" of the church's relation to cultural life around it, Gilkey says, "is a dialectic or tension between transcendence and relevance." *Church*, p. 56.

33. *Whirlwind*, p. 288. Italics mine.

34. Ibid., p. 287.

35. *Society and the Sacred*, p. 55.

36. *Whirlwind*, p. 288.

37. *Society and the Sacred*, pp. 55-56.

38. See Niebuhr, *An Interpretation of Christian Ethics*, chaps. 5-7.

39. Ibid., p. 199.

40. *Society and the Sacred*, p. 55.

41. Langdon Gilkey, *Shantung Compound* (New York: Harper and Row, 1966), pp. 119-122.

42. Others were Fuchs, Gilleman, and members of the neo-Thomist school in Europe. On this see Charles Curran's informative foreword in Timothy E. O'Connell, *Principles for a Catholic Morality* (New York: Seabury Press, 1978), pp. ix-xii.

43. Appearing in German in 1959-1963, the books came out in English in 1961-1966 under the imprint of the Newman Press, Westminster, Maryland.

44. "Twenty-five years after completing my three-volume work, *The Law of Christ*, I attempt anew," Haering writes, "to offer a comprehensive presentation of Catholic moral theology." Bernard Haering, *Free and Faithful in Christ*, Vol. I: *General Moral Theology*; Vol. II: *The Truth Will Set You Free*; Vol. III: *Light to the World* (New York: Crossroad, 1978-81).

The quote is from Vol. I, p. 1. Each volume is cited after this simply by volume number.

45. I, p. 6.

46. See, e.g., I, pp. 6, 85.

47. See I, pp. 17, 60, 67.

48. I, p. 5.

49. I, pp. 2, 67, 69.

50. On the first point see, e.g., I, pp. 137-138, 368-369; and II, p. 374. On the second, see I, p. 306.

51. I, p. 308.

52. I, pp. 122f. Cf. III, p. 454.

53. Of Christ, Haering writes, "We can have no share in his creative liberty unless we follow him in fidelity." I, p. 74.

54. I, pp. 65-66.

55. I, p. 330. See also I, pp. 22-23, 60, 74.

56. I, pp. 22-25, 75-76.

57. I, pp. 330-331.

58. Haering writes that Christ's "co-humanity," his "total being-with-us and for us, is the glory of God's infinite freedom to love." I, p. 116.

59. I, p. 117; II, p. 444.

60. I, pp. 15-17; III, pp. 391-393.

61. I, p. 5. Cf. Gal. 6:2, to which Haering appeals.

62. III, p. 280; I, p. 77.

63. II, p. 432.

64. I, p. 17; II, pp. 479, 432.

65. I, pp. 83-84.

66. I. p. 83.

67. I, p. 364. Against Joseph Fletcher and with Paul Ramsey, Haering insists there are more unbreakable rules than the rule of love, though none exists apart from love. I, p. 341.

68. I, pp. 343-344.

69. III, pp. 395-396. He disputes the claim that violent solutions to conflict may be justified by appealing to the words of Jesus about the sword. The word *sword* on Jesus' lips is sometimes a symbol for conflict, as in Matt. 10:34 and Luke 22:36. Passages such as Luke 22:49-51 and Matt. 26:52 show clearly that Jesus did not advocate the use of the sword by his disciples.

70. I, p. 118; III, p. 396.

71. II, p. 340; cf. III, pp. 264-266.

72. II, p. 267.

73. III, pp. 139-140. Haering is quoting Matt. 5:13-14.

74. III, p. 409.

75. III, p. 266.

76. III, pp. 363-364.

77. III, p. 378.

78. III, p. 378.

79. I, p. 165.

80. Haering appears, however, to be opposed absolutely to the use of nuclear weapons. See III, p. 407.

81. I, p. 5.

82. I, p. 318.

83. I, pp. 318, 327, 330.

84. The quotations in this and the preceding paragraph are all from I, pp. 319-324.

85. I, pp. 313-314.

86. I, pp. 236, 325.

87. I, pp. 312-330. The first quoted phrase is from p. 327. The second is from p. 313. Haering bases the claim about Scripture on Matt. 25 and Rom. 2.

88. I, pp. 327-328. Italics mine.

89. III, p. 329.

90. I, p. 100; III, pp. 420, 129.

91. See, e.g., I, pp. 79, 369; II, p. 453; III, p. 131, 352, 369.

92. I, p. 114.

93. II, p. 454.

94. III, pp. 374, 337. Haering cites Paul and Matthew on divorce to justify this latter point.

95. See John Macquarrie, *Principles of Christian Theology* (New York: Charles Scribner's Sons, 1966), pp. 444-446. See also his *The Concept of Peace* (New York: Harper & Row, 1973), p. 3, and his *Three Issues in Ethics* (London: SCM Press, 1970), p. 87. These works appear after this as *Principles*, *Peace*, and *Three Issues*.

96. See *Peace*, pp. 70-74, and *Principles*, pp. 71-72, 92.

97. *Principles*, pp. 247, 249.

98. *Three Issues*, pp. 45-52. *Principles*, p. 66. *Peace*, pp. 26-27.

99. *Principles*, p. 444. See also Macquarrie's discussion of the "metaphysics of peace" in *Peace*, pp. 63-74.

100. *Principles*, chap. 12.

101. Ibid., pp. 198, 249, 289, 214.

102. Ibid., p. 444.

103. *Three Issues*, p. 21.

104. Ibid., pp. 88-89.

105. *Principles*, pp. 248-249, 289.

106. Ibid., p. 306. See also pp. 286, 291.

107. *Three Issues*, p. 89.

108. *Principles*, p. 341.

109. Ibid., p. 16.

110. See John Dillenberger and Claude Welch, *Protestant Christianity Interpreted Through Its Development* (New York: Charles Scribner's Sons, 1954), pp. 73-74, 99.

111. Ibid., p. 341.

112. Ibid., p. 9.

113. Ibid., pp. 10-11.

114. Ibid., pp. 15-16, 342.

115. Quoted ibid., p. 16.

116. Ibid., p. 341.

117. Ibid., p. 342.

118. *Three Issues*, p. 109.

119. John Macquarrie, *Paths in Spirituality* (London: SCM Press, 1972), p. 113.

120. *Principles*, p. 291.

121. See, e.g., *Peace*, p. 73, and *Principles*, p. 448.

122. *Three Issues*, pp. 103-110. Cf. *Principles*, p. 448. The natural law is the "tendency to actualize selfhood" and "authentic community." It directs us toward "letting-be," which is our "highest potentiality" and the "essence" of God.

123. *Three Issues*, p. 20. See also p. 82.

124. *Three Issues*, p. 22, and *Principles*, p. 449. On this latter see also *Three Issues*, p. 89.

125. *Principles*, p. 348.

126. Ibid., pp. 349, 396, 452.

127. Ibid., p. 393.

128. Ibid.

129. Ibid., pp. 457-458.

130. See, e.g., *Peace*, pp. 21, 26, 33, 36.

131. Ibid., p. 36.

132. Violence occurs, Macquarrie says, when "all means, including the infliction of death and injury, are used for the subjection of the other side. War is the most massive and excessive of all forms of violence." *Peace*, p. 41.

133. Ibid., p. 51.

134. Ibid., p. 52.

135. Ibid., pp. 52-53.

136. Ibid., pp. 53-54.

137. Jacques Ellul, *Violence* (London: SCM Press, 1970), p. 70. Violence is a "necessity" in existing societies, but the role of Christians in society, Ellul says provocatively, is to "shatter fatalities and necessities" (pp. 84, 129).

138. *Peace*, p. 54.

139. Ibid., p. 55.

CHAPTER FOUR

1. Gustavo Gutierrez, *A Theology of Liberation*, translated by and edited by Sister Caridad Inda and John Eagleson (Maryknoll, N.Y.: Orbis Books, 1973) p. 82; after this cited as *Theology*. See also Gustavo Gutierrez, "Liberation Praxis and Christian Faith," in *Frontiers of Theology in Latin America*, ed. by Rosino Gibellini (Maryknoll, N.Y.: Orbis Books, 1979), pp. 9-18; after this cited as "Liberation Praxis."

2. See, e.g., Gustavo Gutierrez, *The Power of the Poor in History*, translated by Robert R. Barr (Maryknoll, N.Y.: Orbis Books, 1983), p. 104. Cited after this as *Power*.

3. *Power*, p. 186.

4. Ibid., pp. 27, 39.

5. Ibid., p. 189.

6. Ibid., p. 190.

7. Ibid., p. 199.

8. Ibid., p. 79.

9. Ibid., p. 191.

10. Ibid., p. 37.

11. "*Liberation Praxis*," pp. 22-24.

12. *Power*, p. 103.

13. Ibid., p. 94; see pp. 91-94 and also p. 212. Although Gutierrez makes this general criticism of modern Catholic and Protestant theology, he does give qualified praise to some theologians (e.g., Dietrich Bonhoeffer) and to the political theology of such writers as Johannes Metz and Jurgen Moltmann. Of the latter he writes, "Today political theology has entered into fruitful dialogue with the theology of liberation, and interesting points of convergence are emerging" (*Power*, p. 185).

14. *Power*, p. 93.

15. Gustavo Gutierrez and Richard Shaull, *Liberation and Change* (Atlanta: John Knox Press, 1977), p. 86. Cited after this as *Liberation and Change*. See also *Theology*, p. 15.

16. *Power*, pp. 31-33.

17. Ibid., pp. 13-14.

18. Ibid., p. 13; *Theology*, p. 228.

19. *Theology*, pp. 227-229.

20. Ibid., pp. 175-176.

21. Ibid., pp. 231-232.

22. *Liberation and Change*, p. 83. See also *Power*, p. 13.

23. *Power*, p. 96.

24. Ibid., p. 14. See also *Liberation and Change*, p. 83.

25. See, e.g., "Liberation Praxis," pp. 9-11.

26. Quoted in *Power*, p. 197.

27. *Power*, pp. 197, 213. See also *Liberation and Change*, pp. 62-66.

28. *Theology*, p. 143.

29. *Theology*, pp. 258-262.

30. *Liberation and Change*, pp. 92-93.

31. *Power*, p. 50. See also *Liberation and Change*, p. 93.

32. *Power*, p. 52.

33. *Theology*, p. 138.

34. *Power*, pp. 16-18. See also *Liberation and Change*, p. 88.

35. *Theology*, pp. 269-270. See also pp. 91, 117.

36. Or as he puts it, history is "conflictual." See, e.g., *Theology*, pp. 36, 273.

37. *Power*, p. 70.

38. Gutierrez seems to approve the distinction between just and unjust violence offered in one document by Latin-American clergy that he cites. He in other places suggests that violence is necessary in liberation praxis. I believe that he nowhere criticizes the socialist revolution for its use of violence. See, e.g., *Theology*, pp. 108-109; *Power*, p. 48; and "Liberation Praxis," pp. 10-12.

39. See, e.g., chap. 7 in *Theology* and chaps. 4 to 6 of *Power*. Here the pivotal document is the statement of the Latin-American bishops at Medellin, Colombia, in 1968.

40. See *Theology*, pp. 138-139.

41. *Power*, p. 69.

42. *Theology*, p. 238.

43. Rosemary Radford Ruether, *The Church Against Itself* (New York: Herder and Herder, 1967). Cited after this as *Church*.

44. Rosemary Radford Ruether, *Liberation Theology* (New York: Paulist Press, 1972), pp. 17, 106. Cited after this as *Liberation*.

45. *Liberation*, p. 6; and Rosemary Radford Ruether, *To Change the World: Christology and Cultural Criticism* (New York: Crossroad, 1981), p. 66. Cited hereinafter as *Change*.

46. *Liberation*, pp. 16-19.

47. *Liberation*, p. 116.

48. *Liberation*, p. 22. See also *Change*, pp. 66-69, and Rosemary Radford Ruether, *Sexism and God-Talk: Toward a Feminist Theology* (Boston: Beacon Press, 1983), pp. 232-233, in which the next-to-last quotation appears. This latter work is cited after this as *Sexism*.

49. In her latest book, Ruether suggests *God/ess* as a nonsexist written symbol to be preferred over *God*. See *Sexism*, p. 71. I have stayed by her earlier practice in this exposition.

50. Rosemary Radford Ruether, *The Radical Kingdom* (New York: Harper & Row, 1970), p. 287. Cited after this as *Radical Kingdom*.

51. See, e.g., *Church*, pp. 92-93. See also Ruether's highly sympathetic accounts of Barth and Reinhold Niebuhr in chap. 7 of *Radical Kingdom*, and of Gabrial Vahanian, in chap. 10.

52. See, e.g., remarks in *Change*, p. 14, and *Liberation*, p. 54.

53. See, e.g., *Change*, p. 69.

54. See, e.g., *Liberation*, pp. 26-27; and *Sexism*, pp. 239-245.

55. *Radical Kingdom*, p. 9.

56. *Change*, p. 1.

57. Ibid., p. 5.

58. Ibid., p. 3.

59. Ibid., pp. 7-15.

60. Ibid., p. 15. If later there occurred the "patriarchalization" of Christology in which the maleness of Jesus was used to buttress a social system of male dominance, the fact remains that Jesus himself renounced all systems of domination, including the domination of women by men. Women, a particular object of his concern, are for him, she says, "the oppressed of the oppressed." See *Sexism*, p. 136.

61. *Change*, p. 1.

62. Ibid., p. 24.

63. Ibid., p. 31.

64. Ibid., pp. 38-39, 43. See also *Liberation*, pp. 92-93, 190-191.

65. *Church*, pp. 226-227

66. Ibid., pp. 61, 147.

67. Ibid., p. 226.

68. Ibid., p. 61.

69. Ibid., p. 228.

70. "Christ, the liberated humanity, is not confined to a static perfection of one person two thousand years ago," Ruether writes in a 1983 publication. "Rather, redemptive humanity goes ahead of us, calling us to yet incompleted dimensions of human liberation" (*Sexism*, p. 138).

71. Ibid., p. 221.

72. *Liberation*, pp. 40-41.

73. Ibid., pp. 44-45.

74. Ibid., p. 43.

75. *Church*, pp. 204-208, 237.

76. *Liberation*, p. 155.

77. Ibid., pp. 30-34.

78. *Church*, pp. 232-237.

79. Besides *Sexism*, see, e.g., Rosemary Radford Ruether, *Mary—The Feminine Face of the Church* (Philadelphia: Westminster Press 1970), and her *New Woman New Earth: Sexist Ideologies and Human Liberation* (New York: Seabury Press, 1975). See also *Church*, chap. 4, and *Liberation*, chaps. 7 and 8.

80. See *Church*, pp. 53-56. See also *New Woman New Earth*, pp. 63-66. For a recent statement of whether a male Savior can save women, see *Sexism*, chap. 5.

81. See, e.g., *Church*, p. 29; *Liberation*, pp. 184-186; and *Radical Kingdom*, pp. 123-125.

82. See the remarks by Haering and Macquarrie in the previous chapter and those by Hauerwas and Yoder in the next. See also Martin Hengel, *Victory over Violence: Jesus and the Revolutionists* (Philadelphia: Fortress Press, 1973).

83. *Church*, p. 220.

84. Col. 1:13.

85. Johann Baptist Metz, *Faith in History and Society: Toward a Practical Fundamental Theology*, translated by David Smith (New York: The Seabury Press, 1980). Cited after this as *Faith*.

86. Ibid., pp. 34-47.

87. Ibid., p. 34.

88. Ibid., p. 43.

89. In this paragraph I am relying, too, on chap. 1 of Johann Baptist Metz, *The Emergent Church*, translated by Peter Mann (New York: Crossroad, 1981). Cited after this as *Church*.

90. *Faith*, p. 45.

91. We may in fairness note what Metz fails to note, namely, that liberal Christianity in, for example, England and the United States came to be far more critical of prevailing social values than in the Germany with which Metz is most familiar. See, e.g., Rosemary Radford Ruether, *The Radical Kingdom* (New York: Harper & Row, 1970), chap. 5.

92. Johannes B. Metz, *Followers of Christ: The Religious Life and the Church*, translated by Thomas Linton (New York: Paulist Press, 1978), p. 68. Cited after this as *Followers*.

93. Johannes B. Metz, *Theology of the World*, translated by William Glen-Doepel (London: Burns & Oates, 1969), p. 21. Cited after this as *World*.

94. Ibid., pp. 57-59.

95. Ibid., p. 60.

96. Ibid., pp. 84, 72.

97. Ibid., pp. 63-67. The biblical quotation is from 1 Tim. 6:16.

98. Ibid., p. 51.

99. Ibid., pp. 91-95.

100. Ibid., pp. 72-73.

101. Ibid., p. 52.

102. Ibid., pp. 86, 89.

103. Ibid., p. 90.

104. Ibid., pp. 51-55.

105. See, e.g., *Faith*, chap. 10, and *Followers*, chap. 4.

106. *Faith*, p. 172.

107. Ibid., pp. 171-172, 176.

108. The quoted phrase, from one Fr. Arrupe, is given in *Followers*, p. 80.

109. Johann Baptist Metz, *The Emergent Church*, translated by Peter Mann (New York: Crossroad, 1981), p. 27. Cited after this as *Emergent Church*.

110. *Faith*, p. 165. See also *World*, p. 42.

111. *Faith*, p. 165. See also pp. ix-x.

112. *Followers*, pp. 33-34.

113. *Faith*, p. 51.

114. Ibid., p. 212.

115. Ibid., p. 90.

116. Ibid., p. 213.

117. Ibid., p. 90.

118. Ibid., p. 166.

119. "The church exists for the sake of the world," Metz writes in *World*, p. 50.

120. Ibid., p. 93.

121. *Faith*, p. 90.

122. Johannes B. Metz, "The Church's Social Function in the Light of a 'Political Theology,'" in *Faith and the World of Politics*, Concilium Series, no. 36, edited by Johannes B. Metz (New York: Paulist Press, 1968), pp. 8, 10. Cited after this as "The Church's Social Function."

123. *Church*, p. 86.

124. Ibid., pp. 64, 87.

125. Ibid., pp. 36, 40.

126. Ibid., pp. 35, 45.

127. Ibid., pp. 61, 72.

128. "The Church's Social Function," p. 14.

129. Ibid., and *Church*, p. 97.

130. *Church*, p. 98.

131. "The Church's Social Function," p. 14.

132. *Faith*, p. 90.

CHAPTER FIVE

1. Stanley Hauerwas, *A Community of Character* (Notre Dame: University of Notre Dame Press, 1981), p. 6. Cited after this as *Community*.

2. Ibid.

3. In addition to *Community*, the books are *Character and the Christian Life* (San Antonio: Trinity University Press, 1975), cited after this as *Character*; with Richard Bondi and David B. Burrell, *Truthfulness and Tragedy* (Notre Dame: University of Notre Dame Press, 1977), cited after this as *Truthfulness*; and *Vision and Virtue* (Notre Dame: Fides/Claretian, 1977), cited after this as *Vision*.

4. See *Truthfulness*, p. 16; *Community*, pp. 77, 149, 171; and *Vision*, p. 34.

5. *Truthfulness*, p. 20.

6. *Character*, p. 113. See also *Community*, p. 113.

7. See especially *Vision*, pp. 30-47. See also *Truthfulness*, pp. 54 and 82-98.

8. *Truthfulness*, p. 92.

9. Ibid., pp. 54, 95-96.

10. Ibid., pp. 51-52.

11. Ibid., p. 45.

12. Ibid., pp. 44, 49, 56.

13. *Character*, p. 125, and *Truthfulness*, p. 47.

14. *Character*, p. 121.

15. Ibid., p. 125.

16. On the question of an "ethics of obligation" versus an "ethics of virtue," Hauerwas writes that "our obligations make sense only as they are part of ways of life, both communal and individual. In effect this means that we need neither an "ethics of obligation" nor an "ethics of virtue" as if those were discrete alternatives. *Obligation* and *virtue* are but reminder terms that help us mark off aspects of our moral existence." *Truthfulness*, p. 52.

17. Ibid., p. 83.

18. For Hauerwas we acquire character mainly through the "beliefs and dispositions we have come to possess," but "it may be confirmed and qualified" through our decisions (Ibid., p. 20).

19. See, e.g., ibid., p. 24, and *Community*, p. 97.

20. See *Community*, p. 10.

21. *Truthfulness*, p. 25.

22. Ibid.

23. Ibid., p. 73. See also *Character*, p. 210, and *Vision*, p. 69.

24. John Dewey, *Theory of the Moral Life* (New York: Holt, Rinehart and Winston, 1967), p. 150, quoted in *Vision*, p. 81.

25. *Truthfulness*, pp. 20, 52.

26. See, e.g., ibid, pp. 55-56, where Hauerwas takes issue on this matter with philosopher William Frankena.

27. From Hampshire's "Morality and Pessimism," *The New York Review of Books*, January 25, 1973, p. 29, quoted in *Truthfulness*, p. 52.

28. *Truthfulness*, pp. 27-33.

29. *Vision*, p. 107.

30. This sentence may raise a question about the principle of universalizability, considered in much modern philosophical ethics to be the criterion of morality. In accepting the truth of relativism, Hauerwas does not deny this principle. Everyone, to be moral, must accept it, regardless of one's own peculiar history. But the basic commitment it expresses is that all human beings deserve just treatment "regardless of their particular merits, culture, or station." The moral practices we adopt in attempting to embody the principle still reflect, however, the point of view of some community and its narrative. What *counts* as "lying" or "killing," for example, will vary as a function of this point of view. See ibid., pp. 82-89. See also *Truthfulness*, pp. 18-21.

31. See, e.g., *Community*, p. 101, and *Vision*, p. 69.

32. *Community*, p. 103. The phrase is from Bernard Williams, on whom Hauerwas relies.

33. Ibid.

34. By contrast, a merely "notional confrontation"—the phrase again is from Bernard Williams—is one in which the alternative way of life does not address the persons involved powerfully enough to raise the question of adopting it.

35. The example is Gilbert Harman's. See *Community*, p. 102.

36. Hauerwas's *Character* is, of course, a book-length treatment of this matter, though it is a central concern in his other works as well.

37. See *Character*, p. 210, and *Community*, pp. 90-94.

38. See *Community*, pp. 49-50.

39. See ibid., pp. 53-71 for a discussion of the authority of the Bible.

40. Ibid., pp. 48, 50.

41. Hauerwas has some reservations about the image of "transformation," but they do not by any means count decisively against its use. See ibid., p. 246.

42. *Vision*, p.190.

43. Ibid.

44. *Community*, p. 44.

45. Ibid., p. 68.

46. Ibid., p. 2.

47. Ibid., p. 85.

48. Ibid., p. 2.

49. Ibid., pp. 50, 86, 107.

50. Ibid., pp. 133, 141.

51. Ibid., pp. 44, 106.

52. Donald G. Bloesch, *Essentials of Evangelical Theology*, Vol. I: *God, Authority and Salvation*; Vol. II: *Life, Ministry and Hope* (San Francisco: Harper and Row, 1978-79), I, p. 18. Cited after this as *Essentials*.

53. Ibid., I, p. xi. See also, e.g., II, p. 169, and Donald G. Bloesch, *The Invaded Church* (Waco, Texas: Word Books, 1975), p. 14. This latter is cited after this as *Invaded Church*.

54. Carl F. H. Henry, *The Uneasy Conscience of Modern Fundamentalism*, p. 32.

55. I do not suggest more than is expressly stated. These writers would not agree in all details of the doctrine of Scripture.

56. *Essentials*, II, p. 167, and *Invaded Church*, p. 39.

57. Donald G. Bloesch, "The Challenge Facing the Churches," in Kevin Perrotta, ed., *Christianity Confronts Modernity* (Ann Arbor, Mich.: Servant Books, 1981), pp. 214-215, 221. Cited after this as "Challenge."

58. *Essentials*, II, p. 166.

59. *Invaded Church*, p. 37. On this paragraph see also, e.g., pp. 9, 22-26, and "Challenge," pp. 205-222.

60. Bloesch distances himself in more than one way from popular evangelicalism—as, e.g., by criticizing dispensationalist eschatology and denying the *total* inerrancy of Scripture. See, e.g., *Essentials*, I, pp. 20, 66-67. And he appreciates the liberal tradition not only for its social concern but also for its "self-critical spirit," its "earnest desire to communicate to the world outside the church," its "openness to truth wherever it appears," and its "readiness to learn from other religious persuasions." Ibid., I, p. 15.

61. Ibid., I, pp. 54-55.

62. Ibid., I, pp. 69, 75.

63. Ibid., I, pp. 62-63.

64. Ibid., I, p. 56.

65. "Challenge," p. 208.

66. *Essentials*, II, pp. 156-157. See also *Invaded Church*, pp. 103-105.

67. *Essentials*, I, p. 19.

68. *Invaded Church*, p. 88.

69. See ibid., pp. 85-87, and *Essentials*, II, p. 163.

70. See, e.g., *Invaded Church*, pp. 31, 91, 98-99, and *Essentials*, II, p. 169.

71. *Invaded Church*, p. 123.

72. Ibid., p. 56, and *Essentials*, II, p. 86.

73. Ibid., II, p. 168. Bloesch cites Niebuhr's analysis of Christ and culture numerous times—beginning as far back as 1964—in his *Centers of Christian Renewal* (Philadelphia: United Church Press, 1964), p. 113.

74. *Invaded Church*, p. 113, and *Essentials*, II, p. 168.

75. *Invaded Church*, p. 56.

76. Ibid. and *Essentials*, II, p. 170.

77. *Invaded Church*, p. 57.

78. Ibid., pp. 13, 70.

79. See ibid., p. 104, and *Essentials*, II, p. 149.

80. Ibid., II, p. 151.

81. See *Invaded Church*, p. 10, and *Essentials*, II, p. 149.

82. See *Invaded Church*, pp. 70, 88, and "Challenge," p. 211.

83. See *Essentials*, II, pp. 147, 150.

84. *Invaded Church*, pp. 60, 10. See also *Essentials*, pp. 148-150.

85. *Essentials*, II, pp. 148, 150.

86. The quoted phrases are from ibid, II, p. 148. See also pp. 149-150 and *Invaded Church*, pp. 60-64.

87. *Invaded Church*, pp. 64-65.

88. Ibid., pp. 108-111.

89. Ibid., p. 97.

90. Ibid., p. 40.

91. Ibid., pp. 110-111.

92. Ibid., pp. 57, 61. See also *Essentials*, II, pp. 148-149.

93. *Invaded Church*, p. 89. See also Donald Bloesch, *Wellsprings of Renewal* (Grand Rapids: Eerdmans, 1974), p. 111. Cited after this as *Wellsprings*.

94. "Challenge," pp. 221-222.

95. *Essentials*, II, p. 59.

96. *Wellsprings* and Donald G. Bloesch, *Centers of Christian Renewal* (Philadelphia: United Church Press, 1964), cited after this as *Centers*.

97. *Centers*, pp. 5-6.

98. Ibid., pp. 13-14.

99. See chap. 10 of *Centers*. The quoted phrase is from p. 145. The list draws on material in the whole book.

100. Ibid., pp. 145-146, and *Wellsprings*, pp. 111-112.

101. Ibid., p. 17. See also pp. 144, 151.

102. Ibid., pp. 15, 152.

103. *Essentials*, II, p. 34.

104. See John H. Yoder, "*Christ and Culture*: A Critique of H. Richard Niebuhr," pp. 6-16. This is a privately circulated paper, drafted in 1976 and available from the library of the Associated Mennonite Biblical Seminaries in Elkhart, Indiana. For other references to H. Richard Niebuhr see John Howard Yoder, *The Politics of Jesus* (Grand Rapids: Eerdmans, 1972), pp. 18, 103 (cited after this as *Politics*), and Yoder's unpublished Stone Lectures, given at Princeton Theological Seminary (and also as the Jaymes Morgan Lectures at Fuller Theological Seminary) in 1979, I, p. 16; II, pp. 13, 30, 33, 38; III, p. 13. There are five typed lectures. I will cite them after this as "Lectures," referring as now to the specific lecture by Roman numeral and the specific page or pages by Arabic numerals. Yoder does, incidentally, compliment Niebuhr for being a "Christological" pacifist, but this is faint praise since he considers him wrongly to play down the authority of Christ. "Lectures," II, p. 33.

105. John Howard Yoder, *The Christian Witness to the State* (Newton, Kans.: Faith and Life Press, 1964), cited after this as *State*.

106. *Politics*, p. 101.

107. See John H. Yoder, *The Original Revolution* (Scottdale, Pa.: Herald Press, 1971), p. 138. Cited after this as *Revolution*.

108. See "Lectures," I, p. 9.

109. See *Politics*, pp. 15-19.

110. Ibid., p. 12.

111. Ibid., p. 25. See also p. 12.

112. Ibid., p. 27.

113. Yoder argues that for Jesus' listeners the phrase *acceptable year of Jahweh* in Luke 4:19 meant the Jubilee year—when economic inequities would be undone. Ibid., pp. 36-38.

114. Ibid., p. 39.

115. Ibid., pp. 39-40.

116. For this detail Yoder relies on John 6, which, he says, brings out better than Luke the link between the several events of Luke 9:1-22. He depends here on recent resurgence of confidence in the historicity of the Fourth Gospel. He invokes here the authority of Maurice Goguel, saying he has "justifiably taken" the account in John 6 "to have serious historical value." Ibid., p. 42.

117. Ibid., pp. 43-44.

118. Ibid., p. 45.

119. Ibid., p. 46.

120. Some have argued that Jesus used violence in the temple cleansing, but Yoder invokes recent New Testament scholarship to refute this. Ibid., pp. 50-51.

121. Ibid., pp. 52-53.

122. Again, according to John. Ibid., p. 55.

123. Ibid., p. 59.

124. Ibid., pp. 60-61.

125. Ibid., p. 63.

126. Ibid., p. 134.

127. See "Lectures," II, pp. 4, 30-31, and III, pp. 12-16, 23. Yoder's views about power have changed over the years. Earlier essays tend to draw a stark contrast between power and servanthood. However, in the "Lectures," servanthood is the Christian form of power. It is how Christians attain their ends. Cf. *Revolution*, p. 29, and "Lectures," III, pp. 12-16.

128. See *Revolution*, pp. 155-156; *Politics*, p. 238; and John H. Yoder, *What Would You Do?* p. 34.

129. "The cross of Christ," Yoder writes, "is the model of Christian social efficacy, the power of God for those who believe." *Politics*, p. 250.

130. See, e.g., "Lectures," I, p. 7. See also *Revolution*, p. 57; and *State*, pp. 28-29.

131. *Politics*, pp. 15-19. See also "Lectures," I, p. 10.

132. *Politics*, pp. 42-46, 115-134. See also *Revolution*, pp. 38-40.

133. "Lectures," I, p. 9.

134. Ibid., I, pp. 10-11.

135. Ibid., I, p. 33. See also I, p. 10.

136. Ibid., pp. 10-15.

137. "Lectures," II, p. 25, and *Revolution*, p. 128.

138. *Politics*, p. 25.

139. See, e.g., *Revolution*, pp. 48, 82. On the first of these pages Yoder remarks that the term *nonresistance* goes back to Christ's words in the Sermon on the Mount: "Do not resist one who is evil. But if any one strikes you on the right cheek, turn to him the other also" (Matt. 5:39, RSV).

140. Ibid., p. 56.

141. Ibid., p. 72.

142. Ibid., p. 57. Yoder is alluding to 1 John 4:17.

143. Ibid., p. 62; *Politics*, p. 204n, and also chapter 5 of this book, where Yoder writes approvingly of the nonviolent resistance by Jews against Pilate reported in Josephus.

144. Yoder, *What Would You Do?* p. 40. In this book Yoder considers how the Christian should respond to aggression by a violent criminal.

145. Yoder does argue, however, that the traditional understanding of the nature of war in the Old Testament "needs revision from every angle." (See his introduction to Millard Lind's *Yahweh Is a Warrior* [Scottdale, Pa.: Herald Press, 1980], pp. 17-19.) "Christian interpretations of the meaning of the Old Testament are generally warped when the effort is to derive direct moral guidance from the ancient stories. This is nowhere more clear than in the reverse legalism with which majority Christianity has argued that killing must not be wrong for Christians since it was once proper for Hebrews, and God must not change." Ibid., p. 18.

146. *Revolution*, pp. 86-104, 112. See also "Lectures," I, p. 19.

147. *Revolution*, pp. 65-66. See also "Lectures," I, pp. 4, 21, 22. The quoted phrase is from this latter, p. 21.

148. *Revolution*, pp. 68-69.

149. Yoder says the identification of the church with particular power structures is a "fundamental structural error" of Constantinianism. *Revolution*, p. 148. See also pp. 149-150.

150. *State*, pp. 6-7, 12, 24, 29, 72.

151. Ibid., pp. 12, 47, 75, 77, 80-81. See also, e.g., chap. 10 of *Politics*.

152. *State*, pp. 7, 12, 75-77.

153. Ibid., pp. 74-77; *Politics*, p. 214.

154. Ibid., p. 8.

155. *State*, p. 38.

156. Ibid., pp. 42, 50.

157. Ibid., p. 72.

158. Ibid., pp. 38-39, 73. After terminology used at the 1948 General Assembly of the World Council of Churches in Amsterdam, Yoder used the term *middle axiom* to refer to

prescriptions offered by the church to the state. Ibid., p. 33n. It does not seem a particularly apt term, nor does Yoder's exposition always seem coherent. In light of what I have just reported it is baffling, for example, why Yoder should say that Christian social judgments "will usually coincide with the best informed secular analysis." Ibid., p. 45.

159. Ibid., pp. 16-21.
160. Ibid., p. 17.
161. Ibid., pp. 18-21.
162. "Lectures," II, pp. 23, 26-27; III, p. 13.
163. Ibid., II, pp. 23, 31.
164. Ibid., I, p. 34.
165. *Politics*, pp. 238-246.
166. *State*, p. 44. See also "Lectures," II, p. 4.

CHAPTER SIX

1. This claim is based on his overall corpus, recognizing its development over time. It also involves weighing the logical trajectory of his thought against individual statements that may sound contrary to this thesis.

2. Niebuhr's metaphor of Christ as "focusing point" appears in his *Christ and Culture* (New York: Harper and Row, 1951), p. 29. To avoid clutter in this chapter, I will, except in a few cases such as this one, normally footnote only those quotations and references not previously footnoted in the earlier chapters.

3. For Niebuhr, Christ is clearly linked with the Jesus who lived on earth. In his *The Purpose of the Church and Its Ministry* (New York: Harper and Row, 1956), p. 31, he speaks, for example, of "the identity of the historic with the risen Lord." At the close of his career he again links Christ with the "historical" figure whose story the gospel tells in *The Responsible Self* (New York: Harper & Row, 1963), pp. 154-157. All this reaffirms the similar point made earlier in his *The Meaning of Revelation* (New York: Macmillan, 1941), p. 32.

4. H. Richard Niebuhr, *Radical Monotheism and Western Culture* (New York: Harper & Row, 1970), p. 59.

5. H. Richard Niebuhr, "The Doctrine of the Trinity and the Unity of the Church," *Theology Today*, III (1946), pp. 371-384.

6. H. Richard Niebuhr, "The Responsibility of the Church for Society," in *The Gospel, the Church and the World*, ed. by Kenneth Scott Latourette (New York: Harper and Brothers, 1946), p. 117. For the metaphor of Christ as "focusing point," see Niebuhr, *Christ and Culture*, p. 29. Gustaf Aulèn, though not himself in the radical tradition, is helpful on these matters. He denies that Christocentrism draws attention away from God and in doing so employs a metaphor similar to Niebuhr's. Through Christ, he says, God's "image" appears as "clearly as it is possible under the conditions to which human life is subject," Gustaf Aulèn, *The Faith of the Christian Church*, translated by Eric H. Wahlstrom (Philadelphia: Fortress Press, 1960), p. 54.

7. See H. Richard Niebuhr, *The Responsible Self* (New York: Harper and Row, 1963), p. 154. This was Niebuhr's last book.

8. In addition to Niebuhr's *Radical Monotheism and Western Culture*, pp. 59-60 and "The Doctrine of the Trinity and the Unity of the Church," pp. 371-384, see his *Christ and Culture*, pp. 51-65.

9. John Macquarrie, *Three Issues in Ethics* (London: SCM Press, 1970), p. 20. See also p. 82.

10. On this see Alasdair MacIntyre, *A Short History of Ethics* (New York: The Macmillan Company, 1966), p. 95. For a similar point, see also his *After Virtue* (Notre Dame: University of Notre Dame Press, 1980), pp. 178-180.

11. Ruether also relativizes Christ's authority by urging that Christianity is not the only pathway to salvation and calling for the embrace of "existing human pluralism." I do not here consider this in detail except to note that it is one thing to show love and respect for those who

differ from us and another to mute the particular witness of Christian faith. This latter is what the radical vision would not abide.

12. John 16:13-14 (RSV).

13. Niebuhr, "The Doctrine of the Trinity," pp. 382-383. The biblical text is Rom. 8:9, here quoted from the RSV. Niebuhr makes a similar point about Christ as criterion of the Spirit in *The Responsible Self*, p. 155.

14. From Yoder's Stone Lectures and Jaymes Morgan Lectures, V, p. 7. For further bibliographical detail, see footnote 104 in chapter five.

15. Langdon Gilkey, *Society and the Sacred* (New York: Crossroad, 1981), p. 148.

16. Ibid., p. 147.

17. John Howard Yoder, *The Politics of Jesus* (Grand Rapids: Eerdmans, 1972), p. 134. See all of chapter seven for Yoder's impressive backing of this claim.

18. Quoted in Walter Klaassen, ed., *Anabaptist in Outline: Selected Primary Sources* (Scottdale, Pa.: Herald Press, 1981), p. 86.

19. Yoder, *The Politics of Jesus*, p. 101.

20. Perhaps all the virtues are social. One effect of Stanley Hauerwas's essays is to cast doubt upon the conventional distinction between personal and social ethics. On his account, for example, sexual fidelity, which is conventionally placed in the domain of personal ethics, turns out to be a social virtue. See chapter 10 of his *A Community of Character* (Notre Dame: University of Notre Dame Press, 1981).

21. The writers "at the center" of recent Christian social doctrine do not, it is true, emphasize the explicit political intention of Jesus, but neither do they deny it emphatically. They certainly do not suggest a hierarchy of church concerns with the "spiritual" elevated above the social and political.

22. Cited from the RSV.

23. See Luke 4:18-21.

24. Richard J. Cassidy. *Jesus, Politics and Society: A Study of Luke's Gospel* (Maryknoll, N.Y.: Orbis Books, 1978). Cassidy is arguing against the well-known thesis of Hans Conzelmann that according to Luke, Jesus did not oppose the existing political order and his followers should not do so either. The phrases quoted here are from pp. 34, 48.

25. Bloesch faults liberation theology for doing this, but he is not precisely correct. We saw in chapter 4 how Gustavo Gutierrez acknowledges the importance of personal conversion and life in eternity with God. See his *A Theology of Liberation*, trans. and ed. by Sister Caridad Inda and John Eagleson (Maryknoll, N.Y.: Orbis Books, 1973), pp. 231, 232.

26. Yoder, *The Politics of Jesus*, p. 226.

27. John B. Cobb suggests that the relation between these interests is reciprocal. "Do we change individuals through structural social changes?" he asks. "Or do we change society through changing individuals? The answer, of course, is that neither can occur effectively except in interaction with the other." See David Tracy and John B. Cobb, Jr., *Talking About God* (New York: The Seabury Press, 1983), p. 90.

28. Mark 11:18 (RSV). The quotation is from Isa. 56:7.

29. Jack T. Sanders, *Ethics in the New Testament* (London: SCM Press, 1975), p. 100.

30. Hans Leopold, quoted by J. Winfield Fretz, "Brotherhood and the Economic Ethics of the Anabaptists," in Guy F. Hershberger, ed., *The Recovery of the Anabaptist Vision* (Scottdale, Pa.: Herald Press, 1957), p. 197.

31. On the Anabaptist commitment to evangelism, see chapter four, on "The Great Commission," in Franklin Littell, *The Origins of Sectarian Protestantism* (New York: Macmillan, 1964).

32. Stephen Charles Mott, *Biblical Ethics and Social Change* (New York: Oxford University Press, 1982), p. 172. Mott quotes the summarizing phrase from an essay by William Beardslee.

33. Yoder himself is wary about any appeal to altruism in this regard. "This apparent altruism" can really be "an altruistic form of egoism when I defend *my* wife or *my* child because they are precisely *my own* . . . . True, the potential victim is my neighbor and thus deserving of my help. But the attacker also becomes at that moment a neighbor, and any attempt to distin-

guish between these two and say that the nearness of my family member as preferred neighbor takes precedence over that of my attacker is also a form of egoism. This cannot be sufficient basis for Christian ethical decision-making" (*What Would You Do?* pp. 20-21).

34. Ibid., p. 175.

35. Matt. 5:2, 14-16.

36. See 1 Pet. 2:11-25.

37. E.g., Isa. 42:1-9, 43:10-12, 49:1-6, 53:2-12. On this point see J. Lindblom, *Prophecy in Ancient Israel* (Philadelphia: Fortress Press, 1962), pp. 379, 400-401, 428-430. On p. 429, Lindblom says that the "individualistic interpretation" of the servant theme in Deutero-Isaiah involves "insoluble difficulties, which have often been demonstrated." With this theme, he says, the prophet is defining Israel's task as a community. On this point see also pp. 268-269 of Lindblom's book.

38. Here I rely in part upon Luise Schottroff, "Non-Violence and the Love of One's Enemies," in Luise Schottroff, et al., *Essays on the Love Commandment*, translated by Reginald H. and Ilse Fuller (Philadelphia: Fortress Press, 1978), pp. 22-27.

39. Cassidy, *Jesus, Politics and Society*, pp. 123, 198-199.

40. No one, to my knowledge, doubts that the festival was indeed being celebrated at the time of Jesus. Among comments on the reference in John, see, e.g., Barnabas Lindars, *The Gospel of John* (Grand Rapids: Eerdmans, 1972), p. 366; John Marsh, *Saint John* (Philadelphia: Westminster Press, 1968), p. 403; and C. K. Barrett, *The Gospel According to Saint John*, 2d ed. (Philadelphia: Westminster Press, 1978), p. 379.

41. Luke 23:19, 25.

42. See Matt. 26:51-54 and John 18:36.

43. Two commentators who make this connection are J. C. Fenton, *Saint Matthew* (Philadelphia: Westminster Press, 1963), p. 425; and H. Benedict Green, *The Gospel According to Matthew* (Oxford: Oxford University Press, 1975), p. 215.

44. Matthew 26:31, 54.

45. Floyd Filson suggests this in remarks on Matthew 26:52-54 in his *A Commentary on the Gospel According to Matthew* (London: Adam and Charles Black, 1960), pp. 280, 281.

46. See Matt. 10:24-25, 38. I wish here to acknowledge the help of Ernest Bursey, who among other things has pointed out a helpful article by Birger Gerhardsson, "Confession and Denial Before Men: Observations on Matt. 26:57—27:2," *Journal for the Study of the New Testament*, no. 13 (1981), pp. 46-66. Though this article focuses on the passage just following the account of Peter's violent act, it helped me see the connection with Matt. 10.

47. Mott, *Biblical Ethics and Social Change*, p. 181.

48. John 18:37.

49. See, e.g., John 13:16-17, and 15:20.

50. On the Sabbath, see Mark 2:23-28 and parallels. On divorce see Matt. 5:31-32 and parallels. Though many scholars believe that Matthew's "unchastity" exception has been added to a saying that originally did not include it, this is "open to debate," as W. F. Albright and C. S. Mann remark in *Matthew*, The Anchor Bible (Garden City, N.Y.: Doubleday, 1971), p. 65. For Paul's statements about divorce see 1 Cor. 7:10-15.

51. See 1 Cor. 11:23—15:28. For explicit mention of the *imminence* of transformation, see Paul's comments in Rom. 13:11-12.

52. Niebuhr, *Christ and Culture*, pp. 66-68.

53. H. Richard Niebuhr, "The Responsibility of the Church for Society," in Kenneth Scott Latourette, ed., *The Gospel, The Church and the World* (New York: Harper and Brothers, 1946), p. 124.

54. Quoted in Walter Klaassen, ed., *Anabaptism in Outline: Selected Primary Sources* (Scottdale, Pa.: Herald Press, 1981), p. 112.

55. Niebuhr, "The Responsibility of the Church for Society," pp. 130-132.

56. A recent classic illustration of this, not mentioned by Yoder, is the Vietnam War.

57. These last two paragraphs depend heavily upon remarks in Bernard Williams, *Morality: An Introduction to Ethics* (New York: Harper and Row, 1972), pp. 104-107, in refuta-

tion of utilitarianism.

58. John H. Yoder, *What Would You Do?* (Scottdale, Pa.: Herald Press, 1983), p. 40.

59. Ibid., p. 28.

60. See, e.g., Num. 9:1-14. I am grateful to Jon Dybdahl for this interesting example.

61. John H. Yoder, *The Original Revolution* (Scottdale, Pa.: Herald Press, 1971), p. 56. This remark was written in the 1950s.

62. Matt. 23:23 and Luke 11:42.

63. Matt. 12:18-21 quotes somewhat loosely from Isa. 42:1-4. I have quoted (from the RSV) Isaiah's substantially similar wording. On Luke and Isaiah, see, for example, 4:18-19 of the Gospel, where Isaiah 61:1-2 and 58:6 are quoted.

64. See, e.g., Isa. 58:6-7 and 59:15-16. A detailed discussion of biblical justice occurs in Mott, *Biblical Ethics and Social Change*, chap. 4.

65. H. Richard Niebuhr, "The Grace of Doing Nothing," *Christian Century*, March 23, 1932, p. 379.

Bibliography

WORKS BY OR ABOUT H. RICHARD NIEBUHR

Frei, Hans W. "The Theology of H. Richard Niebuhr." In *Faith and Ethics*, pp. 65-116. Edited by Paul Ramsey. New York: Harper and Row, 1957.

Godsey, John. *The Promise of Richard Niebuhr*. New York: J. B. Lippincott, 1970.

Hoedemaker, Libertus A. *The Theology of H. Richard Niebuhr*. Philadelphia: Pilgrim Press, 1970.

Kliever, Lonnie. *H. Richard Niebuhr*. Waco, Texas: Word Books, 1977.

Mount, Eric, Jr. "Realism, Norm, Story, and Character: Issues in the Civil Religion Discussion." *Journal of Church and State* 22 (1980): pp. 41-52.

Niebuhr, H. Richard. *Christ and Culture*. New York: Harper and Row, 1951.

_____. "The Doctrine of the Trinity and the Unity of Church." *Theology Today* 3 (1946): pp. 371-384.

_____. "The Ego-Alter Dialectic and the Conscience." *The Journal of Philosophy* 42 (1945): pp. 352-359.

_____. "The Grace of Doing Nothing." *Christian Century*, March 23, 1932, pp. 378-380.

_____. "Introduction to Biblical Ethics." In *Christian Ethics*, pp. 10-45. Edited by H. Richard Niebuhr and Waldo Beach. New York: Ronald Press, 1955.

_____. *The Meaning of Revelation*. New York: Macmillan, 1941.

_____. *The Purpose of the Church and Its Ministry*. New York: Harper and Row, 1956.

_____. *Radical Monotheism and Western Culture*. New York: Harper and Row, 1970.

_____. "Reformation: Continuing Imperative." *Christian Century*, March 2, 1960, pp. 248-251.

_____. *The Responsible Self*. New York: Harper and Row, 1963.

_____. "The Responsibility of the Church for Society." In *The Gospel, the Church and the World*, pp. 111-133. Edited by Kenneth Scott Latourette. New York: Harper and Brothers, 1946.

_____. *The Social Sources of Denominationalism*. New York: World Publishing Company, 1972.

Ramsey, Paul. *Nine Modern Moralists*. Englewood Cliffs, N.J.: Prentice-Hall, 1962.

Yoder, John Howard. "*Christ and Culture*: A Critique of H. Richard Niebuhr." Available from the library of Associated Mennonite Biblical Seminaries in Elkhart, Indiana.

WORKS OF NINE
POST-NIEBUHRIAN THEOLOGIANS

Bloesch, Donald. *Centers of Christian Renewal.* Philadelphia: United Church Press, 1964.

_____ . "The Challenge Facing the Churches." In *Christianity Confronts Modernity*, pp. 205-223. Edited by Kevin Perrotta. Ann Arbor, Michigan: Servant Books, 1981.

_____ . *Essentials of Evangelical Theology.* 2 vols. San Francisco: Harper and Row, 1978-79.

_____ . *The Invaded Church.* Waco, Texas: Word Books, 1975.

_____ . *Wellsprings of Renewal.* Grand Rapids: Eerdmans, 1974.

Gilkey, Langdon. *How the Church Can Minister to the World Without Losing Itself.* New York: Harper and Row, 1964.

_____ . *Maker of Heaven and Earth.* Garden City, N.Y.: Doubleday, 1959.

_____ . *Reaping the Whirlwind: A Christian Interpretation of History.* New York: Seabury Press, 1976.

_____ . *Shantung Compound.* New York: Harper and Row, 1966.

_____ . *Society and the Sacred.* New York: Crossroad, 1981.

Gutierrez, Gustavo. "Liberation Praxis and Christian Faith." In *Frontiers of Theology in Latin America*, pp. 9-18. Edited by Rosino Gibellini. Maryknoll, N.Y.: Orbis Books, 1979.

_____ . *The Power of the Poor in History.* Translated by Robert R. Barr. Maryknoll, N.Y.: Orbis Books, 1983.

_____ . *A Theology of Liberation.* Translated and edited by Sister Caridad Inda and John Eagleson. Maryknoll, N.Y.: Orbis Books, 1973.

Gutierrez, Gustavo, and Shaull, Richard. *Liberation and Change.* Atlanta: John Knox Press, 1977.

Haering, Bernard. *The Law of Christ.* 3 vols. Westminster, Md.: Newman Press, 1961-66.

_____ . *Free and Faithful in Christ.* 3 vols. New York: Crossroad, 1978-81.

Hauerwas, Stanley. *Character and the Christian Life.* San Antonio: Trinity University Press, 1975.

_____ . *A Community of Character.* Notre Dame: University of Notre Dame Press, 1981.

_____ . *Truthfulness and Tragedy.* Notre Dame: University of Notre Dame Press, 1977.

_____ . *Vision and Virtue.* Notre Dame: Fides/Claretian Press, 1977.

Macquarrie, John. *The Concept of Peace.* New York: Harper and Row, 1973.

_____ . *Paths in Spirituality.* London: SCM Press, 1972.

_____ . *Principles of Christian Theology.* New York: Charles Scribner's Sons, 1966.

_____ . *Three Issues in Ethics.* London: SCM Press, 1970.

Metz, Johannes Baptist. "The Church's Social Function in the Light of a 'Political Theology.' " In *Faith and the World of Politics*, Concilium Series, no. 36, pp. 1-18. Edited by Johannes B. Metz. New York: Paulist Press, 1968.

_____ . *The Emergent Church.* Translated by Peter Mann. New York: Crossroad, 1981.

_____ . *Faith in History and Society: Toward a Practical Fundamental Theology.* Translated by David Smith. New York: Seabury Press, 1980.

_____ . *Followers of Christ: The Religious Life and the Church.* Translated by Thomas Linton. New York: Paulist Press, 1978.

_____ . *Theology of the World.* Translated by William Glen-Doepel. London: Burns and Oates, 1969.

Reuther, Rosemary Radford, *The Church Against Itself.* New York: Herder and Herder. 1967.

_____ , *Liberation Theology.* New York: Paulist Press, 1972.

_____ . *Mary—The Feminine Face of the Church.* Philadelphia: Westminster Press, 1970.

_____ . *New Woman New Earth: Sexist Ideologies and Human Liberation.* New York: Seabury Press, 1975.

_____ . *The Radical Kingdom.* New York: Harper and Row, 1970.

_____ . *Sexism and God-Talk: Toward a Feminist Theology.* Boston: Beacon Press, 1983.

_____ . *To Change the World: Christology and Cultural Criticism.* New York:

Crossroad, 1981.
Yoder, John Howard. "*Christ and Culture*: A Critique of H. Richard Niebuhr." Available from the library of the Associated Mennonite Biblical Seminaries in Elkhart, Indiana.
_____ *The Christian Witness to the State*. Newton, Kans.: Faith and Life Press, 1964.
_____ *The Original Revolution*. Scottdale, Pa.: Herald Press, 1971.
_____ *The Politics of Jesus*. Grand Rapids: Eerdmans, 1972.
_____ Stone Lectures, presented at Princeton Theological Seminary in 1979. Also presented at Jaynes Morgan Lectures at Fuller Theological Seminary in the same year.
_____ *What Would You Do?* Scottdale, Pa.: Herald Press, 1983.

OTHER CITED WORKS

Albright, W. F., and Mann, C. S. *Matthew*. The Anchor Bible. Garden City, N.Y.: Doubleday, 1971.
Aulèn, Gustaf. *The Faith of the Christian Church*. Translated by Eric H. Wahlstrom. Philadelphia: Fortress Press, 1960.
Bainton, Roland H. *Christian Attitudes Toward War and Peace*. New York: Abingdon Press, 1960.
Barrett, C. K. *The Gospel According to Saint John*. 2d ed. Philadelphia: Westminster Press, 1978.
Barth, Karl. *Church Dogmatics*. 13 vols. Translated by G. W. Bromiley. Edinburgh: T. and T. Clark, 1957-1969.
_____ *The Epistle to the Romans*. Translated by Edwyn Hoskins. 6th ed. New York: Oxford University Press, 1968.
Cassidy, Richard J. *Jesus, Politics and Society: A Study of Luke's Gospel*. Maryknoll, N.Y.: Orbis Books, 1978.
Childress, James F. "Scripture and Christian Ethics." *Interpretation* 34 (October 1980): pp. 356-370.
Cobb, John B., Jr., and Tracy, David. *Talking About God*. New York: Seabury Press, 1983.
Curran, Charles. Foreword to *Principles for a Catholic Morality*, by Timothy E. O'Connell. New York: Seabury Press, 1978.
Deppermann, Klaus; Packull, Werner O.; and Stayer, James M. "From Monogenesis to Polygenesis: The Historical Discussion of Anabaptist Origins." *Mennonite Quarterly Review* 49 (April, 1975): pp. 83-121.
Dewey, John. *Theory of the Moral Life*. New York: Holt, Rinehart and Winston, 1967.
Dillenberger, John, and Welch, Claude. *Protestant Christianity*. New York: Scribners, 1954.
Durnbaugh, Donald. *The Believers' Church*. New York: Macmillan, 1968; Scottdale: Herald Press, 1985.
Ellul, Jacques. *Violence: Reflections from a Christian Perspective*. London: SCM Press, 1970.
Fenton, J. C. *Saint Matthew*. Philadelphia: Westminster Press, 1963.
Filson, Floyd. *A Commentary on the Gospel According to Matthew*. London: Adam and Charles Black, 1960.
Forel, George, ed. *Christian Social Teachings*. Garden City, N.Y.: Doubleday, 1966.
Frankena, William. "Is Morality Logically Dependent on Religion?" In *Religion and Morality*, pp. 295-317. Edited by Gene Outka and John P. Reeder, Jr. Garden City, N.Y.: Doubleday, 1973.
Friedmann, Robert. *The Theology of Anabaptism*. Scottdale, Pa.: Herald Press, 1973.
Gadamer, Hans-Georg. *Philosophical Hermeneutics*. Berkeley: University of California Press, 1976.
_____ *Truth and Method*. New York: Seabury, 1975.
Gerhardsson, Birger. "Confession and Denial Before Men: Observations on Matt. 26:57—27:2." *Journal for the Study of the New Testament* no. 13 (1981): pp. 46-66.
Green, H. Benedict. *The Gospel According to Matthew*. Oxford: Oxford University Press, 1975.
Heidegger, Martin. *Being and Time*. Translated by John Macquarrie and Edward Robinson.

New York: Harper and Row, 1962.

Henry, Carl F. H. *The Uneasy Conscience of Modern Fundamentalism*. Grand Rapids: Eerdmans, 1947.

Herberg, Will. *Protestant, Catholic, Jew*. Garden City, N.Y.: Doubleday, 1960.

Hershberger, Guy F., ed. *The Recovery of the Anabaptist Vision*. Scottdale, Pa.: Herald Press, 1957.

_____. *War, Peace and Nonresistance*. Scottdale, Pa.: Mennonite Publishing House, 1944.

_____. *The Way of the Cross in Human Relations*. Scottdale, Pa.: Herald Press, 1958.

Hengel, Martin. *Christ and Power*. Philadelphia: Fortress Press, 1977.

_____. *Victory over Violence*. London: SPCK, 1975.

_____. *Was Jesus a Revolutionist?*. Philadelphia: Fortress Press, 1971.

Hillerbrand, Hans J. "Anabaptism and the Reformation: Another Look." *Church History* 29 (1960): pp. 404-23.

Klaassen, Walter, ed. *Anabaptism in Outline: Selected Primary Sources*. Scottdale, Pa.: Herald Press, 1981.

_____. "The Anabaptist Critique of Constantinian Christendom." *Mennonite Quarterly Review* 55 (July, 1981): pp. 218-230.

Lindars, Barnabas. *The Gospel of John*. Grand Rapids: Eerdmans, 1972.

Lindblom, J. *Prophecy in Ancient Israel*. Philadelphia: Fortress Press, 1962.

Littell, Franklin. *The Origins of Sectarian Protestantism*. New York: Macmillan, 1964.

Marsh, John. *Saint John*. Philadelphia: Westminster Press, 1978.

McClendon, James Wm., Jr., and Smith, James M. *Understanding Religious Convictions*. Notre Dame: University of Notre Dame Press, 1975.

MacIntyre, Alasdair. *After Virtue*. Notre Dame: University of Notre Dame Press, 1981.

_____. *A Short History of Ethics*. New York: Macmillan, 1966.

Mergal, Angel M., and Williams, George H, eds. *Spiritual and Anabaptist Writers*. Philadelphia: Westminster, 1957.

Mott, Stephen Charles. *Biblical Ethics and Social Change*. New York: Oxford University Press, 1982.

Niebuhr, Reinhold. *An Interpretation of Christian Ethics*. London: SCM Press, 1936.

Osborn, Eric. *Ethical Patterns in Early Christian Thought*. New York: Cambridge University Press, 1976.

Sanders, Jack T. *Ethics in the New Testament*. Philadelphia: Fortress Press, 1975.

Schottroff, Luise, et al. *Essays on the Love Commandment*. Translated by Reginald H. and Ilse Fuller. Philadelphia: Fortress Press, 1978.

Tillich, Paul. *Christianity and the Encounter of the World Religions*. New York: Columbia University Press, 1963.

_____. *The Protestant Era*. Chicago: University of Chicago Press, 1957.

_____. *Systematic Theology*. 3 vols. Chicago: University of Chicago Press, 1951-1963.

Troeltsch, Ernst. *The Social Teachings of the Christian Churches*. New York: Harper and Row, 1960.

Verhey, Allen. "The Use of Scripture in Ethics." *Religious Studies Review* 4 (January 1978): pp. 28-37.

Weaver, J. Denny. "Discipleship Redefined: Four Sixteenth Century Anabaptists." *Mennonite Quarterly Review* 54 (October, 1980): pp. 255-79.

Williams, Bernard. *Morality: An Introduction to Ethics*. New York: Harper and Row, 1972.

Williams, George H. *The Radical Reformation*. Philadelphia: Westminster, 1962.

Yoder, John. *The Legacy of Michael Sattler*. Scottdale, Pa.: Herald Press, 1973.

Index

Abraham, 153-154
Alienation, 107-109
Anabaptists, Anabaptism: and Christ, 11, 28; and the church, 181, 184, 196nn.26, 34; and twentieth-century authors, 30-31, 127, 146, 159, 161-162; overview of, 20-26; and Scripture, 33; and social structures, 170, 197nn.38, 42
Apocalyptic, 25-26, 110, 120-121, 186, 191
Aquinas, Thomas, 19, 51, 82, 145
Aristotle, 28, 51
Ascetic communities, evangelical, 144-145
Augustine, 19, 27-29, 197n.48
Aulèn, Gustaf, 213n.6
Authority of Christ, 17, 28-29, ch. 2, 160, 161-167, 193; in Bloesch, 138; in Gilkey, 70-75; in Gutierrez, 103; in Haering, 77-78, 82-85; in Hauerwas, 134-136; in Macquarrie, 88-89, 91-92, 96; in Metz, 122-123; in Ruether, 111-112, 164, 213n.11; in Yoder, 31, 146-147, 151, 153

Barth, Karl, 29, 31-32, 118
Bender, Harold, 30
Benedict of Nursia, 45
Bible. *See* Scripture
Bloesch, Donald, 136-146, 167-169, 173-174, 179, 186
Bonhoeffer, Dietrich, 32, 118
Brown, William Adams, 88
Bultmann, Rudolf, 41, 115

Caesar, 150
Calvin, John, 19, 24, 142, 145

Capital punishment, 28-29
Cassidy, Richard, 169, 176, 213n.24
Celsus, 26-28
Character, 127, 129-130, 133, 193
Christ: Anabaptist view of, 21-26; ethics of, 40-41, 56, 78, 102, 111-112, 134, 139, 148-150, 174-178; and the historical Jesus, 42, 213n.3; as mediating God, 87-88; and revelation, 53-54. *See also* Authority of Christ
Christ and culture, problem of, 18-20, 29, 31-32, 34-35, ch. 2, 160, 192
Christocentrism, 28, 92, 163-166, 213n.6
Christology, H. R. Niebuhr's, 163
Church: as alternative society, 181-184, 193; Anabaptist view of, 20-26; as body of Christ, 93, 180-181; and sect, denomination, 67; and state, 24, 27, 142-144, 147, 154-155, 171, 182-183, 214n.158; and surrounding culture, 63, 160, 180-192; and surrounding culture, in Gilkey, 67-68, 69-72, 75; and surrounding culture, in Haering, 85-86; and surrounding culture, in Macquarrie, 93-94, 96-97; and surrounding culture, in Gutierrez, 104-107; and surrounding culture, in Ruether, 113-115; and surrounding culture, in Metz, 123-125; and surrounding culture, in Hauerwas, 133-136; and surrounding culture, in Bloesch, 138-144; and surrounding culture, in Yoder, 146-147, 152, 156; as transformative example, 184-192, 193. *See also* Community

Cobb, John B., 214n.27
Community, Anabaptist view of, 25, 171, 172. *See also* Church
Conscientization, 105
Constantine, Constantinianism, 26, 28, 114, 154, 182, 212n.149
Creation. *See* World, created
Cross, and social ethics, 151, 153, ch. 6
Culture: definition of, 199n.45; and religion, Gilkey on, 68-69; *See also* Christ and Culture, problem of; Transformation of Culture

Day, Dorothy, 32
Discipleship, 22-23, 29, 122, 196n.16, 197n.57
Denck, Hans, 23, 167, 195n.9
Denomination, 67-68
Descartes, 108
Dewey, John, 131
Didache, The, 43
Dualism, 108

Ellul Jacques, 32, 95
Enlightenment, 116-118
Ethics, H. R. Niebuhr and, 39, 58-60, 61, 199n.46
Evangelicals, Evangelicalism, 136-138
Evangelism, 93, 105, 172

Faith, H. R. Niebuhr on, 55, 60
Faithfulness. *See* Fidelity, Haering on
Forel, George, 30
Frei, Hans, 54
Festival of Dedication, 177
Fidelity, Haering on, 78, 81, 85-86, 203n.53
Frankena, William, 198n.86
Freedom, Haering on, 77, 81

Gadamer, Hans-Georg, 34
Gandhi, Mahatma, 187
Gilkey, Landon, 66-76, 165, 182
God, H. R. Niebuhr on, 40-41
Gospel, and politics, 168-170, 214n.24
Guevara, "Che," 100
Gustafson, James, 127
Gutierrez, Gustavo, 98-107, 172, 205n.13, 206n.38

Haering, Bernard, 76-87, 164, 170, 173, 179, 181, 185, 203nn.53, 69
Hampshire, Stuart, 132
Harnack, Adolph von, 40
Hartmann, Nikolai, 57

Hauerwas, Stanley, 12, 32-33, 126-136, 185, 209nn.16, 30
Heidegger, Martin, 34
Hengel, Martin, 32
Henry, Carl F. H., 33, 137
Herod, 149, 176
Hershberger, Guy, 30
Historicity, human, 82, 130, 132, 162, 193; in H. R. Niebuhr, 49, 54, 57-58, 200n.49. *See also* Human person, Relativity
Hitler, Adolf, 77, 129
Human person, the, 49-53, 58, 87-88, 130-131, 133, 162. *See also* Historicity, human
Holy Spirit, the, 23, 78, 112-115, 164-165, 167
Hooker, Richard 89

Josephus, 176
Judas the Galilean, 175-176
Judas Maccabeus, 176

Kant, Immanuel, 51, 57-58
King, Martin Luther, 32, 187
Kingdom of God, 73-74, 111, 141

Las Casas, Bartolome de, 103
Law, 57, 59-60, 78, 201n.97. *See also* Natural law
Legalism and nonviolence, 179, 188-192
Liberation: in Haering 89; theology of, 98-116, 137
Love, 29, 40-41, 79-81, 153, 173
Loyalty, 200n.68. *See also* Universal loyalty, virtue of
Luther, Martin, 19, 21-24, 142, 145

Maccabean War, 176
MacIntyre, Alasdair, 59
Macquarrie, John, 87-97, 163, 173, 180, 204nn.122, 132
Man. *See* Human person, the; Historicity, human
Maritain, Jacques
Marx, Karl, 80
Marxism, 119
Maurice, F. D., 19, 47
Mariategui, Jose Carlos, 99
Mead, George Herbert, 49, 51
Menahem, 176
Mennonites, 30, 196n.45
Method of this study, 35-36
Metz, Johannes Baptist, 116-125, 185-186
Monotheism, in Anabaptist perspective, 162. *See also* God, H. R. Niebuhr on

Morality, "standard account of," 128, 131, 162

Mott, Stephen Charles, 174-178

Narrative: and ethics, 161-167, 193; in Hauerwas, 127, 130-131, 134; in Metz, 116, 122-123, 125; in H. R. Niebuhr, 53-56, 58, 61-62; in Yoder, 152-153

Nationalism, 170-171

Natural law, 82-84, 92, 164, 204n.122

New Life, Anabaptists on, 23

Niebuhr, H. Richard, 11-13, 28, ch. 2, 127, 146 ch. 6; authority of Christ in, ch. 2; and Bloesch, 137, 140, 144; Christ and culture in, 18-20, 26, 29, 35, ch. 2; Christ, ethics of, in, 40-41, 56; Christ and historical Jesus in, 42-43, 213n3; Christ and law in, 57, 59-60, 213n.13; ethics and theology in, 39, 61, 199n.46; God in, 40-41; human historicity in, 49, 54, 57-58, 200n.49; human person in, 50-51, 58; loyalty in, 55, 200n.68; narrative in, 53, 55, 60-62; obedience in, 41, 43; responsibility in 50-52, 55, 60, 62, 200n.59; revelation in; 53-55, 57-58, 62

Niebuhr, Reinhold, 11-12, 29-30, 66, 71, 73 79, 115

Nonresistance, 153-154

Nonviolence: Anabaptists and, 24, 32; in Haering, 80-81, 86, 203n.69; virtue of, 173-180; in Yoder, 150, 152-153, 212n.139. See also Legalism, nonviolence and; Violence

Obedience, 23, 29, 41, 43, 91, 196n.16

Origen, 26-28

Pacifism, 11, 74, 95, 143, 173, 188-189. See also Nonviolence

Peace, 94

Pfistermeyer, Hans, 195n.14

Pilate, 150, 175, 178

Pluralism, cultural, 62, 71, 82, 160. See also Historicity, human; Relativity

Political engagement, virtue of, 167-170

Political theology, 116-125, 137, 205n.13

Power, 151, 212n.127

Radical Reformation, 12, 36. See also Anabaptists

Radical vision, 11, ch. 6

Riedeman, Peter, 184

Reason: and historicity, 49, 57, 61; and revelation, 39, 57; in Macquarrie, 90, 92

Relativity, human, 59-60, 83, 132-133. See also Historicity, human

Relevance, Gospel and, 58, 72, 202n.7

Religion, and culture, 68-69, 202n.12; and ethics, 34, 131

Responsibility: in moral life, 50-53, 55-56, 60, 62, 76, 162-163, 200n.59; for society, 74, 179, 185-186

Resurrection, 151, 187

Revelation: and Holy Spirit, 78; and natural law, 82-84; H. R. Niebuhr on, 39, 53-55, 57-58, 62

Revolution, 80-81, 101, 103, 105, 124-125, 143, 172

Rothmann, Bernhard, 23

Royce, Josiah, 200n.68

Ruether, Rosemary Radford, 107-116, 164, 182, 185, 213n.11

Rules in morality, 79-80. See also Legalism, nonviolence and

Salvation, 101-102, 104, 110, 138, 168-170

Sanders, Jack, 33, 171

Sattler, Michael, 196n.29

Schweitzer, Albert, 40

Scripture: Anabaptist view of, 22; in Bloesch, 136, 138; in Hauerwas, 134; in Macquarrie, 90-92; in H. R. Niebuhr, 58-59; in recent ethical reflection, 32-34

Schleitheim Confession, 196n.29

Sect, 67, 75

Self, the. See Human person

Sermon on Mount, 11, 59-60, 124, 174-178

Simons, Menno, 24, 26

Socrates, 57

Solidarity with Christ, 21-26, 77-79, 159, 165, 167, 181

Speer, Albert, 129

Story. See Narrative

Tertullian, 28, 43-46

Temple, William, 90

Tillich, Paul, 32, 66, 68-69, 71, 202n.12

Tolstoy Leo, 45

Torres, Camillo, 100

Tradition, 34, 77, 90, 92, 112-113

Transformation of culture: in Bloesch, 139-141, 144-145; in Gilkey, 68-69, 75; in Gutierrez, 101, 103-107; in Haering, 85; in Hauerwas, 133-136; in Macquarrie, 93-94, 96-97; in Metz, 122-124; in Niebuhr, ch. 2; in post- Niebuhrian world, 12; as properly Anabaptist, 20,

26, 180-192; relation of society and individual in, 214n.27; in Ruether, 109, 113-115; in Yoder, 156-157
Trinity, 165
Troeltsch, Ernst, 32, 38, 67. 198n.3

Universalizability, principle of, 209n.30
Universal loyalty, virtue of, 55, 170-173

Value, 50, 55
Vatican II, 76, 104, 106, 181
Violence, 27, 29, 94-95. 105, 115, 124, 143, 204n.132, 206n.38, 211n.120. *See also* Nonviolence
Virtue(s), 129, 133, 167-180, 190, 193, 209n.16
Vision, 129-130
Voltaire, 117

War, 28-29, 95, 212n.145
Witness, 23-25

Wittgenstein, Ludwig, 34
World, created, 107, 109-110, 118-120

Yoder, John Howard, 146-158; and Anabaptism, 30, 32, 146, 159; authority of Christ in, 31, 146-147, 151, 153, 165-167; church and state in, 147, 154, 213n.158; church and surrounding culture in, 152, 156-157, 168, 184; on Constantine and Constantinianism, 154, 212n.149; ethics of Christ in, 148-149, 158, 168; and Hauerwas, 127; and nationalism, 170-171; and H. R. Niebuhr, 12, 42, 146; nonresistance in, 153-155, 212n.139; nonviolence in, 150, 152-153, 179, 188-190, 211n.120; power in; 151, 212n.127; resurrection in, 151, 158, 187; on War in Old Testament, 212n.145

Zealots, 174, 176-177
Zwingli, Ulrich, 20-22, 24

THE AUTHOR

Charles Scriven was born into a minister's home in the state of Oregon in 1945. After training for the pastoral ministry at Walla Walla College (Washington) and at Andrews University (Michigan), he edited a Seventh-day Adventist youth magazine, *Insight,* from 1969-1973. He taught journalism at Walla Walla College in 1974. He then moved to St. Helena, California, where his wife,  Marianne, taught music at a nearby college and he was a househusband and graduate student at the Graduate Theological Union in Berkeley, California.

Under James Wm. McClendon, Jr., Scriven studied theology, ethics, and the philosophy of religion at the GTU, finally writing a doctoral dissertation on the relation of the church and the world. He taught in the religion department of Walla Walla College from 1981 to 1985.

He is presently the senior pastor of the Sligo Seventh-day Adventist Church, a congregation of 3,300 in Takoma Park, Maryland.